T0311376

Winifred Sanford

SOUTHWESTERN WRITERS COLLECTION SERIES
The Wittliff Collections at Texas State University–San Marcos
Steven L. Davis, Editor

THE
LIFE
AND
TIMES
OF A
TEXAS
WRITER

Winifred Sanford

BETTY
HOLLAND
WIESEPAPE

UNIVERSITY OF TEXAS PRESS, AUSTIN

The Southwestern Writers Collection Series originates from the Wittliff Collections, a repository of literature, film, music, and southwestern and Mexican photography established at Texas State University–San Marcos.

Information in Chapters 4 and 5 previously appeared in "The Manuscript Club of Wichita Falls: A Noteworthy Literary Club," *Southwestern Historical Quarterly* 47, no. 4 (April 1994): 643–659.

Copyright © 2012 by the University of Texas Press
All rights reserved
First paperback edition, 2023

Requests for permission to reproduce material
from this work should be sent to:
Permissions
University of Texas Press
P.O. Box 7819
Austin, TX 78713-7819
utpress.utexas.edu/rp-form

The paper used in this book meets the minimum requirements of ANSI/NISO Z39.48-1992 (R1997) (Permanence of Paper). ∞

LIBRARY OF CONGRESS CATALOGING-IN-PUBLICATION DATA

Wiesepape, Betty Holland.
Winifred Sanford : the life and times of a Texas writer / by Betty Holland Wiesepape.
p. cm.
Includes bibliographical references and index.
ISBN 978-1-4773-2800-2 (pb : alk. paper)
1. Sanford, Winifred M., 1890–1983. 2. Authors, American—20th century—Biography. 3. Authors, American—Texas. I. Title.
PS3537.A696Z95 2012
813'.52—dc23
[B]
2012008448
doi:10.7560/742963

FRONTISPIECE: Winifred Sanford shortly before she and Wayland moved from Duluth, Minnesota, to Wichita Falls, Texas, circa 1920.

In memory of Helen Jackson Sanford, Keeper of the Ashes.

Contents

Acknowledgments

THE TELLING OF WINIFRED SANFORD'S
story would have been impossible without the cooperation of her three daughters.
Helen Sanford embraced this project from its inception, made her mother's papers available, and gave me access to the family's collection of photographs. Helen,
along with her sisters, Emerett Miles and Mary Gordon, granted numerous interviews and directed me to friends and associates of their mother. These associates
granted additional interviews and supplied further information about Winifred
Sanford's life and the time period in which she lived. Paul Railsback, Winifred's
executor and grandson, allowed me unrestricted use of his grandmother's letters,
photographs, short stories, articles, and unpublished manuscripts.

Former members of the Manuscript Club of Wichita Falls took me to lunch,
shared their memories of bygone years, and read poems and short stories by Manuscript Club members to me. Margaret Dvorken, Jenny Louise Hindman, Peggy
Schachter, Bert Kruger Smith, and Laura Faye Yauger also provided me with documents, newspaper clippings, and invaluable information about this remarkable
group of female writers who met together for more than thirty years.

Reverend John A. Buehrens, minister of the First Unitarian Church of Dallas in
1983, granted permission for the inclusion of remarks that he made when he conducted Winifred's memorial service.

Averil J. Kadis, Rights and Permissions Administrator for H. L. Mencken's literary estate and representative of the Enoch Pratt Free Library, granted permission
for the inclusion of Mencken's letters to Winifred in Appendix A of this book, in
accordance with the terms of Mencken's will. The New York Public Library supplied copies of Winifred's letters to Mencken that reside in the H. L. Mencken and
Sarah Hardt Mencken Collection. Patricia Angelin, literary executrix of the George
Jean Nathan Estate, allowed me to include letters that Nathan wrote to Winifred
when he was coeditor with Mencken of *The American Mercury.*

SMU Press identified Dr. Don B. Graham and Dr. William T. Pilkington as First
and Second Readers of *Windfall and Other Stories,* and Dr. Graham and Dr. Pilkington allowed me to lift quotations from their reports. More recently, Dr. Pilkington's
widow, Betsy Pilkington, and Dr. Graham granted permission for these comments
to appear in this book. George Ann Ratchford of SMU Press granted permission
for the quotation of passages from short stories published in the publically offered
edition of *Windfall and Other Stories.*

The Duluth Public Library supplied photocopies of newspaper articles that per-
tained to the Mahon and Sanford families. Richard Holland, former curator of the
Southwestern Writers Collection at Texas State University, obtained permission
from the Texas Institute of Letters for my research of TIL files, and Steve Davis,
current curator of the Southwestern Writers Collection, honored my request for
photocopies of documents that are now housed in the Winifred Sanford Collection. And the staff of the History and Archives Department of the Dallas Public
Library guided me to newspaper articles and other sources of information about
Winifred's life after she moved to Dallas, Texas.

I also owe debts of gratitude to William H. Vann and to early editors of the
Southwest Review. Vann provided a record of what went on in the organizational
years of TIL's history, and the editors of the *Southwest Review* documented major
concerns of Texas writers of the 1920s and 1930s in the pages of that journal.

Friends, scholars, and family members that are too numerous to name have
encouraged my work on this project, as well. My initial research of Winifred Sanford's life and writing was guided by Dr. Joan Chandler, who chaired my graduate
committee at the University of Texas at Dallas, and by Dr. Frederick Turner and
Dr. Robert Nelsen, who served as members of that committee and awarded my
thesis on Winifred Sanford a special commendation. Dr. Bert Kruger Smith of The
University of Texas Health Science Center at Austin made it her personal mission
to see that a copy of this thesis was placed in the Harry Ransom Center at the University of Texas at Austin.

My dear friend Dr. Lou Rodenberger provided the nudging that I needed to
put other writing projects aside and place the writing of this book at the top of

my to-do list. Steve Davis, acting curator of the Southwestern Writers Collection at Texas State University in San Marcos, read the manuscript and made invaluable suggestions for its improvement. He also brought it to the attention of Allison Faust, sponsoring editor at the University of Texas Press, who shepherded the project through the acceptance and production process and was never too busy to answer my many questions. My husband, Floyd Wiesepape, served as proofreader of numerous drafts of this manuscript and continually assured me that someone, somewhere, would publish this book if ever I finished it.

Finally, I owe a debt of gratitude to Winifred Sanford, whose excellent short stories have inspired me to become a better writer.

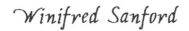

Winifred Sanford

Introduction

MY HUSBAND AND I WERE DRIVING
along the Kona coast of the Island of Hawaii when I spotted the handmade sign. Uneven blue letters scrawled across the length of a weathered board spelled "petroglyphs," and a crooked arrow pointed in the direction of an overgrown field. My husband grimaced, pulled the car to the side of the road, and shut off the motor. This trip to Hawaii was his anniversary gift to me, and after twenty-five years of marriage, he was well aware of my obsession with places other people ignore: dusty attics, neglected cemeteries, dilapidated houses, and overgrown paths that lead to nowhere.

Earlier that week, we had driven twenty miles from our hotel to view a highly advertised petroglyph site in Volcano National Park. There, we hiked five miles in midday heat to a site surrounded by a wooden boardwalk and numerous interpretative signs that explained the significance of nearly invisible markings on the rock outcroppings. After that experience, neither of us had great expectations for a field of petroglyphs marked by one hand-painted sign, but we had an hour to fill before the first leg of our flight back to Dallas.

I shall never forget the rush of adrenalin I felt when I parted the weeds and saw hundreds of distinct carvings on the rocks in front of me. Some figures danced, some carried torches; some marched single file in straight lines, while others crouched low with raised spears. Unable to focus my attention, I ran from one group of figures to another. While my husband took photographs, I inspected the carvings, marveling at their clarity, puzzling over their meaning, and regretting that I had only one hour to spend in this abandoned field.

I stood with the breeze blowing in my face and the afternoon sun roasting my skin and tried to imagine what life had been like for the people who carved the petroglyphs—people who lived out their days between the roar of the Pacific Ocean and the rumblings of an active volcano. What was so important? Why had they spent countless hours with the hot sun beaming down upon their backs as they worked? And who was their intended audience? I felt an intense desire to know what had happened on the island that was so important to the individuals who carved these figures.

When I returned to Dallas, I engaged in some light research on petroglyphs. I learned that the carvings I had seen probably represented the narrative history of a native tribe, that the stick figures arranged in vertical rows beneath the outstretched arms of larger stick figures represented the tribe's genealogical records. Although I might never fully understand what those carvings meant to the people who carved them, as an aspiring writer, I could identify with the tribe's desire to preserve a record of their experiences—to create some kind of narrative about the people they had encountered, the island they inhabited, and the events they had witnessed. I had no way of knowing that soon I would stumble upon another abandoned field—one much closer to my home, but just as unheralded as the field of petroglyphs.

My interest in Winifred Sanford began one Sunday morning the following November when, shivering from my foray into the front yard to fetch the newspaper, I wrapped my fleece robe closer around me, poured a steaming cup of coffee, and sat down to read the Sunday edition of *The Dallas Morning News*. In 1988, the Sunday edition contained a weekly insert entitled *Dallas Life Magazine* that featured stories of particular interest to residents of Dallas and the surrounding Metroplex.

I thumbed through the magazine until I encountered a short story entitled "Windfall." A brief introduction to this story identified the author as Winifred M. Sanford, a woman born in Minnesota in 1890 who moved to West Texas with her lawyer husband during the Burkburnett oil boom. "Windfall" was but one story in a collection of this author's short stories that had been released recently by SMU Press as part of the Southwest Life and Letters series.

As I read "Windfall," a story narrated from the perspective of a West Texas farm wife named Cora, I experienced a similar rush of adrenalin to what I had felt while looking at the petroglyphs in Hawaii. I identified with Cora's ambivalent attitude toward the oil well that had been brought in on her family's farm the previous night. As the wife of a petroleum engineer, I had experienced firsthand the stresses that an association with the oil industry can precipitate on a family. I felt an immediate kinship with the author.

The short biographical sketch that accompanied the story identified Winifred Sanford as a Texas writer whose short stories were published between 1925 and 1931. A majority of these stories had been accepted by H. L. Mencken for publication in *The American Mercury*. I was intrigued by Sanford's connection to the famous editor. In my studies at the University of Texas at Dallas, I had read "Sahara of the Bozart," Mencken's scathing attack on regional writers of the American South, and I wondered how stories written by a Texas housewife had gained the famous editor's approval. I also was surprised that I had never before encountered Winifred Sanford's name in my study of Texas literature.

Determined to learn more about this author and eager to read more of her stories, I drove to the nearest bookstore the following morning to purchase a copy of *Windfall and Other Stories*. Neither the bookstore clerk nor the manager had heard of Winifred Sanford, so they brought out the only short story collection they had in stock that was published by SMU Press and written by a woman author whose last name was Sanford. After I assured them that Annette Sanford was not Winifred Sanford, the manager searched his computer database and found the correct entry. He promised me that he would have a copy of *Windfall and Other Stories* in his store within a few days.

With Annette Sanford's short story collection *Lasting Attachments* in a plastic shopping bag on the seat beside me as I drove home, I wondered how an author whose stories had gained the favorable attention of the leading literary figure of the 1920s and 1930s could fade so completely from the collective literary memory. I also wondered if, fifty years into the future, Annette Sanford and her award-winning short stories would meet a similar fate.

When *Windfall and Other Stories* arrived, I read every story in the collection and searched Emerett Sanford Miles's foreword and Lou Rodenberger's afterword for additional information about the author. Miles's speculation that her mother quit writing because "new interests grew to fill her days, and she went on to other things" only increased my curiosity, as did the encouraging comments from Mencken that Miles quotes. I was just beginning to submit my own short fiction for publication, and I knew that if I ever experienced the level of success that Winifred Sanford had achieved almost instantaneously, I would not stop writing and go on to other things.

I looked for Winifred Sanford's name in secondary sources that Miles and Rodenberger cite and uncovered a few mentions of her in books about H. L. Mencken and *The American Mercury*. My search through Mencken's published letters was fruitless. I did not locate what I mistakenly thought was a single letter from Mencken to Winifred, but I did discover an interesting reference to her in M. K. Singleton's *H. L. Mencken and The American Mercury Adventure*. In a footnote, Singleton identifies Sanford as the mysterious, unnamed female that Mencken's onetime assistant editor, Charles Angoff, wrote about on pages 111–113 of *H. L. Mencken: A Portrait from Memory*:

> Another newcomer was a woman writer of short stories about whom Mencken was almost as excited as he was about [George] Milburn . . . She wrote about life in newly discovered oil lands . . . and did so with a truly astounding perspicacity. She had a . . . sharp eye for the vulgarity of nouveau riche American men, and she also had a very keen ear for the speech . . . these men picked up. Mencken thought that in many ways, she was more gifted in this respect than was Sinclair Lewis.

Angoff tells that Mencken pleaded with this woman to write a novel, but she said the novel form did not interest her. She suddenly stopped submitting stories to the *Mercury* after telling Mencken that she had experienced an emotional disturbance and would probably never write again.

At this point, all the hours that I had spent reading Nancy Drew mysteries and envisioning myself as a private detective when I was an adolescent resurfaced. Solving the mystery of why such a successful short story author would suddenly stop writing became a quest, one that took precedence over several other pending research projects. I was determined to follow every lead until I learned why this had happened. My search led me first to Southern Methodist University, located only a few miles from the Sanford family's former home in Highland Park. When I contacted SMU Press, I was told that Suzanne Comer, the editor who had acquired the rights to the Sanford family's privately published collection of *Windfall and Other Stories*, was deceased. The current editors did not know how Comer had acquired the collection, where the Mencken letters that Emerett Sanford Miles quotes in her foreword might be located, or how the Sanford family might be contacted.

I talked to research assistants at all of the SMU libraries, including the DeGolyer. Although the DeGolyer has an extensive collection of papers by Texas poets and writers of the 1920s, 1930s, and 1940s, the archivist could not find a single reference to Winifred Sanford. She suggested that I contact the SMU Archives. The archivist there vaguely recalled a conversation that she once had with one of Winifred Sanford's daughters, who still resided in Highland Park. Based solely upon a telephone conversation with Winifred's daughter Helen, the archivist had concluded that the author's papers contained nothing that would be of interest or value to the university.

As soon as I hung up the telephone, I located Helen J. Sanford's name and address in the Dallas telephone directory and wrote her a letter telling of my interest in her mother's stories and requesting her help with my investigation. A few days later, Helen contacted me by telephone. She was delighted to learn that I was interested in writing a master's thesis about her mother, and she was eager to aid in my investigation. Despite Helen's willingness, I approached our first meeting with more than a little trepidation. I was concerned about how she might respond to questions about the sudden termination of Winifred Sanford's writing career and to questions about M. K. Singleton's footnote that identifies Winifred as the mystery woman in Charles Angoff's *H. L. Mencken: A Portrait from Memory.*

On February 14, 1989, I drove to Helen J. Sanford's home and conducted a three-and-a-half-hour interview. At the end of the interview, Helen led me up a staircase to the attic of her house, where she had stored her mother's papers. I will never forget the excitement I felt as I carried the cardboard box down the stairs to Helen's living room and removed the lid.

"Oh look," Helen said, reaching into the box. "Here are those Mencken letters right on top." She lifted a bundle of letters still in envelopes addressed to Mrs. Winifred Sanford, untied the string that held the letters together, and placed them in my hands. I had begun to suspect that I might find among these papers the Mencken letter(s) referenced in Emerett Sanford Miles's foreword, but suddenly, what I had expected to be a single letter turned into a collection.

In addition to the Mencken letters, the cardboard box contained over one hundred pieces of information: correspondence between Winifred Sanford and a variety of literary figures, copyrights and receipts for the sales of her short stories, and original copies of *The American Mercury* and other magazines in which Sanford's stories and nonfiction articles had appeared. In the bottom of the box, I found manuscripts of stories that Winifred Sanford had written in her childhood and a couple of stories that her family had not included in *Windfall and Other Stories.* In short, the box in Helen's attic contained everything I needed to solve the mystery surrounding Winifred's abbreviated writing career.

I spent the better part of a year fitting this evidence together with information that I gained from interviews with Winifred's daughters—Helen J. Sanford, Emerett Sanford Miles, and Mary Sanford Gordon—and with surviving members of the writing club that Winifred had helped to organize in the West Texas town Wichita Falls. Manuscript Club members who granted interviews and provided me with other information were Margaret Dvorken, Jenny Louise Hindman, Bert Kruger Smith, Peggy Schachter, and Laura Faye Yauger.

In fall 1992, I submitted my thesis entitled *Winifred Sanford: Her Life And Times* to fulfill requirements for a master of arts in humanities at the University of Texas at Dallas. At the insistence of Dr. Bert Kruger Smith, my thesis was placed in the Harry Ransom Collection at the University of Texas at Austin, and members of my thesis committee, along with Dr. Lou Rodenberger, urged me to turn my thesis into a book, which I fully intended to do at some point. But as so often happens, unplanned events disrupted good intentions, and years have now passed since that Sunday morning when I discovered "Windfall" and first became acquainted with Winifred Sanford's fiction.

So who is Winifred Sanford, and why is a writer whose literary output was limited to fourteen published stories worthy of a biography? Although Sanford did not have a prolific career, scholars who served as readers for *Windfall and Other Stories* pronounced her works, published in leading American magazines in the twenties and thirties, to be on a par with the short stories of Pulitzer Prize-winning Texas author Katherine Anne Porter and superior to all other stories written in Texas during that time period.[1]

In 1926, Edward J. O'Brien listed four of Winifred's stories in *The Best Short Stories of 1926*, making her the only Texas writer at the time—perhaps the only Texas writer ever—to achieve such an accomplishment. Although these stories attracted the attention of leading editors, reviewers, literary agents, and publishing houses, and appeared in a number of anthologies, Winifred never published her stories as a collection. This may account in part for the fact that more than fifty years after these stories first appeared in print in national magazines, until they were published in the SMU edition of *Windfall and Other Stories*, few scholars knew these stories existed.

Even in the twenties and thirties, when Winifred's fiction was attracting such favorable attention nationally, her work received few accolades from literary luminaries in Texas. Her realistic stories differ greatly from the romantic tales of cowboys, desperados, treasure seekers, and Texas heroes that were being produced and promoted by prominent regional writers such as Roy Bedichek, J. Frank Dobie, and Walter Prescott Webb. At a time when arbitrators of Texas culture were engaged in an ongoing debate about what characteristics should define southwestern literature, Winifred Sanford was quietly producing stories that featured characters modeled upon contemporary Texas residents and current events that were taking place on Texas soil.[2]

Today, these stories, written in an ironic mode and set in the oil boom days of the twenties and thirties, have historical and cultural as well as literary significance. The cultural upheaval that occurred in the state's rural societies when oil was first discovered lasted for only a brief period of time, and Sanford's artful stories provide rare glimpses of the historical moment when industrialization in the form of oil exploration came into conflict with the long-standing beliefs and values of an agrarian society. As Sylvia Ann Grider and Lou Rodenberger, editors of the short story anthology *Let's Hear It: Stories by Texas Women Writers,* indicate, "It is important to note that Winifred Sanford was the first among the more gifted Texas writers to recognize that this was a unique experience worthy of literary response."[3]

SMU Press's 1988 release of *Windfall and Other Stories* precipitated a flurry of interest among literary scholars of southwestern literature and culture. Reviewers of the collection commented favorably about the content of the stories and about Winifred's minimalist writing style. Subsequently, contemporary scholars solicited individual stories for soon-to-be-released anthologies, and literary historians began to mention Winifred's accomplishments when they discussed early Texas writing, effectively installing her name in its rightful place in the canon of southwestern literature. In the 1990s, when most of the literature produced in Texas in the twenties and thirties had been relegated to dusty basements or dimly lit shelves in the back rooms of university libraries, Winifred Sandford's short fiction was enjoying resurgence, not only in Texas but also in Hollywood. *Windfall and Other Stories* appeared on the reading lists of book clubs and on syllabi for college and university courses on southwestern culture and literature. Clint Eastwood's production company, Malpaso Productions, collaborated with veteran actor Robert Duvall to make a movie based on Winifred's short story "Luck." This movie, a 1995 release entitled *Stars Fell on Henrietta,* was shown in literary festivals and movie theaters throughout the United States.

MY BIOGRAPHY OF Winifred Sanford's life illuminates circumstances that stimulated her desire to write fiction early on as well as circumstances that impeded her literary production and contributed to the early termination of her brilliant career. Other scholars have puzzled over this sudden end and have lamented the fact that, although Winifred lived to be ninety-three years old, her last short story was published when she was only forty-one. Friends and family members have offered hypotheses as to why she stopped writing, and these suppositions have been repeated as fact by several scholars. For this project, I have made a careful examination, through the primary sources, correspondence, and other related materials that reside among her papers (now located in the Southwestern Writers Collection at Texas State University in San Marcos), of the circumstances surrounding the termination of Winifred Sanford's writing career. I reveal my findings and solve the mystery of her aborted career in the pages of this biography.

Many of the circumstances that impeded Winifred's writing life have been present in the lives of other women writers—in Texas and elsewhere, in the twenty-first as well as the twentieth century. My findings lend support to statements made by Grider and Rodenberger in *Let's Hear It: Stories by Texas Women Writers* that many women writers in Texas have excelled in the short story form because the genre has accommodated the limited amount of time they have been able to devote to their writing.[4] In *Texas Woman of Letters, Karle Wilson Baker,* Sarah Ragland Jackson tells how, although Baker always felt that she would become a novelist, she was unable to do so while rearing her children.[5] And in a 1963 interview with Barbara Thomson Davis that appeared in the *The Paris Review,* Katherine Anne Porter, a woman who had no children, commented on writing her first and only novel, *Ship of Fools:*

> You're brought up with the notion of feminine chastity
> and inaccessibility, yet with the curious idea of
> feminine availability in all spiritual ways, and in
> giving service to anyone who demands it. And I suppose
> that's why it has taken me twenty years to write this
> novel; it's been interrupted by just about anyone who
> could jimmy his way into my life.[6]

In my research of Winifred Sanford's papers, I uncovered irrefutable evidence that she made numerous attempts to publish two novels, and that at one point, she was working on a third. When her literary agent David Lloyd's efforts to place the novels proved unsuccessful, he returned them to Winifred. However, these manuscripts are not among her papers, and Sanford family members whom I interviewed had no knowledge of two of them. Given the superior quality of Winifred's short fiction and the positive comments that readers at various publishing houses made about her novel manuscripts, it is unfortunate that they have not been located and probably no longer exist.

Correspondence that Winifred Sanford exchanged with H. L. Mencken during the years that he was editor of *The American Mercury* reveals a side of the editor that is very different from his often caustic public persona. Finally, and most importantly, Winifred's statements to M. K. Singleton concerning Mencken set the record straight regarding Charles Angoff's account in *H. L. Mencken: A Portrait from Memory* of the mysterious woman who wrote about Texas oil fields. Winifred's comments in her letters to Singleton in 1962 substantiate what Mencken scholars such as William Nolte, Charles Fecher, and Carl Bode have long suspected—that much of what Angoff wrote about his former boss in this unflattering biography was either partly fabricated or greatly exaggerated.[7]

The Story Begins

DULUTH,

MINNESOTA:

1890–1916

THE WIND WAS BLOWING, AND Winifred Mahon and her friend Marguerite Culkin held tight to the skirts of their Gibson Girl dresses as they boarded the streetcar that was the main means of public transportation in Duluth, Minnesota, in the first decade of the twentieth century. Holding skirts in place was an automatic reaction for modest young women in the windy city situated high atop a rock outcropping overlooking Lake Superior. If the literary event that Winifred recalled attending in her 1936 interview with Texas journalist Hilton Greer had taken place in winter, banks of snow would have lined both sides of Superior Street, and fresh snow would have clung to the branches of pine trees so tall they seemed to brush the poster-blue sky above the city.

On the coldest of days, temperatures in Duluth could plummet as low as minus forty degrees. The surface of Lake Superior turned into a solid sheet of gray ice, and local residents did not venture outside without warm wool undergarments beneath even their most fashionable attire of fur-lined boots, coats, hats, mitts, and mufflers to protect their extremities from frostbite. Even if the literary event that Winifred and Marguerite attended took place in spring or summer, they would have worn warm wraps over their dresses, for even in summer, wind that blew over the surface of the great lake was capable of raising goose bumps on unprotected skin.[1]

Whatever the weather that long ago afternoon, the two high school classmates would have dressed appropriately. They had grown up in Duluth and were as accustomed to the harsh climate as they were to the sight of fish merchants, lumber jacks, cross-country skiers, and men in Native American dress who came into Duluth from nearby reservations to negotiate mineral lease contracts in the law offices of these young women's fathers.

The streetcar passed through the middle of the mercantile district, where shop windows and sidewalk vendors displayed an assortment of wares, from guns, skis, fishing gear, and the red-checkered woolen shirts and caps worn by iron workers, to fur-lined skates, the latest fashions in ready-to-wear and Duluth-manufactured Mackinaws, overcoats that were the rage in cities throughout the country. But on this particular afternoon, even the most fashionable of dresses could not have lured the two young ladies from their seats before the streetcar reached their destination. A young Minnesota native named Sinclair Lewis was scheduled to read from his latest work of fiction, and Winifred and Marguerite were eager to hear him speak. Although Lewis was merely five years older than they, his ironic portrayals of middle-class Midwesterners already were attracting the attention of major literary critics in New York.[2] No doubt, the success of a writer so near Winifred and Marguerite's age fueled their secret aspirations, for both had been composing poems and stories since they were children and had entertained fantasies of becoming writers.

Within ten years, the women would achieve a measure of literary success—Marguerite Culkin Banning as a popular novelist and Winifred Mahon Sanford as the author of short stories. But if Winifred and Marguerite attracted the attention of Sinclair Lewis, the source of that attraction was not the young women's literary talents. As their senior pictures in the Duluth Central High School's 1907 yearbook attest, both Marguerite and Winifred were attractive.

Standing five feet seven inches, with a slim waist, a dreamy smile, a dimpled chin, and dark blond hair piled atop her head, Winifred epitomized Susan E. Meyer's description of Charles Gibson's iconic Gibson Girl in both looks and personality:

> She was taller than the other women currently seen in the pages of magazines, infinitely more spirited and independent, yet altogether feminine. She appeared in a stiff shirtwaist, her soft hair piled into a chignon.... She was poised and patrician. Though always well bred, there often lurked a flash of mischief in her eyes.[3]

Winifred was only five years old when Charles Gibson's idealized pen and ink drawings of American women first appeared on the covers of U.S. magazines, but by the time she entered high school, the Gibson Girl had become a popular icon that represented qualities that were celebrated in America at the time, including independence, resourcefulness, and a love of adventure. At the turn of the twentieth century, the problems associated with the Civil War were in the past, and Americans were looking forward with optimism to a new century, unconcerned about events taking place beyond their country's borders. During the years between 1900 and the start of World War I in 1914, Gibson's drawings decorated everything from wallpaper and china plates to matchboxes and umbrella stands. More importantly, the Gibson Girl became the model for an entire generation of modern American women.

We can only imagine the thoughts that went through Sinclair Lewis's mind when these two attractive females entered the room where he was to speak. By Lewis's own admission, he was an unattractive youth, and although he yearned for the attention of beautiful women, he was shy and uncomfortable in their presence and began to sweat when they came near him. Perhaps when he saw Winifred and Marguerite, he smoothed his already thinning hair over his forehead and covered his acne-scarred cheek with the palm of one hand. Or perhaps, if they had entered quietly and taken seats in the back of the room, he was not aware of the two young women until they were introduced to him at the reception that followed his reading.

Winifred, or "Winnie" as she was affectionately called by her classmates, was accustomed to the attention of male admirers. When she was fourteen, a thirteen-year-old classmate challenged another of her admirers to a duel for her affections. The note sent to Max. A. Pulford by the challenger no longer exists, but Pulford's handwritten acceptance, dated February 25, 1904, reads:

> Dear W. H. [Wayland] Sanford
> Dear Sir, I am most pleased to except [sic] your challenge. We will duel with boxing gloves at 4:30 P.M. Friday in Mr. P. A. Poirier's shack. Hoping to see you at an early hour.
> I remain,
> Your humble servant
> Max A. Pulford[4]

Whether this duel was ever fought is unclear, but the note is a testament to young Winifred's charms.

Not only was she beautiful, the caption beneath her picture in the Duluth Central High School yearbook from her senior year reveals that her classmates and teachers recognized her intelligence: "The manner in which 'Winnie' contrives

Winifred Mahon as she looked during her senior year at Duluth High School, circa 1908.

such a twinkling smile has long since been an insolvable mystery.... [High grades] have been a matter of fact with her ever since March 16, 1890. Here's wishing her every possible success."[5]

Ranked eleventh in a class of 103 students, Winifred graduated from Duluth High School with high honors.[6] Her parents were proud of their eldest daughter's accomplishment, but they could hardly have been surprised, for academic achievement was the norm in the Mahon and Brooks families. Winifred's maternal grandfather, Samuel Brooks, had earned the titles of doctor and reverend, and her grandmother Hannah Elizabeth Balch Brooks was descended from an old and accomplished Massachusetts family. Samuel and Hannah, with their two young daughters, moved from their home state of Massachusetts to Michigan when Samuel accepted a teaching appointment at the University of Michigan.

In "Fannie Baker," a nonfiction story that Winifred composed for the pleasure of her young daughters, she provides a glimpse into the lives of her maternal grandparents. The story revolves around a china doll named Fannie Baker that was handed down through several generations of females in the Brooks extended family. In this story, Winifred portrays her maternal grandparents as genteel, religious, well educated, and prosperous enough to travel by train to Boston and to vacation at a lakeside resort each summer. The father in this story is a minister, and the mother does not sew on Sunday because doing so would violate the family's religious beliefs. The entire family attends church services twice each Sunday, and the children are discouraged from bringing Fannie Baker to church because she might cause them to be inattentive to their father's sermon.[7]

Winifred's paternal grandparents endured circumstances that were quite different from those of her maternal grandparents. George Charles Mahon and Sarah L'Estrange Mahon migrated to the United States from King's County, Ireland, after suffering the effects of one of Ireland's severe economic depressions. When George Mahon, his wife, and their two young sons moved to Detroit, Michigan, Winifred's father, Henry, was only two years old. A short time later, the family relocated to Boston to be near Harvard University, where George Mahon hoped to enroll his sons when they were old enough to attend college. But long before the Mahon boys reached college age, their father changed his mind about the appropriateness of a Harvard education for his sons and moved the family back to Michigan.

In "A Victorian Grandmother," Winifred portrays her paternal grandmother as a stern, hard-working woman who valued thrift, disdained luxuries, and had a strong sense of right and wrong. Born ten years before Queen Victoria ascended to the throne of England, Sarah Mahon clung to traditional European values and customs and never hesitated to express her opinion of modern American lifestyles. She strongly disapproved of the changes that she witnessed taking place in the American family around the turn of the twentieth century. She fretted about the lack of discipline meted out to her grandchildren and disapproved of married women leaving their homes to attend "silly club meetings." Winifred describes Sarah Mahon as a "rock upon which others were dashed to spray," but she balances her portrayal of this stern, high-minded woman with the revelation that, although Sarah Mahon despised sentimentality, she was capable of deep and genuine emotions.[8]

In an action that appears almost out of character for such a frugal couple, Sarah and George Mahon purchased a vacation cottage in the Michigan resort of Charlevoix. It was in Charlevoix that the Mahon family met the Brooks family when the latter came to the resort with a group of Baptists to conduct a Chautauqua meeting. Samuel and Hannah Brooks enjoyed their stay at the resort so much that they returned the following summer and eventually purchased a vacation cottage. Thus Helen Marie Brooks and Henry Symes Mahon renewed their acquaintance each year.

Eventually, they fell in love and became engaged, and on October 24, 1888, they married in Kalamazoo, Michigan. Soon after the wedding, the newlyweds moved to Duluth, Minnesota, where Henry, a recent graduate of the University of Michigan Law School, set about establishing a prosperous law practice. His practice became so successful that the young couple was able to enjoy a comfortable, upper-middle-class lifestyle in a bustling community that had emerged only recently from its frontier period. They enjoyed boating on Lake Superior, attending social functions at the Duluth Yacht Club, taking part in church services at the First Baptist Church, and participating in numerous social, cultural, and philanthropic activities.

On March 16, 1890, a year and a half after Henry and Helen Mahon married, their first child was born. The baby was a girl with blue eyes and blond curls, and the couple named her Winifred Balch Mahon. Just four days after Helen gave birth to Winifred, a birth of a different sort took place in New York, when representatives of sixty-one women's clubs from around the country came together to organize the General Federation of Women's Clubs. This nonpartisan, nondenominational association of women would provide the Mahons' new baby and other females of her generation with educational and service opportunities that had been unavailable to previous generations of American women.

When Winifred was just eighteen months old, Helen Mahon gave birth to a boy baby, George Brooks Mahon, whose constitution was so weak that he died before his first birthday. Within a year of George's death, Helen became pregnant once again. Winifred was three years and seven months when Helen Elizabeth Mahon was born, and from the beginning, Winifred adored her little sister and was soon composing stories in which "Baby Helen" was a major character. In "Memories," a composition that Winifred wrote in a childish cursive script on lined paper, Helen is a one-year-old toddler with brown eyes and brown hair. In this story, Helen and three-year-old Winifred accompany their parents to the train station to meet their maternal grandparents, who are traveling from Kalamazoo, Michigan, to Duluth to see Baby Helen for the first time. On the way to the train station, Winifred picks a bouquet of pretty grasses to present to her grandmother, and when the grandparents arrive, they give Winifred a souvenir glass from the 1893 Chicago World's Fair, where they had stopped off on their way to Duluth.[9]

In a second manuscript, also entitled "Memories," a slightly older Winifred takes a summer trip to Kalamazoo with her mother and sister. During this visit to see her grandparents and extended family, Winifred attends kindergarten for the first time with her cousins and enjoys a trip to the lakeside resort in Charlevoix with her mother's family. In a third segment of "Memories," Winifred recalls a trip to Kalamazoo, when she was five years old, that didn't turn out quite like she had expected. She had expected to accompany her father on a business trip to Chicago before going on to Kalamazoo to visit her grandparents. Speaking of herself in the third person, Winifred tells about meeting Mr. and Mrs. Pulford, friends of her father's who lived in Chicago:

> When they arrived at Chicago, her father left her at the hotel, while he did his business. She went to the window and looked out, but the crowds of people frightened her so that she staid [sic] in the other part of the room all the rest of the time. It seemed very long to Winifred before her father came back. He told her that he had found it necessary to remain at Chicago, but he knew of someone who would take her on to Kalamazoo. This man was very good to her and bought a lovely dinner on the train. It was very late when she arrived at her destination, where Grandma and Grandpa meet [sic] her. She had expected to stay here only a few days, but it was four months before she arrived safely at home with a friend of her mother's.[10]

These three childhood accounts of life in the Mahon household portray a loving and emotionally stable family. Pictures of the Mahon home and the nursery that Winifred shared with Helen provide additional evidence that the Mahon children were brought up in an environment that was financially as well as emotionally secure. Even during the Panic of 1907, when more than four million Americans were unemployed, the Mahon family continued to participate in the social and cultural life of Duluth, to maintain an extensive library of books, and to attend plays, parties at the yacht club, and concerts put on by the local orchestra. Henry Mahon maintained his membership in the Duluth Yacht Club and continued to participate in competitive water sports and to enjoy hunting trips into the nearby Minnesota forest.

When Winifred and Helen reached school age, their parents enrolled them in Duluth public schools, where they received an excellent public school education. The faculty pictured in the Duluth Central High School's 1907 yearbook held degrees from some of the most prestigious universities in the United States, and course listings in the yearbook indicate that Duluth Central High School students received a classical education. Because American literature was not taught in U.S. high schools and universities until the 1920s, the Mahon sisters' formal education did not include the study of American literature. However, letters that Winifred exchanged with Helen when they were adults indicate that from an early age they were avid readers whose formal schooling was supplemented by further exploration at home.

But as ideal as Winifred's and Helen's childhood appears to have been, neither a loving family nor a patrician lifestyle could shield them from the tragedy that befell the Mahons a few days after Winifred's high school graduation. One Sunday

Winifred and her baby sister, Helen, with their parents, Helen and Henry Mahon, in the front yard of the Mahon home in Duluth, Minnesota.

Helen and Winifred Mahon, circa 1897–1898.

morning in June 1908, Henry Mahon suffered a fatal heart attack. Articles printed in Duluth newspapers at the time of Henry's death told that he had practiced law in Duluth for twenty-two years and that he was a respected community leader who had appeared to be in excellent health and who had participated rigorously in local sporting events. One of Henry's close friends said he was the highest type of private citizen, and another newspaper reported that the death of a forty-eight-year-old man who was so robust and active was a shock to the entire community.[11]

Henry Mahon's sudden death had an even more devastating effect on his wife and children and his widowed mother, who was visiting the family when he died. Dealing with her own loss and watching the people she loved suffer theirs left a lasting impression upon the Mahons' oldest daughter—one that contributed to the development of what Mary Sanford Gordon described in an interview as "Mother's great empathy for the human condition." This family tragedy also provided Winifred with experiences that would later enable her to portray fictional characters who exhibit great dignity in the face of tragic circumstances.[12]

Less than three months after Henry Mahon's death, Winifred left Duluth to attend Mount Holyoke College in South Hadley, Massachusetts. Leaving home for the first time can be a difficult experience for a teenager under the best of circumstances, and with Winifred's separation from her family and friends coming only three months after her father's death, the stresses of adjusting to her first year of college were amplified. Recalling the difficulties that she had experienced during her freshman year in conversations with her daughters many years later, Winifred said she felt like an outsider in New England. She not only missed her mother and sister, she missed Duluth's diversity that she was accustomed to encountering in Duluth, a city that encompassed a variety of nationalities and social classes. Her Holyoke classmates thought Duluth was the hinterlands, and they expressed surprise that someone who came from such a place could exhibit sophisticated manners and dress in fashionable attire, as Winifred obviously did. These classmates were even more surprised to learn that Winifred had purchased her wardrobe in Duluth. Being the center of this kind of attention was an uncomfortable experience for the reserved teenager.

Winifred remained at Holyoke until the end of her freshman year. Then she returned to Duluth, where her grandmother Mahon and grandfather Brooks were now living with her mother and sister. Winifred stayed in Duluth until fall 1910, when she resumed her education at the University of Michigan. A year later, after Helen graduated from Duluth Central High School in 1911, she and her mother also moved to Ann Arbor, Michigan, and the three Mahon women lived together in a rented apartment near the university campus, where Winifred and Helen continued their education.[13]

The list of activities that appears under Winifred's picture in the 1911 *Michiganensian* indicates that her college experience at the University of Michigan was much happier and more productive than her freshman year at Mount Holyoke. Winifred consistently earned A's at the University of Michigan; she pledged Alpha Phi Sorority, was elected to Mortar Board, and became a member of the service organization Wyvern. As a member of the writing club Stylus, she composed poems and short stories and wrote a scholarly article entitled "England and the Home-Rule Question" that appeared in the *South Atlantic Quarterly* in October 1913. The focus of this article was the legislative independence of Ireland and the Home Rule bill that was introduced in the British Parliament in 1912. This was a subject that would have been of particular interest to this granddaughter of Irish immigrants.

Winifred also was active in the University of Michigan's chapter of the Women's League, an organization that campaigned for the passage of the Nineteenth Amendment to the U.S. Constitution—an amendment whose ratification in 1920 granted American women the right to vote. According to Winifred's daughter Helen, from the time Winifred served as president of the college chapter of the Women's League in 1913 until her death in 1983, she remained "a quiet feminist" who actively supported the causes of independent women.[14]

After graduating from the University of Michigan in 1913 with an AB degree in English and a Phi Beta Kappa key, Winifred accepted a teaching position in Sault Ste. Marie, Michigan, one of the oldest and snowiest cities in the United States. Located on the U.S. side of the Canadian border, Sault Ste. Marie was separated from its twin city of the same name, in Ontario, by the St. Mary's River. When Winifred recalled her first teaching assignment in conversations with her daughters, she recounted mostly positive experiences. She loved the children in her classes and quickly bonded with their parents, many of whom spoke both French and English. In fact, many years after Winifred left Sault Ste. Marie, she returned to attend a school reunion so that she might renew acquaintance with her former students.

Despite her satisfaction with this teaching assignment, for some unknown reason, Winifred resigned her position in Sault Ste. Marie after only three years and accepted a teaching position in Idaho. Her experiences in this second location were neither pleasant nor rewarding. She later told her daughters that her class in Idaho was made up almost entirely of "hulking boys twice her size." She felt isolated from the rural community, and by the end of the school year, she had tired of teaching school and was ready to explore other career opportunities.[15]

CHAPTER

TWO

A Wonderful Time

NEW YORK,

NEW YORK,

1916–1918

NOW IN HER MID-TWENTIES, UNEM-
ployed, and with no immediate prospects for marriage, Winifred took advantage of
the opportunity to travel. Mary Sanford Gordon explained that her mother came
of age at a wonderful time in American history for women, a time when young
single women of the middle class enjoyed freedoms that had not been available
to their mothers and grandmothers. With the advent of railroad cars, and with an
ever-increasing number of railroad tracks crisscrossing the country, a young single
woman could travel about in relative comfort and safety.

If Winifred recorded her travel experiences during this period of her life, those
writings have long since been destroyed or lost. But like many young people who
had an interest in the arts and came of age in the early modern period, Winifred
was attracted eventually to New York City. She applied and was accepted into a
course of study for prospective librarians offered by the New York Public Library.
And just as they had done when Winifred moved to Ann Arbor to attend the University of Michigan, her mother and sister also relocated to New York. For a time,
the three Mahon women shared a rented apartment in a new apartment building
at 1455 Undercliff Avenue in the Bronx, located east of the Harlem River in the
vicinity of the Washington Bridge. This apartment building was surrounded by a

bustling middle-class neighborhood that had experienced rapid growth after the installation of the New York subway system in 1904 connected the previously rural area to Manhattan.[1]

Although some parts of the Bronx retained their rural charm, in 1916, Morris Heights was a suburban neighborhood with paved streets and newly constructed apartment buildings that offered the latest in modern conveniences. Gas and electricity and, in some apartment buildings, elevator service and central heating were available to residents. Refrigerators, kitchen ranges, and bookcases were standard features in two-bedroom apartments that rented for as little as twenty dollars a month, and some landlords provided access to a centrally located telephone, an unheard of luxury in many parts of the country. And for subway fares as low as a nickel, Bronx residents could travel on the subway system's elevated tracks to jobs in Manhattan. Conveniences and amenities such as these were unheard of in Europe, and as a result, many middle-class European immigrants, primarily of Irish, German, or Jewish descent, settled in the South Bronx in the early decades of the twentieth century. Consequently, the area surrounding Winifred's apartment building encompassed the ethnic diversity that she had missed when she left Duluth to attend Mount Holyoke.[2]

The Bronx had much to offer residents in the way of cultural and recreational opportunities. The New York Botanical Garden, the New York Zoological Garden (the Bronx Zoo), and a branch of the New York Public Library were all located there, and a colonnade on the campus of New York University offered a beautiful view of the Harlem River Valley. Numerous parks and playgrounds offered outdoor activities like golfing, sailing, and boating, as well as opportunities to attend athletic events, such as track meets, running marathons, and semiprofessional baseball games. Ice skating on area lakes and ponds was a popular outdoor activity in wintertime, and restaurants and shops along subway lines offered year-round dining and shopping for residents and visitors alike.[3]

Several famous literary figures had lived in the Bronx after the turn of the century. In 1901, Samuel Clemens moved his family to a rented country estate where he hoped country living would restore his wife's deteriorating health. In 1903, the novelist Theodore Dreiser and his wife lived there in a small, furnished apartment, while Dreiser worked as a laborer on the railroad and recovered from a mental breakdown after the scathing reception of his first novel. And for a short time in 1917, the Russian author Leon Trotsky and his wife occupied one of the newly constructed apartment buildings before they moved back to Russia to take part in the Bolshevik Revolution. No evidence exists that Winifred was acquainted with any of these authors, but many well-known and would-be writers resided in or visited

New York City during the years that Winifred lived and worked there. Because she was employed by the public library, where many literary events took place, it is not unlikely that she came into contact with prominent literary figures like H. L. Mencken, or renewed her acquaintance with Sinclair Lewis.[4]

By all accounts, the years Winfred lived in New York were some of the happiest in her life. Wayland Sanford mentioned her pleasure with suburban living several times in his letters to her during the early months of her stay there. More than once he teasingly expressed jealousy that she was so enchanted with life in New York that she sometimes neglected to answer his letters. He addressed many to Miss Winifred Balch Mahon, 1455 Undercliff Ave., New York, New York, between 1916 and 1919, and it is these letters that supply many of the details about Winifred's sojourn in New York City.[5]

A 1912 graduate of Amherst College, Wayland had graduated from Duluth High School one year after Winifred, and he was in his first year of law school at the University of Michigan when he began to correspond with her. His early letters are filled with news of activities that were taking place on the University of Michigan campus and with reports on his academic progress. His tone in these letters is friendly, teasing, and completely devoid of romantic declarations. In one letter, he confided that he had a new girlfriend who was "most attractive." In another, he told Winifred that he wouldn't consider her to be a confirmed New Yorker until she added smoking cigarettes and drinking cocktails to her list of accomplishments.[6] In letters dated November 27, 1916, and March, 5, 1917, Wayland mentioned his infatuation with two different co-eds and declared that he was enjoying a "most romantic year." In one of these letters, he asked Winifred to relay his congratulations to her sister Helen, who recently had married Maurice Toulme, one of Winifred's University of Michigan classmates. In this letter, Wayland referred to the bride and groom, who were approximately his age, as "children." This is a clear indication that Wayland was not anticipating his own marriage in the near future.[7]

In several of Wayland's early letters to Winifred, he either apologized for not having written sooner or he lamented the fact that she had neglected to write to him.[8] His concerns in these letters are typical of a college student in that they focus upon local and national events that affected student life on the University of Michigan campus—prohibition, the university president's retirement, and "the recent replacement of venerated law professors by legal theorists." Of even greater concern to him was news that graduates of the University of Michigan Law School would no longer be admitted to the bar without taking an examination. Wayland complained because he would be one of the first law school graduates in the United States required to take the test. However, in this same letter, he reported that he

Winifred shortly before she moved to New York City and got her hair bobbed, circa 1916.

had received high academic marks and warned Winifred that, in the near future, she might not be the only one with a Phi Beta Kappa key. Wayland's prediction came true a few months later when he, too, was selected for membership into the prestigious honor society.[9]

In a letter written on November 27, 1916, Wayland indicated that both he and Winifred had made investments in the stock market. He told her that he and a friend had invested in ten shares of U.S. Steel on a ten point margin and wrote, "That outrageous German U-boat came over here and sank a ship within a stone's throw of American waters, a panic struck the market, and we sold out at 112, after the stock had dropped to 109." Wayland was probably referring in this letter to an incident that took place in early October 1916, when a U-boat under the command of Hans Rose sank a Canadian ship in international waters off the coast of New England. Although the United States had maintained a position of neutrality in the European conflicts for two years, U-boats patrolled the eastern seacoast and ventured into U.S. waters from time to time. Their presence, when it occurred, precipitated a flux in the price of stocks. Wayland also commented in this letter on the rising price of Nevada Consolidated stock, which Winifred apparently owned. He asked her how it felt to be rich.[10] In another of Wayland's letters, in which he responded to Winifred's words of encouragement regarding his lack of job offers as he approached graduation, he made his first mention of oil properties. "I have no more news from Duluth," he wrote, "except that father has gone to Oklahoma to look for an oil well!"[11]

The subject of war first appeared in a letter that Wayland wrote to his mother on April 8, 1917, when he reported that he and other male students at the University of Michigan were engaged in "more or less haphazard military training." In January 1917, American military personnel had intercepted a telegram sent from Germany's Foreign Secretary Arthur Zimmerman to the foreign minister of Mexico. In this telegram, Zimmerman promised that in exchange for Mexico's aid in defeating the Allies, Germany would return the lands that Mexico had ceded to the United States at the conclusion of the Mexican-American War. In February and March 1917, German submarines targeted several American ships, killing passengers as well as seamen. In response to these acts of aggression, President Woodrow Wilson went before Congress and requested a declaration of war. Although both houses of the legislature approved the president's request, war was not officially declared until December 27, 1917. At the time of President Wilson's request, the United States had only a small volunteer army that lacked experience in the kind of warfare that was being waged in Europe. Before the country could play a significant role in the Allied effort, troops had to be drafted and trained, thus the haphazard training that Wayland mentioned in his letter to his mother. In words that reveal both Wayland's idealism and his patriotism, he argued with his mother regarding her negative attitude toward U.S. involvement in the war.[12] Their disagreement is indicative of the division that occurred in the United States in the months that preceded the country's entry into World War I.

Ten days after writing this letter to his mother, Wayland asked Winifred if people in "urban New York" were as excited about the declaration of war as people in "provincial Ann Arbor."[13] He soon learned that Winifred shared his mother's opinion that the United States should maintain a position of neutrality.

In a letter written on April 8, 1917, Wayland answered his mother's questions about a job offer that he had received from a leading law firm in Detroit and told her of his wish to return to Duluth and open an independent law firm. He expressed the opinion that his hometown offered great opportunity for a young lawyer right out of law school.[14] Located on the shores of a lake so big that it had oceanic tides, Duluth was a large industrial seaport and a major exporter of American goods such as timber from northern Minnesota forests and iron from one of the largest iron ore deposits in the world. In addition to economic opportunities, the Duluth area offered young men of Wayland's age and disposition recreational opportunities such as boating, skiing, and hunting.

In a letter dated April 18, 1917, Wayland sought Winifred's opinion of the job offer in Detroit. He noted that Winifred's course of study at the New York Public Library would soon be ending. He invited her, along with her mother, to attend commencement exercises at the University of Michigan, where he was slated to deliver the valedictory address. However, in a letter written a few weeks later, Wayland expressed doubts that there would be much of a commencement ceremony because military affairs were now "occupying the entire stage." He worried that his fraternity might be forced to disband because so many fraternity members were signing up for military duty. And in a statement that indicated that his friendship with Winifred had become romantic, Wayland referred to a recent misunderstanding between them and wrote that he was "casting about for the attitude of reconcilement most appropriate for unrequited lovers."[15]

By May 2, 1917, Winifred had completed her course of study at the public library and had begun a new job as a librarian. In a letter written to her on this date, Wayland congratulated her on her satisfaction with the job and expressed his hope that she wouldn't turn into a "chronic New Yorker." In a comment that indicates that Wayland was beginning to think of a future that included Winifred, he wrote that although he had not yet decided where he was going to practice law, New York City was automatically eliminated from his list of possible locations. He had determined that he could not afford the high cost of living there for the five or six years it would take to build a profitable law practice.[16]

With Winifred settled into a new career, her mother may recently have returned to Duluth, for in a letter that Wayland wrote to Winifred on June 16, 1917, he mentioned that her mother was no longer in the city.[17] Questions regarding Wayland's military enlistment appeared in his letters to Winifred and in letters to his mother after the U.S. Congress enacted military conscription through selective service in May 1917. With military service now a requirement instead of an option, his mother encouraged him to enlist in the navy. She reasoned that the country needed more ships and that his knowledge of boats and sailing could be useful to the war effort. After much deliberation, Wayland followed his mother's advice and enlisted in the navy. On May 31, 1917, he sent Winifred a Western Union telegram from Newport, Rhode Island, telling her that he was to start military training the following Monday and would like to pay her a visit when he passed through New York City.[18]

In a letter that he wrote to Winifred a few days after his visit, he told her that he had had a more difficult time saying goodbye to her than to anyone in Duluth or Ann Arbor, and that if he had stayed with her longer, he might have said things that he ought not to have said. He promised to return to New York at his first opportunity and expressed the hope that she would be happy to see him when he did.[19] Apparently she was, because less than a month later, he and Winifred became engaged—the development of their romance hastened, no doubt, by Wayland's impending deployment.

On June 28, 1917, Wayland expressed relief that Winifred's mother approved of their engagement.[20] Helen Mahon's approval probably came as a surprise to no one except the prospective groom. Wayland and Winifred had been friends since they were in elementary school. Both their fathers were lawyers, and both their families were respected members of the Duluth community. Although Wayland could not yet provide the kind of lifestyle to which both he and Winifred were accustomed, he was the top graduate of the University of Michigan Law School class of 1917, and as such, his economic prospects were good. Of equal importance to Winifred's future happiness, Wayland was not threatened by his fiancée's intelligence, for he had grown up in the presence of a highly intelligent woman. His mother was an alumnus of Oberlin College who had gone on to take graduate level courses at the Harvard Annex (which later became Radcliff College). Correspondence that Wayland and his mother exchanged indicates that the two often engaged in intellectual discussions that were as deep as they were far ranging.

Wayland's letter to Winifred on July 1, 1917, contains the words of a man unreservedly in love: "The days when letters come from you are bright and joyful, whether the sun shines or not, and whether other things go right or wrong . . . I take back all I ever said about lovers being foolish. They live in another world, where things are different."[21]

In his next letter to Winifred, Wayland referred to difficulties (probably sexual in nature) that the young lovers were experiencing in their relationship because the war had forced the postponement of their wedding: "If it weren't for this blasted war—but what is the use of speculating?" Wayland wrote. "We'll just have to do our best with things as we find them ... I'm no advocate of a 'laissez-faire' code of morals in ordinary times—but anything else in the present situation is simply useless."[22] Wayland confessed that he had been dreaming of "things as they might be" if it were not wartime, and said, "The time is coming when we'll make those dreams come true!" He told Winifred that when naval officers had asked for volunteers for general service, he had been tempted to stay safely on guard duty, but knowing that Winifred would want him to do what his "better nature told him to do," he had volunteered. His better nature told him that if he refused to serve, either he had enlisted in order to be exempt from the draft or he was too selfish to serve his country. In Wayland's mind, such motivation would be judged immoral by Kant's "Categorical Imperative," Kipling's "If," and what Wayland referred to as "Sanford's common sense."[23]

Despite the seriousness of Wayland's remarks to Winifred, he revealed his impish nature by playing a trick on his mother when he wrote to tell her he was engaged. He provided the name of his fiancée in Morse code, something he knew his mother couldn't decipher, and hinted at the young woman's identity by telling his mother that one of his fiancée's names was Balch. Mrs. Sanford, who apparently didn't know that Winifred's middle name was Balch, mistakenly concluded that Wayland was marrying a college classmate of his from Buffalo whom she did not like. According to Wayland's report of this incident to Winifred, his mother thought this young woman was "a vampire on the trail of [her] susceptible son."[24]

Wayland corrected the misunderstanding when he wrote to his mother on July 4, 1917. In this letter, he assumed a more serious tone when he confided that he considered himself most fortunate that Winifred had agreed to marry him:

Winifred has been the one bright star in the sky for me ever since I can remember ... As a matter of fact, I never did have much hope. I always thought of Winifred as being away out of reach—way above what I could ever hope for. But when I compared the other girls I knew to her, and always with the same result—there never was any real comparison—I kept thinking that I would just ask her, anyway, when things got straightened around; not with any idea that she'd have me, but because any of the others would have been substitutes, at best.[25]

Wayland also confessed that the real reason he had signed up for training at the naval academy in Annapolis was so he could be close to Winifred. Then he recounted the events that had led to their engagement. He had arrived at Winifred's apartment early on a Sunday morning but hadn't been able to muster up the courage to propose until Sunday evening. To his astonishment, she didn't laugh at his proposal. He told his mother that both he and Winifred were opposed to long engagements and he expressed his hope that she would take the news of their engagement as well as Winifred's mother had taken it.

In a letter that Wayland wrote to Winifred that same day, he mentioned that she had changed jobs once again and had begun working in "the telephone building," doing work that was clerical instead of literary. This change may have occurred because Wayland encouraged his fiancée to seek a better-paying job, for he also expressed guilt that she was stuck in "hot New York, working in an office from morning till night, coming home all tired out, just to go back and read about rate-fixing all the next day . . . ." In letters that he wrote to Winifred on July 3 and 6, Wayland indicated that both he and she were in the process of conveying the news of their engagement to their friends, and more importantly, to "former suitors."[26]

In these and subsequent letters to Winifred, Wayland expressed conflicting feelings about signing on for general military service. He attempted to alleviate Winifred's fears about his safety, assuring her that he was more likely to be assigned to a ship than to a trench. In one letter, he confessed that when the opportunity to take an honorable discharge had presented itself, his sense of honor had prevented him from doing so, and on August 6, 1917, he wrote, "I have no 'lust to kill,' nor do I long for the smoke of battle. But now that I'm definitely in the war, and in it to stay, the quicker I get into the middle of it the better I'll like it."[27]

Winifred was just as eager to be married to Wayland as he was to be married to her, if not more so, for on August 9, 1917, he responded to her suggestion that she also sign up for naval service. "I'm afraid the navy is no place for you as a yeowoman [sic]," he told her. "We'd probably be shipped miles apart after about a week, and then we'd be worse off than we are now." He was more amenable to Winifred's suggestion that they move their wedding date forward. "Would you really be 'game' to get married now?" he asked. "We'll have to consider the matter. When I come to New York [on] Labor Day . . . maybe we'll decide to hie [sic] ourselves to a justice of the peace and do it—what do you say?"[28]

On August 10, Wayland wrote that he had been recommended for an officers' training school that was soon to be established and suggested that Winifred stop worrying about torpedoes and start worrying about how they would live on a military salary of $150 a month. He begged her not to be disappointed that his entry into the officers' training school would delay their marriage. He told her that in

Wayland Sanford
in his World War I
naval uniform,
circa 1917.

future years she would be more comfortable telling people that her husband had served his country as a naval officer during the Great War than having to explain why he was practicing law while other men were serving their country.[29]

Despite his comment that his admission into training school would delay their marriage, on August 22, Wayland responded favorably to pressure from Winifred to get married as soon as he could take a weekend leave. He asked her how much a marriage license would cost and told her that his real objection to marrying so soon had more to do with their future than with the present. When his military service was finished, he would still have to establish himself as a lawyer.[30] And when he wrote to Winifred again on August 25, 1917, he made sure that she understood the reality of his financial situation:

I'm not only poor—I'm destitute—I left college owing about $800, borrowed to enable me to complete my education; and all the funds I have in the world are the $41 I received yesterday for my monthly pay. It is a jolt not only to my pride but to my conscience to think of getting married under such conditions—and I want you to think it over very carefully. You see it isn't simply a question of not having much money—it's a question of not having *any*. So I want you to be sure you understand just what the situation is before you decide . . . I have no property or income to which we could turn—our sole support must be my earning power. I'm urging this upon you simply so you'll know what you're getting into. Under ordinary conditions I wouldn't even think of getting married under such circumstances. Under present conditions—well, if you still want to rush in where angels would fear to tread, it's simply a question of when I get to New York.[31]

These comments indicate that Wayland held traditional views concerning the roles and responsibilities of married men and women, but despite his misgivings, he and Winifred proceeded to make plans to wed at the first opportunity. On August 29, he gave his consent for her to accept a gift of money from her mother to finance a short honeymoon. He wrote that he had applied for a leave but did not know yet if it would be granted. When he wrote again two days later, he was still unsure that his request would be granted. Concerning the news that she was shopping for a trousseau, he wrote, "Too bad that I can't provide myself with a trousseau, too, but . . . the regulation USN wardrobe will have to suffice for my wedding raiment, inasmuch as the regulations forbid my wearing anything else, and I couldn't afford to buy my clothes if they didn't." He added, "Do tell me what a negligee is, though!"[32]

Two weeks after Wayland wrote this letter, his application for a weekend leave still had not been granted. Rather than keep Winifred in a state of uncertainty, he suggested that they postpone their wedding and urged her to make alternate plans for her vacation rather than waste it. When, by September 13, his request for a leave was still pending, he told Winifred to enjoy her vacation. The very next day, his application for a five-day pass was granted.[33]

What happened next became a favorite story that Winifred would repeat in later years for the entertainment of her friends, her children, and later, her grandchildren. When Wayland attempted to contact Winifred at her apartment, she had already departed and was on her way to spend the weekend with a friend on Long Island. The friend had no telephone so, hoping to intercept Winifred before she boarded the train, Wayland called Grand Central Station and had her paged. As she passed through the ticket line, she heard a voice over the loudspeaker say, "Miss Winifred Mahon, calling Miss Winifred Mahon." Winifred heard her name and thought, Imagine that! Someone else in New York has a name the same as mine!

The family story ends there, and none of the remaining Sanfords know if Winifred finally realized she was the one being paged, or if Wayland managed to contact her some other way. But the two did connect somehow, for in a letter that Wayland wrote to his mother on September 8, he told her that he and Winifred had married at 12:30 p.m. on September 7 in New York City, in a "regular wedding" at The Church of the Transfiguration.[34]

The Church of the Transfiguration had a long, romantic history. Its first rector had sheltered escaped slaves during the Civil War and had also maintained a bread line for the needy. In 1870, when a highly respected New York minister refused to conduct the funeral of the actor George Holland, Holland's friends said, "The little church around the corner does that kind of thing." As a result of its reputation for compassion, The Little Church Around the Corner—as The Church of the Transfiguration came to be known to native New Yorkers—developed a close association with the Actors Guild. By the time Winifred and Wayland were married there, it had become a popular site for weddings and other ceremonies.

On the day of Wayland and Winifred's wedding, Winifred—whose parents and grandparents were Baptists and did not believe in christening babies—was baptized. Her baptism may have been required by the Episcopal diocese or by the priest who performed the wedding ceremony. Wayland had already been christened as an infant in the Pilgrim Congregational Church in Duluth, Minnesota.

After what Wayland described as a "regular wedding" with his and Winifred's friend Mary Bonner serving as bridesmaid and the husband of one of Winifred's Holyoke roommates (a Mr. Fox) serving as best man, Winifred's mother hosted a luncheon with a "real wedding cake" for the bride and groom and their guests. Besides Mary Bonner and the best man and his wife, the guest list included several of Winifred's New York friends and three great aunts from the Balch family. After the wedding luncheon, the newlyweds departed for Long Beach, where they spent their short honeymoon at the Hotel Nassau in a room that overlooked the sea. On September 8, Wayland penned the following words to his mother: "Dear Mother— Well, I little thought when I left Ann Arbor to join the navy that I'd be taking a wedding trip so soon—but here I am, and here *she* is—you have a daughter-in-law."[35]

When Wayland's five-day leave came to an end, he returned to the naval base in Newport, Rhode Island, and Winifred returned to her apartment on Undercliff Avenue in the Bronx. Just two weeks later, Wayland received confirmation of his selection for the officers' training school at the naval academy in Annapolis. Although he was pleased to have qualified and grateful to receive the pay raise that would accompany this appointment, he was concerned that becoming a naval officer might lengthen his military service and further delay the start of his law career. His appointment may also have meant that he and Winifred had to keep their recent marriage a secret. So for the first six months of their marriage, Winifred remained in New York and Wayland lived on the naval base in Annapolis.

The newlyweds spent as many weekends as possible together, either at Winifred's New York apartment whenever Wayland could take a leave or at Newport Beach, where Winifred stayed with married friends who lived near the naval academy. As Wayland remarked in one of his letters, Newport was a tiresome place to reach by train, and the couple's travels, probably conducted under a cloak of secrecy, sometimes resulted in a comedy of errors. The first time Wayland spent a weekend in New York, he misread the departure schedule and missed his train back to Annapolis. Another weekend, after Winifred had stayed with him in Newport Beach, Wayland left her on the train platform with a ticket in her hand, and neither of them realized that she had left her purse at their friend's house until she reached Grand Central Station and discovered that she had no money for the subway ride to her apartment. On still another weekend, the train from Newport Beach to New York City was delayed for eight hours and Winifred was forced to spend the night in a Pullman car.

Finally, in early March 1918, after some indecision on Winifred's part, she agreed to take a leave of absence from her job so that she and Wayland could spend as much time together as possible before he was deployed. Winifred sublet her apartment in the Bronx and rented one in Wollaston, Massachusetts, that was located a short distance by trolley from where Wayland was now stationed in Boston.[36]

But when Wayland wrote to Winifred on July 17, 1918, she was back in her apartment at 1455 Undercliff Avenue. The return address stamped on the envelope of Wayland's letter read "European Waters." In his first letter to Winifred after he was deployed, Wayland, who had recently been promoted to Navy Lieutenant, complained of seasickness. This malady continued to plague him until a benevolent captain arranged for Wayland to trade jobs with an ensign who had been assigned to shore duty. Although he was forbidden from directly disclosing his location, when he wrote to Winifred on August 10, 1918, he described a scene in which he was sitting on the porch of a Mediterranean Club sipping John Collins while a band played the Hungarian Rhapsody. When he wrote again on August 21, he was permitted to disclose that he was stationed in Gibraltar. Although he was embarrassed by his seasickness and subsequent shore assignment, his transfer to a relatively safe location must have been a great relief for Winifred as well as for Wayland's parents. Recently, they had received word that their younger son, Dwight, had enlisted for military duty with the army.

On September 7, Wayland wrote that he was spending the first anniversary of their wedding rereading Winifred's letters. He asked her to supply more details about her new position with the Vulcan Company, a job that paid twenty-five dollars a week, involved a lot of filing, and required that she supervise a staff of assistants.[37]

On October 8, 1918, Wayland, who was taking lessons in Spanish, wrote that he had been spending a great deal of his time reading the Spanish newspapers. He sensed from what he read that the war might be entering its latter stages. German submarine bases in the North Sea appeared to be doomed, the ones in the Mediterranean appeared to be in grave danger, and Bulgaria had pulled out of its alliance with Germany. Although Wayland didn't think it paid to be too optimistic, these signs indicated to him that the war might be coming to an end. He wrote that since he wouldn't be home for Christmas, he was sending Winifred some pieces of hand-made Spanish lace that he had bought for her in Valencia.[38]

When Wayland wrote again a month later, he reported that he was in the midst of "great excitement." For the first time since he signed up for military service, he was close to the fighting, and as he told Winifred, the war was "ending with a flourish." He and his associates were awaiting word that the conflict was over when a superior officer interrupted Wayland's letter-writing with an order that had to be carried out immediately. Wayland finished the letter to Winifred the following day, after the armistice with Germany had been signed. Although World War I had officially ended, Wayland expressed doubts that he would return to the United States for at least another year.[39]

In letters that he wrote to Winifred after the armistice, the focus of his attention shifted from military service to plans to establish himself as a lawyer as soon as possible. He told Winifred of his intention to take the bar exam at the first possible opportunity and reiterated his desire to set up an independent law practice in Duluth. In one letter, he asked if she would be agreeable to living in his parents' temporarily vacant house. At that time, his parents were living in Kansas so that his father could pursue his interests in the oil business. In what had become a reoccurring theme in Wayland's letters to Winifred during the couple's first year of marriage, he reminded her of just how poor they would be until he got his law practice underway. In a letter dated November 19, 1918, he used a phrase that would become something of a mantra in the years to come. He told her that he was "depending on the good Lord and the Sanford luck" to bring a quick resolution to the couple's financial problems.[40]

In response to Winifred's report that a disastrous fire had burned much of the forest surrounding their hometown of Duluth, Wayland wrote, "That was a dickens of a thing, wasn't it? I can't imagine a fire traveling that way through the lightly wooded sections near Duluth. It must have been as dry as timber. And the fact that it happened on a weekend made it so much worse for Duluth people."[41]

The fire began on October 12, 1919, when sparks from a train engine ignited vegetation near the railroad tracks after a season of hot, dry weather. The blaze spread quickly from Sturgeon Lake to the shore of Lake Superior just north of Duluth destroying thirty-eight suburban communities. Over 52,000 people were injured or displaced, 1,500 square miles of timberland were blackened, and six ships in the harbor, along with three at nearby Grassy Point dock, were destroyed. The death toll from this fire rose to more than 1,000 people, and although the city of Duluth sustained no damage, morgues were set up there to contain the bodies of the suburbanites who had perished.

This fire was probably Winifred's inspiration for a short story entitled "The Forest Fire," which was published in *The American Mercury* in April 1925. The story is set in a boarding house in a pine forest like the ones that surrounded Duluth, and its central incident is an out-of-control fire. The character through whose consciousness the story is narrated is Hattie Griggs, co-owner of the Griggs Hotel—and unlike the unreliable narrators in some of Winifred's other stories, Hattie is keenly aware of the danger that an uncontainable forest fire represents. In this story's first section, she watches smoke in the distance through her kitchen window, and when a young man asks if there is danger of the fire coming their way, she replies, "You can't tell about forest fires . . . It depends on the wind."[42]

Hattie is a strong woman whose main concerns are for the comfort, safety, and propriety of the hotel's residents. In one scene, she knocks on the door of a room from which she has heard a loud commotion, and when one of the occupants opens the door partway and Hattie catches a glimpse of a "thick arm waving a bottle, a glass lying on its side, [and] a jumble of bedclothes," she tells the rowdy boarders, "I can't have such goings-on in my place. If you've got to make a saloon out of a decent hotel, you've got to do it quietly." And when a young couple appears at the hotel late at night and requests a room, Hattie hesitates to rent one to them until the girl shows a "narrow platinum wedding ring fitting so snugly against its jeweled mate."[43]

In the second section of the story, Hattie rises at 5 a.m. to prepare breakfast for her boarders, and with amazing economy, Winifred portrays a vivid picture of the men who inhabit the Griggs Hotel: "All of them ate with their noses in their plates, sipping coffee while their mouths were full, still chewing as they folded their napkins. Afterwards they filled their pockets at the toothpick bowl, and walked around digging at their gums."[44]

Hattie shows particular concern for the new bride, whose youth and vulnerability Winifred captures through a description of the young woman's hands. When a telephone call alerts the characters that the fire is headed in the direction of the hotel, the men depart to set a backfire while Hattie and the girl remain inside the hotel. As the fire approaches, Hattie moves about the property stamping out firebrands with her feet or beating them out with a wet broom. When the blaze comes dangerously close to the hotel, Hattie tells the young woman to get in her car, drive to the beach, and get into the water.

Hattie's courage and determination become even more apparent in the story's final scene, when she climbs to the roof of the hotel to remove a burning branch. Once again, Winifred uses few words to paint a vivid picture:

> The sparks were falling all around them, as they used to fall on Fourth of July nights a long time ago from Roman candles. A piece of wood no bigger than Hattie's thumb fell on the broad branch of a spruce tree behind her, and immediately the needles sizzled and blazed and shriveled. Then the next limb caught and the next.[45]

Just when it appears that the fire will devour the Griggs Hotel, the wind shifts and the fire alters course. The men return, and Hattie tells the groom his wife is down by the beach, before resuming her regular duties. But as Hattie cleans a particularly messy room, empties slop jars, and prepares to make dinner for the hotel's residents, the memory of the fire mingles in her mind with the memory of the young woman's white hand "hanging like a blossom from her arm, with the jewel gleaming red and blue and orange in the lamplight."[46]

Through her characterization of these women, Winifred contrasts Hattie's circumstances with the young bride's. Hattie has had to work hard and be strong in order to survive, while the younger woman has not yet been tested. In the bride's youth and vulnerability, Hattie sees, perhaps wistfully, what her life might have been. But irony comes into play when the reader realizes that the source of Hattie's strength is the difficult circumstances she has had to endure.

CONTRARY TO WAYLAND'S earlier prediction that he would be required to remain in Europe for at least a year after the fighting ceased, when he wrote to Winifred again on November 28, 1918, he was awaiting the arrival of a ship that would transport him back to the United States. Although Wayland and Winifred would spend another Christmas holiday apart, they now knew they would soon be reunited. Just four days after Christmas, Winifred received the cablegram she had been anticipating. It read: "LEAVING TOMORROW HOME MIDDLE JANY."[47]

The details of Wayland's homecoming and the young couple's post–World War I reunion will forever remain a private affair, but this experience and the understanding that Winifred gained about the mix of emotions that accompany such homecomings provided the experience she needed to write "Two Junes," a story that appeared in the November 1931 issue of *Household Magazine*.

In a letter that Winifred wrote to S. Omar Barker (an editor who had solicited one of her stories for inclusion in a textbook) on May 18, 1940, she said that this story about a blind World War I soldier's return home from war began as a writing exercise in which she attempted to appeal to senses other than sight:

> Then I hit upon the idea of . . . two parts, the first of which should depend upon sight, and the second of which should depend upon the other senses, and suddenly it became a story. Another thing about it which pleases me was that the second part is practically the first part in reverse. Most readers . . . are quite unaware of the technical problem, and judge it as a story pure and simple, which is the way a story should be judged.[48]

When this story begins, a young farmer named Martin is saying goodbye to his wife, Thelma, and thinking about all the things about her that he will miss when he is at war in France—"the way her hair was drawn over her ears like a hood . . . the way her lashes made shadows on her eyes . . . the way her nose wrinkled when she laughed." As he leaves the house, suitcase in hand, his eyes linger on various items about his property that he wishes to remember—the front step that he recently made out of new pine boards, his bird dog beating its tail against the ground, chickens scratching in the dust, a pump with its long black handle and tin cup, newly planted peach trees no bigger than sticks. He stops at the top of a rise and surveys the entire farm, wanting to memorize its features, especially the new house with white curtains over the parlor windows and Thelma's honeysuckle bush that is just beginning to bud.

As he walks toward the gate, he sees the clock tower on the granite courthouse in town, the willow tree that grows beside the creek at the corner of his property, and the ruts in the road ahead. Part I of this story ends with the approach of the train that will take Martin away to France. He takes another quick look around and says to no one in particular, "I'm a-coming back and I'm a-going to see it all again someday."

Part II begins with the train approaching the same station that Martin departed from two years earlier. Martin, who is now blind, has pulled his hat down over his forehead in hopes that no one he knows will recognize him. Thelma will not be at the station to greet him because he has not notified her, or anyone, of his homecoming. Neither has he told Thelma about his injury because he is apprehensive about how she will react to his blindness.

As soon as Martin departs from the train, he is greeted by familiar smells of his hometown: "the warm dusty wind . . . the sweaty people . . . the mules." As he makes his way down the road, carefully keeping to the side, where weeds catch at

the legs of his pants, he encounters other familiar smells and sounds: water drip-
ping from a water tank, steers moving about a loading pen, the smell of the steers.
When he leaves the town and enters the countryside, he can smell the plowed fields
and the wheat dust. He can hear the roar of a threshing machine. Further along, he
gets a whiff of peaches and hears the song of a mockingbird and the gurgle of the
creek at the corner of his property. Knowing that he is almost on his own land, he
starts to run but stubs his toe on the bridge and falls to his knees. This is not how
he had imagined his return. He had pictured himself striding down the road until
he reached his land, his house, and, "if everything was all right . . . Thelma"—not
falling on his face like a fool.

He feels an overpowering need to reach his land, for if the property is well cared
for, perhaps everything else will be all right. He edges himself into the ditch at the
end of the bridge, climbs up the far side, and fumbles through the grass until he
reaches a fence post. On his hands and knees, he crawls through the barbed wire
fence and feels his way along the ground. The cotton stalks are three feet high, the
soil around their roots is loose, as it should be, and as he is following the fence line,
he trips over a pile of sticks and rocks that someone has used to fill a washed-out
place. These signs that the land has been cared for give him hope, and he hurries
along until he reaches the gate. Once there, he hesitates, postponing the encounter
that he both dreads and desires.

As he approaches the house, he stumbles over a baby chick, smells honeysuckle, trips on the front step, and hears his dog barking as it runs to greet him. He
hears Thelma's footsteps, "quick and young," moving across the kitchen floor to
the door. Then she is standing in front of him, for he feels "her bare arms, her hands
pulling his face down to her breast, her lips, and her warm cheek." The story ends
with Martin saying, "So you was a-waiting for me," and Thelma telling him, "I been
a-waiting for you all the time."[49]

CHAPTER THREE

Keeping House

DULUTH,

MINNESOTA,

1919–1920

WAYLAND HAD BEEN BACK IN THE
states less than a month when he wrote to Winifred from the railroad station in
Chicago. He was waiting for a train that would take him back to Duluth when he
remembered that he had forgotten to bring his diploma from Amherst College.
With this letter, Wayland sent Winifred the key to a tin box he had left in her apartment, along with instructions on how to unlock the box. He told her to remove
his diploma and send it to him in Duluth, with the key for the tin box, "for good
reasons, which you will doubtless understand." This comment may have been an
indication that Winifred's mother, who was visiting Winifred at her New York
apartment at the time, was not averse to snooping.[1]

When Wayland wrote to Winifred again on January 25, 1919, he had arrived in
Duluth and was disappointed that the temperature in the middle of winter was
only thirty degrees. Duluth lawyers who were friends of his had painted a dismal
picture of job prospects in the city, but he noted that "none of them seem to be
starving." He indicated that he had not changed his plans to take the bar exam as
soon as possible and to begin practicing law in his hometown.[2]

By February 7, 1919, Wayland had completed all thirty-four bar exams and was
awaiting his discharge papers from the navy. These papers arrived three days later,
and he sent Winifred a telegram requesting that she forward his civilian clothes to

Duluth as soon as possible.[3] In subsequent letters, Wayland revealed his restless-ness and complained that he had nothing to do while he awaited the results of the exams. And when he wrote to her again on February 19, he was in Neodesha, Kansas, visiting his parents. Wayland's interest in his father's oil ventures is evident in this letter. "Were it not for the mud and the snakes and the people I think even mother would like it," he wrote, adding, "I would be tempted to get into the oil business myself if it weren't that mother would be disappointed. If we don't make a go at the law business, we can try it later."[4]

Two weeks after Wayland received his discharge papers from the navy, Win-ifred resigned her job in New York, made arrangements to ship her belongings to Duluth, vacated her Bronx apartment, and boarded a train back to her hometown. For the first time in their marriage, Wayland and Winifred Sanford would share the same mailing address—2432 East First Street in Duluth, Minnesota. No doubt the anticipation of living together on a day-to-day basis, along with the knowledge that they were returning to familiar surroundings, tempered Winifred's regrets about leaving New York City.

In the weeks that Wayland had been in Duluth without Winifred, he had re-newed acquaintance with several of his and Winifred's friends and classmates who still resided in the city, many of whom were now married and starting families. As soon as Winifred arrived, she, too, was reintegrated into Duluth society. While Wayland concentrated on establishing himself as a lawyer, Winifred assumed the socially approved role of stay-at-home matron, and in addition to performing the usual domestic duties, she entertained and enjoyed being entertained by friends at luncheons and bridge parties. Given her interest in literature, she also probably participated in one or more of the women's clubs that were active in Duluth in the 1920s.

Although Winifred had been employed for most of her adult life—first as a school teacher, then as a librarian, and finally as a lower-level business manag-er—she made a quick and happy adjustment to married life. From the time of her return to Duluth in 1919 until her death in Dallas in 1983, she consistently wrote "housewife" whenever she listed her occupation. As her daughters and Manuscript friends explained in personal interviews, to do otherwise would have reflected poorly upon her husband.

Approximately three months after Winifred and Wayland returned to Duluth, Winifred discovered that she was pregnant, and on January 18, 1920, she gave birth to the couple's first child, a baby girl with blue eyes and blond hair, whom Winifred and Wayland named Emerett Spencer Sanford. It is through Winifred's written correspondence that the details of Emerett's birth and Winifred's life as a young wife and mother have been preserved. In a letter addressed to "Dear 'Aunt' Helen" shortly after Emerett's birth, Winifred wrote the following to her sister while recuperating in the hospital:

> They are letting me sit up in bed like a regular fellow. I feel perfectly able to get up and do the work, but there's a conspiracy against me. Both mothers are half disappointed to think I am taking this affair so lightly. They kept telling me beforehand how weak I would feel . . . and here I have more pep than they.

In this letter, Winifred also apologized to Helen for not giving birth to a nephew and wrote, "I knew the baby was going to be a girl and so wasn't disappointed." This statement reflects the gender preference of a majority of Americans in the early twentieth century, but the words that follow also reveal Winifred's delight over the birth of a near-perfect baby girl: "She's getting too cute for anything." While the emotions she expressed are typical of a new mother and first-time parent, her description of her daughter's appearance at birth is devoid of sentimentality: "The first two days she was awfully homely—her head went up to a point, her chin went in . . . except when she cried," Winifred wrote, adding, "Then she was exactly like Father Sanford."[5]

By the end of Winifred's two-week hospital stay, the baby's head had assumed a more regular shape, the folds of her face had filled out, and she had begun to gain weight. Although Wayland had insisted for months during Winifred's pregnancy that he hated babies, Winifred told her sister that the new father was in awe of his daughter, whose only apparent flaw was the absence of ringlets.

Winifred also reported that she and Wayland had a "great time over names." While Helen was the obvious choice (both Winifred's mother and sister were named Helen), Winifred had rebelled at the thought of adding another Helen to an "already overloaded supply." "You probably won't like the one we have finally decided on—Emerett," she wrote, and proceeded to explain that Emerett was the name of Wayland's paternal grandmother and the name that his parents would have given his sister if they had ever produced a daughter. "The Sanford family, including myself, all like [the name]," she continued, "but I find that it strikes others as peculiar. Personally I like unusual names." Winifred's comments about the naming of the baby illustrate both her independent nature and her resistance to the impositions of tradition.

Winifred included a very personal detail about her body's response to motherhood in this letter to her sister. "I have unsuspected resources in the food line," she wrote, "so much so that they had to jump some out last night—which went toward the support of a little premature baby down the hall." She also expressed concern about a pregnant friend who had not yet delivered her baby, writing, "I'm afraid she will have a hard time, because she has scarcely stirred out of the house for two months—and has a maid that does all the work while she sits and sews." Winifred contrasted her friend's activities with her own, presenting a list of all the things that she had accomplished on the day preceding Emerett's birth:

> Got up for breakfast. Helped with dishes. Brushed up & dusted entire downstairs as well as our room & bathroom. Made sponge cake & washed dishes I used. Did lunch dishes. Entertained Susan, Marg & Elaine at bridge, serving tea and cake.
> Walked down to 15th and Superior with Elaine and back (nearly 2 miles.)
> Helped get dinner. Played Razzle Dazzle with . . . W. H., my mother and Mother S[andford] until after 10 when we went to bed.

Noticeably absent from this letter is any mention of Winifred's engagement in any kind of literary composition. She may have been so happy, so busy, and so fulfilled at this time in her life that she had little opportunity or desire to write. However, it is also possible that while in Duluth, she composed early drafts of some of the short stories that she later reworked and submitted to H. L. Mencken for publication.

In the same letter in which Winifred expressed her happiness with her new baby and her new role as a mother, she also told Helen about Wayland's increasing dissatisfaction with practicing law in Duluth and his growing attraction to the Texas oil fields:

> Has Mother ever mentioned our Texas scheme? We don't say much about it especially to Duluth because of business reasons. Wayland has been getting more and more restless here. He is already getting as much salary as he dares hope for some time—(a good deal more than most beginner's [sic] get) and besides the oil business is in his blood. "Buzz" Catlett, one of his best [Ann Arbor] friends, who has been in Wichita Falls since spring is making all kinds of money in oil and keeps begging W[ayland] to come down with him. Father S[anford] has a scheme for oil leases which could be combined with law practice. Lawyers are scarce in new country like that and fees high. Another reason we are considering going is that W[ayland] has a cold all the time in this climate (he only weighs about 135) and the family is all worried about him. Nothing may come of it, but we talk daily of touring down there in the summer in Father S[anford]'s car, putting up an Aladdin house, and starting our career . . .

What Winifred meant by "besides the oil business is in his blood" was that Wayland's father, a lawyer who operated a title and abstract company in Duluth and had long been involved in leasing mineral rights, had in recent months been engaged in oil exploration in Kansas, Texas, and Oklahoma. The elder Mr. Sanford employed several of his Sanford relatives, including Wayland's younger brother, Dwight, in his drilling ventures. Winifred's reference to "starting our career" indicates that she was an active and willing participant in Wayland's decision to relocate to West Texas. Her main concern about departing Duluth was the prospect of leaving her mother alone, for as she told her sister, she knew that Helen Mahon would never willingly consent to relocate to Texas. Winifred indicated this when she referred to her mother as "the fly in the ointment."

A few weeks after Winifred wrote this letter, Wayland left Duluth to join his law school friend Buzz Catlett in Wichita Falls, where the Burkburnett oil boom was in full swing. This boom had begun two years earlier when an oil well called "Fowler's Folly" erupted producing a flow of twenty-two hundred barrels of oil per day. News of this occurrence spread rapidly, and within a few weeks, fifty-six oil derricks towered above a West Texas landscape littered with oil-field equipment and hastily erected tent cities. Now surrounded by producing oil fields, Wichita Falls became the headquarters for the region's oil production. People from an assortment of cultures flocked to the West Texas town to take advantage of the economic opportunities that a major oil boom precipitated. By the time Wayland Sanford arrived there, housing had become scarce and real estate values had tripled.[6]

With Wayland living in Texas and Winfred and Emerett remaining in Duluth, the couple resumed writing letters to each other. Once again, only Wayland's side of the correspondence has been preserved. On May 7, 1920, he mailed a letter to Winifred from Rochester, Minnesota, where he had stopped on his way to Wichita Falls to undergo a physical examination. In this letter addressed to "Dearest family," he wrote, "I have been X-rayed, and blood tested, and felt and prodded and tapped by a dozen or so different mechanics. And the upshot of it all was that they told me if I had anything wrong with me it must be all in my eyes, so they are going to let me wear glasses."[7]

When Wayland wrote to Winifred again on May 10, 1920, he had arrived in Wichita Falls on a rainy Sunday afternoon, and after a quick visit to his new law office, he had secured temporary lodging in what he described as a "palatial downtown hotel." He told Winifred that Wichita Falls looked pretty much as it had the last time he was there. Interest in the West Texas oil fields was as "intense as ever," the trees were in "full leaf," and the lawyers all appeared to be busy. The weather, a major concern for Winifred, was warm but not hot. Corn was six inches tall, and wheat was a foot or more. Wayland told Winifred of his plan to buy a straw hat as soon as the stores opened on Monday, and when his trunk arrived, he intended to discard his winter suit in favor of lighter clothing.[8]

Wayland mentioned the weather favorably once again on May 12, 1920:

Wish you could help enjoy this delightful evening—that is, as delightful as could be expected without you. The temperature, humidity, wind velocity, visibility, etc. are beyond reproach. I am spending a few days just getting acclimated. It has rained hard part of the time since I got here, and the roads have been too bad to go over to Clay County."[9]

And again, he remarked on the high cost of living in a hotel and complained about the difficulty of finding suitable housing. He told Winifred repeatedly how much he missed her and Emerett and asked her to send him a picture of the baby shaking a rattle, which was her most recent accomplishment. While they were apart, Winifred sent Wayland many pictures of Emerett so that he would not miss any important steps in their baby's development.

When Wayland wrote to Winifred again on May 15, the West Texas weather was no longer so agreeable. Rain was falling and the balmy spring that he had mentioned in his earlier letters had turned so cold that he had been forced to don an overcoat. He was now living in a one-room apartment that he shared with another man for sixty dollars a month. This apartment had modern conveniences and the landlady was pleasant, but the arrangement was temporary because the landlady was planning to take a trip to California in the near future. As part of a continuing attempt to convince Winifred that West Texas was not devoid of culture, Wayland reported that he had attended a vaudeville show at the Orpheum Theater that was "a better bill than I ever saw in Duluth."[10]

The rain had not abated when Wayland wrote to Winifred four days later, but despite poor road conditions, he had accompanied his brother, Dwight, to the Sanford family's oil lease in Clay County. Rain had fallen for two days prior to this trip and the dirt roads were in "frightful shape," with standing water covering them to a depth of six feet in some places. Prospects for making a flowing well were not promising, and Wayland expressed gratitude that Winifred did not have to depend solely on his 1/80 share of the well's proceeds to buy Emerett baby shoes. Wayland was referring here to money he had invested in an oil well that his father had financed and that his brother Dwight was drilling. On a more encouraging note, he told Winifred that he had a "prospective law client."[11]

When Wayland mentioned the Sanford well again on May 25, 1920, it was in a "highly interesting stage," and he was more optimistic about the prospect of bringing in a good well. In fact, he was so interested in what was going on at the site that he had spent three straight days and nights at the lease, coming into town only once to see if he had any additional clients. Wayland told Winifred that he and Dwight had mixed business with pleasure by going hunting. "I am really enjoying it here," he wrote, "more than I expected, and would be quite happy if you and Emerett were here." He now had two law clients but had not yet collected any fees.[12]

In Wayland's next letter, written on May 29, 1920, he advised Winifred to collect a debt that was owed him by one of his former law clients in Duluth. Wayland indicated that he had worked until midnight the night before in order to finish up his law work so he could leave for the well site in Henrietta by 2:30 in the afternoon. "If the law business keeps up as well as it has begun I shall be satisfied,"[13] he wrote. The hectic schedule that Wayland recounted in this letter should have indicated to Winifred the amount of time her husband would devote to his oil ventures in the future.

In anticipation of Winifred and Emerett's impending relocation to Wichita Falls, Wayland purchased a five-room house on a corner lot for $4,600. The house was a year old, with "fairly large rooms," and was located in a "respectable but far from swell neighborhood." As Wayland told Winifred in his next letter, he would not want to live there permanently, but it would "serve as shelter from the rain" until they could find someplace more suitable. Although the $600 down payment and the $100 monthly payment would be a financial stretch for the young couple, Wayland felt that buying a house was wiser than renting, and he assured Winifred that he would do his best to purchase the furniture that she had indicated they would need by the time she and Emerett arrived.[14]

Although Winifred had been an activist for women's voting rights while in college, her attention was so focused on the approaching move that when the U.S. Congress ratified the Nineteenth Amendment to the Constitution on August 18, 1920, neither she nor Wayland made a single comment about the event in their letters. In Wayland's last letter to Winifred before she departed from Duluth, he told her that his father had offered to bring her and Emerett as far as Kansas when he traveled there on business a couple of weeks hence. Wayland urged Winifred to come even though the furniture would not be delivered for several more weeks. He promised to meet her in Kansas City and to arrange for temporary housing that would accommodate the family until their new furniture arrived. Wayland estimated that the move would cost approximately one thousand dollars and advised Winifred to collect the remaining debts that people in Duluth still owed him. He also instructed her to sign a deed for a tax title on property near Two Harbors that had recently sold for $400. "Most of this money is, of course, yours," he wrote, "but I suggest that, if it is available before you come down, you use it for the trip. We can take stock and arrange our respective finances after you get here." Just in case Winifred was unable to collect ample funds to finance her move to Wichita Falls, Wayland suggested three alternatives. They could borrow money from his father, sell a couple of liberty bonds, or postpone the move until he collected enough legal fees in Texas to finance the trip. "I am strictly against the third alternative," he wrote. "I love you and Emerett very much, and am anxious to have you get here as soon as possible now. Hurry like anything!"[15]

Wayland's instructions clearly indicate that he trusted Winifred's ability to conduct these business transactions in his absence and also that Winifred was in possession of financial holdings that she kept separate from the couple's community property. Helen J. Sanford confirmed in a personal interview that her mother maintained separate property throughout the couple's marriage and that Wayland was the one who insisted upon this arrangement. However, telephone listings for Wayland's solo law firm in the Wichita Falls telephone directories between 1920 and 1930 indicate that Winifred invested her own money in the firm when he was first getting it established.

As eager as Winifred was to be reunited with her husband, the news that her move to Texas was to take place sooner than she had anticipated must have caused her some anxiety. Paramount were her concerns about leaving her mother in Duluth, but Winifred was also attached to her hometown. Although she would never live in Minnesota again, she would return for extended visits throughout her life, and she would never forget the human dramas that she had observed in the cold, blustery north country of her birth.

Several of the short stories that Winifred later published are set in urban Duluth or in its rural countryside, including "Wreck," "The Forest Fire," and "The Blue Spruce," a story that demonstrates Winifred's ability to create beautiful imagery. The incident at the center of this story is a ski-jumping competition, and the protagonist is Swan Swanson. Although thirty-three contestants are to participate in the competition, the one Swan most wants to defeat is Lars Olson, the man who edged Swan out of first place in the previous year's contest. Although the competition between Swan and Lars is central to the story's plot, Winifred's descriptions of the winter landscape are the story's most outstanding feature.

> Swan Swanson came, after a while to the top of a hill, and he halted for a minute and looked down, because he could see from there, as from nowhere else within miles, the broad, cold surface of Lake Superior. Today it was on fire with the cold. The steam was rolling up from it like smoke. The white ice rimmed the shore. Streaks of white floated on the blue. Swan Swanson laughed. He liked the cold. The tighter the mercury hugged itself in the bulb of his thermometer, the louder he laughed.[16]

When Swan passes through a town on his way to the ski competition, he sees

> sleighs waiting, while their drivers stamp their feet and flap their arms and blow their noses with their fingers into the drifts. Swedes and Norwegians and Finns, laughing and jabbering, were crowded into the sleighs and digging their feet into

the straw which lay in the bottom, and drawing quilts on which they sat over their shoulders, and tucking the bear-skin robes under their knees.[17]

And when he comes to the top of a hill overlooking the ski lift, he sees people in bright-colored sweaters standing in groups "like patterns of bright color on a screen." He draws first jump in the competition, and as he stands at the top of the platform, he observes the country below, "as white and as smooth as a frosted cake, and the evergreens were like candles, ready for the match." Then he sees the blue spruce that is his target, at the foot of the ski run, "planted like a warning in the snow."[18]

Swan makes his first jump and lands three yards short of the spruce. On Lars's first jump, he lands a full yard closer to the target. On the second jump, Swan lands only four feet from the tree, while Lars lands a full yard ahead of Swan and then falls, his skis "spinning like pinwheels on the fourth of July."[19] On his final jump, Swan feels his hand brush the top of the spruce as he descends. When he lands, he struggles to maintain his balance but manages to stay upright and win the contest.

A defeated Lars hitches his team to his sleigh and departs, but Swan stays to enjoy the adulation of the crowd. Then, with his stomach full of refreshments and his prize money weighting the pockets of his Mackinaw jacket, he finally heads home.

It was dark. The sun had gone down under the snow at the edge of the sky. The lavender shadows had deepened to purple and the white snow was a luminous gray. A little moon rolled like a wheel of ice along the treetops whose shadows ribbed the road.[20]

The story ends with Swan's enthusiastic yodel echoing throughout the snowy hills that surround him.

Difficult Adjustments

WICHITA FALLS,

TEXAS,

1920–1925

WINIFRED AND EMERETT JOINED
Wayland in Wichita Falls in late September or early October 1920. Wayland, who was well aware of Winifred's concerns about Texas weather, may have orchestrated the move to occur after temperatures that often registered more than 100 degrees in the summer months had abated. In almost every letter that he wrote to her before she joined him, Wayland mentioned the Texas weather favorably, but upon Winifred's arrival, she did not find the climate to her liking. She was especially troubled by the presence of wind that seemed never to cease blowing. Although she had grown accustomed to Duluth's frigid winds, the earth beneath her hometown was a rock outcropping that stayed put when the wind blew. In Wichita Falls, the soil was a red sandy loam that, despite her best efforts to keep it out of the house, seeped under doors and around windows in what local residents called sandstorms.[1]

In Minnesota, the pine and hardwood trees that grew in abundance offered some protection from the wind, but the trees that grew in West Texas were spindly and sparse. Mesquites and scrub oaks thrived in the sandy soil and arid conditions, but they seldom grew taller than a man on horseback and provided little protection from the heat or the wind. And while Duluth was situated on the shores of one of the largest inland ports in the United States, the most substantial bodies of

water in Wichita Falls were stock ponds that local farmers dug to supply their cattle's need for water. But in ways that were less visible, Wichita Falls, Texas, and Duluth, Minnesota, were not so dissimilar. Both cities, when Winifred and Wayland
resided in them, were approximately thirty years beyond their frontier periods.
A major railroad provided ready transportation in and out of both regions, and
the surrounding countryside in both locations was rich in natural resources—iron
and copper ore in Minnesota, oil and gas in West Texas. And because both cities
held the promise of great economic opportunity, their populations were ethni-
cally, culturally, and economically diverse.

Despite Winifred's initial misgivings about West Texas weather, many elements
of the oil boom society stimulated her intellectual curiosity. It was in West Texas
that she saw her first oil derrick, observed an oil well blowout, and experienced the
rich cultural mix of humanity that made up oil boom communities. Here she came
into contact with drillers, roughnecks, promoters, speculators, and engineers, all
of whose speech was so full of strange terms that applied only to oil production
that it sometimes seemed as if these people were speaking a foreign language. This
language fascinated her so much that it eventually became the focus of a nonfiction article entitled "Derrick Jargon" that she coauthored with Wayland's friend
and business associate Clyde Jackson. The article was published in the April 1934
issue of the *Southwest Review*.[2]

The throng of people that descended on Wichita Falls with the advent of the
Burkburnett oil boom included individuals of sophisticated breeding, like Wayland and Winifred Sanford, but it also included more unsavory characters—hus-
tlers, prostitutes, and bootleggers, as well as drifters and derelicts. Culture clashes
were bound to occur in such an environment as individuals with liberal ideas and
flamboyant lifestyles invaded a region populated by farmers and ranchers who es-
poused traditional beliefs and held to conservative values. Landowners who had
eked out a living prior to the boom were suddenly endowed with great wealth and
sought opportunities to spend their newly acquired fortunes. Famous artists, actors, and traveling companies that performed in Europe and New York were im-
ported by train to Wichita Falls, where they entertained the newly rich citizenry
in sold-out performances at the Wichita Falls opera house. In addition to these
performances, a symphony and a ballet company comprised of local talent put on
shows throughout the year.[3]

The assortment of people, politics, religions, and ethnicities that comprised the
population of Wichita Falls throughout the 1920s provided both the atmosphere
and the associations that would serve as stimuli for Winifred Sanford's writing.
Years after the West Texas oil boom had subsided and the Sanford family had relocated to Dallas, Winifred spoke favorably about the time she spent in West Texas.

She confided to close friends and family members that after moving to Dallas, she missed the eclectic environment of Wichita Falls. However, letters that Winifred wrote to her sister during her early years in West Texas indicate that the young woman who had so loved living in New York City often felt isolated and culturally deprived in the West Texas community.[4]

She was a stranger in a strange land when she first arrived in Wichita Falls. And while Wayland and his law partner, Buzz Catlett, worked long hours at their law office in the Commerce Building downtown, Winifred was confined at home with the couple's infant daughter. At times, Wayland, who sometimes received a percentage of interest in an oil venture as payment for legal services, would spend several days and nights at a well site when a rig on a lease in which he owned an interest was at a critical stage of drilling.[5]

Just six months after Winifred joined Wayland in Wichita Falls, she became pregnant with the couple's second daughter. When the baby was born on January 24, 1922, the couple yielded to family tradition and named her Helen Jefferson Sanford, giving the new baby the same first name as her maternal grandmother and aunt, with a middle name that had been her paternal grandmother's maiden name. Family genealogical records give no indication that the new baby, or her sister, Emerett, was ever christened. This omission may have been an indication of Winifred's growing dissatisfaction with organized religion.

On September 14, 1922, when her second daughter was nine months old, Winifred attended the organizational meeting of the Penwomen's Club at the Wichita Falls Library. Mrs. Walter Robinson, president of the District Federation of Women's Clubs, issued invitations to this meeting, but the idea to form a writing club probably originated among the attendees. The purpose of this gathering appears to have been clear to everyone who came together at the library that day. Wichita Falls needed a venue where women who were interested in writing could associate with like-minded individuals and further develop their writing skills. None of the charter members of the newly formed club were professional writers. Only one or two had achieved any kind of publication, and the rest were novices.[6]

There is no indication that the charter members of the Penwomen's Club were well acquainted. They varied in age, personality, marital status, place of origin, educational background, and socioeconomic circumstances. What bound them together that day, and in the years to come, was their love of literature and their eagerness to advance their knowledge and their writing skills. This eagerness was demonstrated by how quickly the group became organized. Before the women left that first meeting at the library, they had selected a slate of officers, drafted a list of membership requirements, determined rules of operation, and set up a schedule for semimonthly meetings.[7]

Although Winifred was one of the more experienced writers in the group, she was not selected to be an officer. Several explanations for this omission are possible. For one thing, Winfred was a quiet and reserved individual who would not have called attention to her past accomplishments. And as a relative newcomer to Texas, she may not have been as familiar with the organizational procedures of the Texas Federation of Women's Clubs as other women in the group. Furthermore, with a toddler and an infant to care for almost singlehandedly, she may have realized that finding time to write was going to be challenging enough without the additional burden of serving as one of the club's officers.

She probably knew some of the individuals who gathered at the library that day, but others would have been relative strangers. However, as Winifred later told her daughters, the better acquainted she became with this group of women, the more comfortable she felt in their presence. These women were not newly rich, socially elite matrons who joined women's clubs in order to show off their latest fashions, gossip about their neighbors, and boast about their husbands' accomplishments. Instead, these were intelligent, educated, and well-mannered middle-class women who disliked social pretensions. For the most part, they were intellectual equals who shared Winifred's interest in literature. Like her, many of them were newcomers to West Texas who had moved to the region with husbands who were attracted to Wichita Falls by economic opportunity. They came from as far away as Holland and Russia and from a variety of regions in the United States. And like Winifred, most of them were going through a period of adjustment when the club was first organized—to the extremes of Texas weather, to the vast emptiness of the plains, and to a society that was much more conservative than what they had previously encountered.

Younger members of the club had come of age during the early modern period, and they did not hold traditional attitudes toward Victorian conventions and morals. Like Winifred, some of them had campaigned actively for ratification of the Nineteenth Amendment, and the majority was skeptical about organized religion. And because their attitudes were so different from the attitudes of the conservative agrarians who had settled in the region, the Penwomen felt isolated from a community where one of the first questions asked of a newcomer was, "Where do you go to church?"[8]

While the attitudes of a majority of the club's members were unconventional by West Texas standards, matrons in the group conformed to the time period's accepted rules of behavior for married women. They assumed traditional domestic roles and avoided actions that might reflect negatively upon their husbands and children. One former member explained that, although the members admired the independence of members of the Algonquin Round Table in New York, these women would never have adopted that group's lifestyles. Instead, they conformed to traditional standards of conduct but remained "liberated in their souls."[9]

The group's adherence to proper decorum was never more evident than during club meetings. Former members used the following words to describe what went on during critique sessions—"charged," "democratic," "intellectually stimulating"—but they stressed that meetings were conducted in a kindly manner with members showing consideration for the individual whose writing was being critiqued. As a group, they were careful to deliver their criticisms in a lady-like fashion, using proper grammar. Displays of anger, profanity, or other unacceptable behavior could result in the termination of the offender's membership. Although expulsion from the group was rare, such an action did occur on at least one occasion.

Early in the club's history, the Penwomen held meetings in public venues, such as the library, and they conducted business according to established rules of parliamentary procedure. Eventually, the group dispensed with strict parliamentary procedure, and meetings became informal gatherings at the homes of various club members. In the club's fourth year, the group voted to change the club's name from the Penwomen's Club to the Manuscript Club so that men in the community who had expressed interest in attending meetings would feel comfortable doing so.[10]

The Manuscript Club's role in Winifred Sanford's career should not be minimized. Winifred stressed the group's importance in her development as a writer when Hilton Greer interviewed her in 1936. In his feature article in *The Dallas Journal*, he wrote,

> One of the most fruitful literary organizations in Texas has been the Manuscript Club of Wichita Falls. That club was actively, if quietly, at work ... when the Sanfords lived in the West Texas city ... Mrs. Sanford ... acknowledges today that she owes much to the friendly association and the critical give-and-take of this club, which has claims on more than a few Texas writers who have won wide recognition as producers of prose and verse.[11]

Fifteen years after she moved to Dallas, Winifred spoke once again of the effects that the nurturing environment created by Manuscript Club members had on her writing in a letter to New York editor and native Texan Margaret Cousins. Regarding an article by Cousins that had been published in *The Dallas Morning News*, Winifred wrote:

> I am particularly interested in what you had to say about the incentive one receives from meeting with a group of fellow writers ... I think you will agree with me that

a group of that sort is of much more value to a writer than an outsider would suppose. It is so much more than a mere giving and taking of criticism. The air seems thick with ideas whenever you get together. You are put on your mettle; the old competitive spirit rises . . . and you find yourself writing in spite of yourself.[12]

Later in this letter, Winifred writes, "Without [the Manuscript Club] I should never have begun my own somewhat limited career."

The Manuscript Club not only provided Winifred Sanford with intellectual stimulation. It also furnished her with a group of friends who became some of her most trusted confidants. Fania Kruger, Anne Pence Davis, Laura Faye Yauger, and other club members shared Winifred's frustrations, sympathized with her homesickness, and bolstered her spirits when she suffered migraine headaches and bouts of minor depression. And sometimes the issues that Manuscript Club members discussed among themselves inspired one another's literary compositions.

This was probably true of the first story that Winifred submitted for publication. In a short essay entitled "The Method of Irony," which appeared in *The Editor; The Journal of Information for Literary Workers*, Winifred tells that "The Monument" originated with her observation of the different ways that people cope with bereavement. The main character in this story is a recently widowed young woman who is the mother of four children, as well as the sole caregiver for her elderly mother. In the opening scene, Margaret is rocking her restless baby well after midnight, and as she moves about the house checking on her sleeping children, the reader is privy to her memories of her deceased husband, Richard, and to her worries about the family's limited finances. Determined to show her love for Richard by making the best life possible for their children, Margaret has taken in three boarders and is writing a weekly column for the local newspaper in order to support herself and her family.

In the story's second scene, Margaret interacts with her noisy but happy children while dressing to have lunch with Julia Chalmer, a young woman who is also recently widowed. Julia was once engaged to Margaret's husband and has, for some time, lived under the false impression that Richard's heart was broken when she called off their engagement. Richard told Margaret that this wasn't true on several occasions, but he also said, "Oh let her think I feel that way, Margo; it gives her a lot of pleasure."[13]

The story's climactic third scene takes place at the Chalmer home, where the two widows' financial circumstances, as well as the way they are coping with their husband's deaths, are contrasted. Julia, dressed all in black, takes Margaret into her husband's library, where everything remains exactly as he left it, and recounts the unremarkable details of his death. She concludes her recitation, "And afterwards he looked so peaceful and happy," to which Margaret replies, "Oh but dying takes such a minute Julia. It's living that takes the time and courage."[14]

When Julia's son, Jack, enters the room, his quiet demeanor contrasts markedly with the noisy activities of Margaret's four children in the previous scene. Julia mentions that Margaret is bearing up under her loss despite having to worry about finances, and Margaret feels as if this comment is an insult to Richard's memory. When Julia pulls out the design of a monument, Margaret assumes it is Julia's husband's marker. Then she sees Richard's name on the headstone and remembers how much Richard "hated display and ceremony and doing conventional things." But she also notices that for a moment Julia's mask of grief has been replaced by a look that is almost radiant. Remembering Richard's words—"Oh let her think I feel that way, Margo; it gives her a lot of pleasure"—Margaret acquiesces, with a line of dialogue that strains credibility, to Julia's request to have the monument placed on Richard's grave: "It's a wonderful thing for you to do, Julia; of course I am willing."[15]

ACCORDING TO FORMER Manuscript Club members, Winifred's portrayal of the contrast between Margaret's and Julia's grieving processes mirrors the contrast that existed between the way that members of the Manuscript Club thought the grieving process should be carried out and the traditional rituals of longtime West Texas residents.

In formal interviews and in informal conversations with friends and family, members of the Manuscript Club insisted that they had no aspirations to become professional writers. As former club member Peggy Schachter explained, the society in which these women lived placed great value on the domestic role of women. Single females, widows, and women who were unable to have children could work outside the home without gaining the society's disapproval, but if a married woman pursued a career, doing so reflected badly upon her husband, who was expected to be the sole financial provider for his family.[16]

Despite the women's insistence that they had no desire to become professional writers, they began sending stories and poems to magazine editors for possible publication in the second year of the club's existence. Winifred was the first member to achieve publication. In a letter to William Kane at *The Editor*, she indicated that her work had been accepted quickly: "Although the Mon[ument] was the first story I ever sold (on its third trip, by the way) the first of mine to be published was Wreck, which came out in Jan. 25 (1925)."[17] In a letter to M. K. Singleton in September 1964, she wrote, "I simply mailed . . . 'Wreck' on my own."[18]

The central incident in "Wreck" is a shipwreck that takes place during a violent winter storm on a body of water that is undoubtedly Lake Superior. When the story opens, Elsie, a young woman of questionable character, is so angry at her boyfriend, Charlie, for believing a lie that her previous lover told about her that she does not see the freighter miss the turn into the ship channel and run aground. When her sister calls the mishap to Elsie's attention, she moves from a chair beside the fireplace to a window overlooking the channel, and her initial reaction to the scene reveals her self-absorbed and insensitive personality:

> She blinked at the Harvey Jones and then she giggled. Honestly, she couldn't help it. It was too funny to see that great big freighter lying crosswise in the shallow water, with the waves going over her. Guess it must have surprised them some to be picked up by the sea when they thought they were safe in the ship canal.[19]

As she watches the rescue efforts—first from the comfort of her rocking chair near the fire, then from a position near the window, and finally from the shore of the lake—Elsie's main concern is how the shipwreck will affect her date with Charlie, who is a member of the rescue crew.

> It is bad enough, she ruminated, scratching idly at the frost on the window, to have a beau who was on the lifesaving crew, and a fool like Anderson to tell him what he could do and what he couldn't do, without having wrecks to spoil your fun. Everytime they planned anything . . . a wreck or an accident.[20]

In a third scene, Elsie dons her fur coat, hat, muff, and overshoes and joins the crowd of onlookers who are watching the rescue attempt from the shore of the lake. She flirts shamelessly with Charlie in an attempt to divert his attention, while the rest of the rescue team makes repeated but unsuccessful attempts to throw life lines to a group of stranded crew members that includes Elsie's former lover.

In a final attempt to attract Charlie's attention, Elsie returns to the cottage to fetch a pot of hot coffee and two mugs. When she returns to the shore, her renewed efforts to distract Charlie are successful. With a tragedy unfolding nearby, Elsie and Charlie sneak off to a nearby stand of cedars to rekindle their relationship. When Charlie's boss demands that he return to the shore and fetch a pickax, Elsie realizes that the members of the freighter's crew have frozen to the deck of the ship. Recognizing their resemblance to ice statues, she shudders, and with words that reveal that Charlie is even more insensitive than Elsie, he says, "What's the matter? . . . You wanted me to change jobs didn't you? Well, what's the matter with the ice business, eh?"[21]

MEMBERS OF THE MANUSCRIPT CLUB were elated by the news that a story written by one of their members—a story they had critiqued at a Manuscript Club meeting—had attracted the attention of one of the most important editors in the country, H. L. Mencken.[22] Hired to be a reporter for the *Baltimore Morning Herald* when he was in his early twenties, Mencken quickly became the newspaper's star reporter. At the age of twenty-four he was promoted to managing editor, and by the age of twenty-five he was editor-in-chief of the newspaper. When the *Herald* ceased operation in 1906, Mencken accepted an offer to work as a writer and editor for *The Baltimore Sun*, where he quickly distinguished himself as a literary and arts critic, editorial writer, and syndicated reporter of local and national events. Mencken excelled in writing spirited and controversial articles that took aim at bigots, politicians, religious fanatics, and pseudo intellectuals. According to Carl Bode, Mencken's reporting style "raised impertinence to an art" and solidified his reputation as an iconic newspaper figure. In 1924, Mencken, along with his coeditor, George Jean Nathan, added two periodicals—*The Smart Set* and *The American Mercury*—to his resume. During the *Mercury*'s first year of operation, Mencken and Nathan published stories and articles by some of the most important writers in the United States, and in a matter of months, Mencken became one of the most respected and sought after magazine editors in the country.[23]

Just a few months after Mencken and Nathan accepted "Wreck" for publication in *The American Mercury*, Mencken became even more famous when his syndicated reports of the now famous Scopes Trial riveted the nation. The trial was instigated by the American Civil Liberties Union for the purpose of invalidating a Tennessee law that prohibited the teaching of evolution in the state's public schools and universities. A young biology teacher named Thomas Scopes agreed to teach the theory of evolution to test the law. At Mencken's urging, the prominent criminal lawyer Clarence Darrow agreed to defend Scopes against the renowned Democratic orator and politician William Jennings Bryan, who represented the state of Tennessee as prosecuting attorney. For eleven days, Mencken's reports of the trial's daily proceedings appeared in virtually every newspaper in the country, bringing the conflict between science and religion to the forefront of American consciousness.[24]

The American Mercury Adventure

WICHITA FALLS,

TEXAS,

1925–1927

THE *AMERICAN MERCURY* EDITORS' AC-
ceptance of "Wreck" was significant. First published in January 1924, the *Mercury*,
under the direction of H. L. Mencken and George Jean Nathan, quickly became the
leading American magazine. Its success revolutionized the American magazine
industry in the 1920s and had a major effect upon American fiction and literary
criticism, as well. In order to compete with the *Mercury*, magazines such as *Harper's*,
North American Review, and *Scribner's Magazine* updated their formats; editors of new
publications such as *McNaught's Monthly* and *Plain Talk* modeled the *Mercury*'s design; and college publications around the country began to parody the *Mercury*'s
style.[1]

During H. L. Mencken's tenure as editor of the magazine, he became one of
the most influential literary figures in the United States. According to Pulitzer
Prize–winning journalist and commentator Walter Lippman, Mencken exerted "a
powerful personal influence on a whole generation of educated people."[2] The *New
York Times* called him "the most powerful private citizen in America,"[3] and in *H. L.
Mencken: Literary Critic*, William Nolte wrote of Mencken:

His successful battle for realism constitutes one of the major chapters in American
literature. His popularity among writers was larger than that enjoyed by any other

American critic before or since . . . With rare exceptions . . . the writers he praised have lived and the writers he condemned have died.[4]

Mencken's support of new writers is well documented. One fifth of the stories that appeared in the *Mercury* before 1928 were by previously unknown writers, but the editors published only .001 percent of all the unsolicited material they received.[5] It was with these odds that "Wreck" gained the famous editor's favorable attention. According to a review of Sanford's story that appeared in *The Bookman* shortly after "Wreck" was published, it was "the kind of starkly realistic story that Mencken favored."[6]

As a general rule, Mencken favored fiction that directed attention away from the deeds of heroic and exotic subjects and focused instead on the problems of working-class Americans. He preferred writers who chose settings that were contemporary and indigenous and who portrayed middle- or lower-class Americans without authorial interpretation or elaboration. As a general rule, these writers focused attention on the culture of the majority rather than on the peculiarities of a minority. In short, the stories that Mencken published featured characters that resembled everyman engaged in an ongoing struggle for survival.[7]

At the same time that Mencken championed a realistic approach to fiction writing, he had little respect for photographic realism, as he made clear in his essay "Zola":

> Art can never be simply representation. It cannot deal solely with precisely what it is. It must, at the least, present the real in the light of some moral, then at all events some direction. For without that formulation there can be no clear-cut separation of the individual will from the general stew . . . and without that separation there can be no coherent drama, and without that drama there can be no evocation of emotion and without that emotion art is unimaginable.[8]

Mencken was especially critical of writers from the American South who romanticized the region's antebellum past and produced fiction that had little relevance to life in the present.[9] He was fond of fiction by Theodore Dreiser, Sherwood Anderson, and Sinclair Lewis—writers from the Midwest whom critics have often associated with the literary movement known as naturalism. In *H. L. Mencken and The Mercury Adventure*, M. K. Singleton writes that the most typical contributors to the *Mercury* during the years that Mencken was editor were imitators of these better-known writers. Singleton identifies Winifred Sanford as one of three writers whose stories were the most characteristic of the magazine's fiction. He describes these writers as "competent stylists and craftsmen" who wrote "quietly realistic" fiction that was based upon personal experiences.[10]

Singleton's assessment of Winifred's stories is only partially correct. She was a competent stylist who wrote realistic fiction, but her keen sense of observation, her aptitude for thorough research, and her compassion for the human condition enabled her to exceed the limits of her own personal experiences. As the wife of a successful oil and gas attorney, her closest friends and associates were mostly of the upper and upper middle classes, while all but one of her protagonists are members of the working class. With the exception of the main characters in "Mary" and "Fools," the female protagonists in Winifred's stories are farm wives, or they operate boarding houses, or take in washing, or tell fortunes, or clerk in dry goods stores. Her male protagonists are either farmers, oil-field workers, or down-on-their-luck oil speculators.

Mencken may also have been drawn to Winifred's stories because they provided accurate portrayals of life in two rather remote regions of the country—the Southwest and the far North. Mencken and Nathan wanted to promote good literature from all regions of the country, as these words from one of the magazine's early advertisements illustrates: "The aim of *The American Mercury* will be to offer a comprehensive picture, critically presented, of the entire American scene."[11]

On October 21, 1924, George Jean Nathan notified Winifred that the *Mercury* editors were accepting "Wreck" for immediate publication.[12] Nathan's letter was not Winifred's first communication with the *Mercury* staff, however. Her letter to H. L. Mencken, dated July 25, 1924, and Mencken's reply, dated August 3, 1924, are proof that the Texas housewife and the New York editor had corresponded at least three months prior to the magazine's acceptance of "Wreck." Nor was "Wreck" the first story that Winifred had submitted to the *Mercury*. In the letter she wrote to Mencken on July 25, 1924, Winifred mentioned a note that he had enclosed when he returned her last story and expressed frustration that, although she had submitted multiple stories to numerous publications, only one had been accepted by a "ladies' magazine":

The note you enclosed with my last story had me guessing. I couldn't make out whether my offering had been the laughing stock of the editorial staff or whether you were frantically anxious to see another. You didn't say you liked it; neither did you order me back to the dishpan and the kitchen mop. If you decide, after reading "Sick for Home" that I belong in the kitchen, please be good enough to tell me so."[13]

The swiftness of Mencken's reply and the tone of his comments indicate that even though he had rejected Winifred's earlier submissions, he had been impressed by her writing. Concerning the last story he had returned to her, Mencken wrote, "If this story didn't deal with the logging country we'd probably take it. At the moment we have no less than three articles in type, all relating to that region." Then he offered the yet-to-be-published writer the following words of encouragement: "I see nothing wrong at all. You are writing very good stuff. I'll be glad to see it, and soon or late I'll buy some of it."[14]

Although Winifred may not have realized the significance of these comments at the time, Mencken had a reputation for being a tough critic who gave his honest opinion of a piece of writing, even when doing so meant insulting a close friend. Because he was known for being forthright and because he occupied a position of great influence in American literary circles, many well-known authors sought his advice. In a letter that writer Thomas Woolf wrote to Madeline Boyd on February 15, 1929, he indicated the value of Mencken's stamp of approval when he wrote, "I am very much pleased by Mencken's note—his praise was moderate, but I take it at its literal value: I do not believe he writes such notes as a matter of form. And of course his belief in one's work would be of tremendous value to a writer."[15]

By Winifred's own admission, "Wreck" marked a major change in her writing style. In a letter to William Kane of *The Editor* in 1926, she recalled the story's development:

> I remember every step . . . because it marked the beginning of what was for me a new point of view and a new style—the ironic! In everything I had written up to that time the story was told sympathetically: I was, so to speak, press agent for my hero. Since then I have either kept out of the story altogether, or I have purposely taken the unsympathetic side, hoping that the wise will read between the lines. . . . In Wreck [sic], which is a story of a ship foundering at a harbor entrance, I started out to overwhelm the reader with the tragedy of it by direct methods, tragic detail on tragic detail. I made two separate attempts to do it before I had the idea I developed later . . . to tell it indirectly through two good-for-nothing characters who were almost entirely insensible of the tragedy they were witnessing. Whether I succeeded or not, I don't know. At any rate I have followed the method ever since in varying degrees.[16]

In 1987, the writer, scholar, and literary critic Don B. Graham noted that it was Winifred Sanford's use of irony that gave her the distance, the discipline, and the control that enabled her to transcend the limitations of the sentimental magazine fiction that was then being published.[17] However, in 1925, the starkly realistic style that Winifred Sanford employed in writing "Wreck" was not as well received by readers and critics as it was by the editors of the *Mercury*. In a letter to her sister Helen, written some time after "Wreck" appeared in print, Winifred expressed dismay over criticism that had been leveled at her first published short story.

I doubt if you can imagine the idiotic criticisms I have heard on Wreck [sic]. I don't mean to imply that everyone who criticizes it is necessarily idiotic, but no one yet who has criticized it has had the least idea of the point of the story. If they had understood what I intended and blamed me for not managing it properly, it would be a different matter. Oh well, it may be my fault that they don't get it, but-then-why [sic] do others get it alright?[18]

She listed criticism she had received from friends and family members and asked, "Did you see the blasting criticism in the March Bookman [sic]?"

The Bookman, a magazine that published reviews of contemporary literature, regularly aimed sharp criticism at stories that appeared in the *Mercury*, and although Gerald Hewes Carson's review of "Wreck" was not an entirely positive one, Winifred's use of the adjective "blasting" was a distortion, as the following excerpt from the review illustrates:

While a big freighter goes to pieces on the rocks and living men are turned to hideous chunks of ice by the windy seas, Miss Sanford studies the mind of Elsie, a seacoast trollop who titters while her lover struggles futilely to rescue the doomed men—to one of whom she has but recently granted secret favors. This story has all the hard, cold, metallic brilliance which Mr. Mencken admires and his contributors imitate; but for all its mordant observation, it shows a complete absence of vivacity or interest in any but an ugly disagreeable world.[19]

The high regard that Mencken held for Winifred's fiction is evident in all eighteen letters that he wrote to her between 1924 and 1930. His comments about her writing are courteous, respectful, instructional, encouraging, and completely devoid of the acerbic comments for which he was famous. As Winifred told M. K. Singleton in a letter that she wrote to him in 1962, the Mencken she knew "never displayed the flippant, wisecracking side of his nature."[20]

In a letter that Mencken wrote to Winifred on March 18, 1925, after the publication of "Wreck," he asked a question that would become a reoccurring theme in his correspondence with her: "Have you anything in hand or in mind that would fit into the *Mercury*?"[21] No doubt, Mencken's interest in Winifred's writing bolstered her confidence and encouraged her to think of herself as a writer, as the following passage from the letter she wrote to him on March 23, 1925, demonstrates:

Well, if you will have some samples, here you are. "Allie" is, I suspect, too much of a bad thing. "The Forest Fire" I have just this minute concocted, and I don't know how it will taste when the brew settles.

I haven't forgotten the American Mercury [sic], nor what has seemed to me your unparalleled generosity in actually paying for and publishing Wreck [sic]. I wonder what, if anything, has been said to you about it. My own acquaintances are divided into wings: the left write to me as to a major prophet; the right to say to the left that it is too bad I didn't put in a little heroism or self sacrifice, and besides, most lifesavers are not the least bit like Charlie . . . And Mr. somebody or other, reviewing "Wreck" in the Bookman [sic], evidently belongs to the right wing.[22]

Winifred told Mencken that she had not been writing many short stories of late because she was working on a novel. She didn't feel that she could drop it, at this point, even though she couldn't imagine what would become of it when she was finished. "If you don't like either of these works of art I am sending you, I'll try something else," she wrote. "I have dozens in my mind, but it is a long way from my mind to my fingers."

Mencken addressed Sanford's concerns about the criticisms she had received about "Wreck" in a letter dated March 28, 1925: "Everyone I respect thought, 'The Wreck' was excellent stuff. And it undoubtedly was! Don't let imbeciles annoy you!" In addition, he encouraged Winifred to submit the novel she was working on to Alfred A. Knopf, publisher of the Mercury, when she finished it. Mencken also expressed his delight with the two new stories she had sent and told her that he was accepting both of them for immediate publication.[23]

"Forest Fire" (summary appears on 25–26) was published in the Mercury in April 1925, and "Allie" in June 1925. In "Allie," Winifred explored the phenomenon of group psychology and employed a point of view similar to the point of view in William Faulkner's "A Rose for Emily," in that the first-person narrative voice represents the perspective of a larger group, often referred to in the story as "we."

The protagonist, whose misfortunes are the focus of the narrative, is a woman named Allie Wright. In the first section of the story, the narrating voice recounts the tragic events of Allie's past—she grew up without a mother, her lover was killed in a train accident, and her father absconded with the funds in his bank, leaving Allie all but destitute. Once the daughter of the town's leading citizen, Allie has been reduced to living in a furnished room above the pharmacy and working as a clerk in the local dry goods store. As a result of her misfortunes, she has become a tragic figure to her former friends, "we girls." They feel uncomfortable when they are in her presence, as if "a cloud had blown over the sun." Through no fault of Allie's, she has become an object of pity, and while her friends continue to associate with her out of a sense of duty, they joke and gossip about her behind her back.[24]

In the story's second section, the narrator reveals that Allie married her former boss because she was pregnant with his child, and although the union was never a happy one, she idolizes the couple's only child, a boy she named Lloyd. Allie's husband died quite suddenly, leaving her a widow, and everyone except Allie now knows that he had been having an affair with another woman. Their knowledge of his infidelity causes Allie's friends to feel even more uncomfortable in her presence.

The past events of Allie's life are mostly chronicled by the unnamed narrator, but a climactic scene takes place in the third section, when Allie, who is hosting a women's literary club meeting in her home, decides to read some poems that her son has composed. She discovered these poems while cleaning Lloyd's room and is so proud of them that she reads them to the group—without his permission.

In the story's final section, Lloyd enters the house while Allie is reading and stands where all the club members except Allie can see him. Then, quietly and without Allie ever being aware of his presence, Lloyd leaves. A short time later, a man rushes into the house and announces that "a boy has just shot himself. . . . Right through the head."[25] Allie rushes out of the house, and in an agitated state, the narrator says, "For goodness sake! She forgot her dress!" What the narrator meant to say was that Allie had forgotten her coat. This mistake isn't funny, given the situation, but the club members' reaction is stress-relieving laughter that causes them to feel even more guilt. The narrator concludes, "And now, whenever I see Allie coming, I can't help remembering how we sat in her house and laughed. Probably that's why I always cross the street to avoid meeting her."[26]

ON APRIL 5, 1925, Winifred again expressed her gratitude to Mencken: "You are the most astonishing editor! I am not used to finding editors who are guilty of considering even one story, let alone two." She assured him that if she ever finished the novel, she would send it to Knopf, but she warned him that the novel was more personal, subjective, and intimate than any of her short stories. In answer to the *Mercury* staff's request for biographical information, she wrote that she was born in Duluth, Minnesota, and educated at Mount Holyoke and the University of Michigan; she had taught school for a time after graduating from college and was currently the wife of a lawyer and the mother of "two small and omnipresent daughters."[27]

Having neither a separate office nor full-time child care, Winifred was composing the short stories that so impressed the New York editors in the midst of her household duties and the demands of two small children. In a personal interview, Emerett Sanford Miles expressed wonder that her mother ever managed to write at all during those years. Miles's recollections of Winifred's writing took the form of two separate images. In one, Winifred was sitting at her desk and typing with two fingers on a manual typewriter, with one or both of her preschool

Winifred and Wayland Sanford's daughters Emerett and Helen with the china doll Fannie Baker.

daughters interrupting her progress every few minutes. In the second image, Winifred was lying on the couch in the living room with one arm over her forehead as she attempted to work out a story line. Once again, both children were constantly disrupting her train of thought with a request or a comment. Ironically, despite these almost incessant interruptions, Winifred's most productive writing period occurred during the years that she was the primary caregiver for two active preschool-age children.

Just three and a half months after Mencken accepted "Forest Fire" and "Allie" for publication in the *Mercury*, Winifred sent him an additional story entitled "Saved by Grace." In the letter that accompanied the manuscript, she asked, "Will it do at all?"[28]

The main character in this story is a young, single man named Willard. In the opening scene, Willard is at a tent revival seated in a folding chair between his mother, who is wearing a starched Mother Hubbard dress, and a tall woman with big thighs and no lap who smells of lily of the valley perfume. As the choir sings a familiar hymn and the song leader prances back and forth at the front of the tent, Willard's conflict becomes apparent. The scent of lily of the valley reminds him of his romantic relationship with Myrtle, who works at the perfume counter of a local pharmacy—a relationship that he has kept hidden from his mother. As the revival proceeds, Willard concocts a plan to meet Myrtle after the service is over so he can present her with six bracelets that he has concealed in the pocket of his trousers.

At the same time that Willard is planning a liaison with Myrtle, he is guilt ridden about lying to his mother. When the preacher asks, "Brother, where are you going to spend eternity,"[29] Willard imagines that the preacher is talking directly to him, but his thoughts quickly return to how good Myrtle makes him feel and how she wants to get married and go to Paris. Willard acknowledges to himself that he has made promises to Myrtle that he cannot keep and that his mother will object to the relationship if she finds out about it.

The preacher's sermon includes the following list of sins—greed, lust, gambling, fine clothes, silk stockings, strong drink, and Paris. The very mention of Paris causes Willard's internal conflict to intensify, and when the preacher begins to point around the audience, Willard becomes so conscience stricken that, as he kneels in the sawdust, tears stream down his face. When he reaches into his pocket for a handkerchief to wipe his tears, the six hidden bracelets tumble to the ground in front of his mother. In the last line of the story, Willard cries out, "God, Mama! There *was* a woman."[30]

IN PERSONAL INTERVIEWS, both Helen J. Sanford and Emerett Sanford Miles recalled attending a tent revival with their mother similar to the one in "Saved," and they surmised that she might have been collecting material for the story at that time. In the foreword to the SMU Press edition of *Windfall and Other Stories*, Miles recalls the "fearful emotion evoked in the great tent by the voice of the evangelist" and the "impassioned hymn-singing" that was so different from the formal services at the Episcopal church that the children usually attended.[31]

Along with the manuscript of "Saved by Grace," Winifred also enclosed her latest version of "Sick for Home," a story that Mencken had rejected in an earlier draft. She wrote that "Sick for Home" had now "been the rounds" and had even been accepted for publication and then returned by the editor because he thought the title was misleading. Winifred expressed concern that the beginning and ending of this story had been worked over so many times that the narrative now had an artificiality about it. Nevertheless, she offered to rework it again, if Mencken had any interest in publishing it. She also reported that her work on the novel was continuing. "It goes slowly when the thermometer is at 110," she wrote, "but in time I hope to reach the end."[32]

Although Mencken accepted most of the stories Winifred sent to him, he did not accept "Sick for Home." In a letter dated July 29, he wrote, "I have the feeling, as you have, that 'Sick for Home' is damaged by its machinery." He suggested that she lay the story aside for a month or two before rewriting it. Mencken's response is typical of the way in which he delivered his rejections to Winifred, giving his honest opinion of her latest effort first and then making suggestions for the story's improvement. At the same time that he rejected "Sick for Home," he informed her that he was accepting "Saved by Grace" but felt that the title would be improved if it were cut down to a single word—Saved. Once again, he wished Winifred the best of luck with her novel and told her that Mr. Alfred Knopf Sr. was eager to see it when she finished.[33]

When Winifred next wrote to Mencken on August 6, 1925, she expressed gratitude that he liked the revival story and gave him permission to shorten the title. She also suggested a couple of alternate titles—"The Tent Meeting" and "The Revival"—and told Mencken that "Saved by Grace" carried on the tradition of "Wreck" and "Forest Fire" in that all three had two common elements—the story and a more or less typical incident. "Or am I talking in my old and forsaken role of school teacher?" she asked. She told Mencken that "Sick for Home," the story he had returned to her, contained a similar structure and that she planned to make one more attempt at rewriting it.[34]

Although Mencken had suggested in one of his earlier letters that Winifred might be selecting markets unwisely, her intuition about publishing markets and what styles were suited to which magazines appears to have been keen. In addition to the stories that she deemed suitable for publication in the *Mercury*, she submitted other stories to popular women's magazines. "The Monument," the first of Winifred Sanford's stories to be accepted for publication, appeared in *Woman's Home Companion* in January 1926, more than a year after the editors accepted it. These same editors published "Mary" in *Woman's Home Companion* in May 1926.

The main character in "Mary" is a young single woman of the upper middle class. The narrator is an unnamed member of Mary's extended family. The family's protectiveness of Mary is revealed in the story's first scene, when the narrator says, "We who were older used to watch her as one watches a child learning to walk. We didn't want her to get a tumble. We wanted to let her down very gently into life."[35] The narrator takes the reader through one year of Mary's life, season by season, party by party, adventure by adventure. Recounting how Mary played bridge, swam at the country club, went on shopping excursions, volunteered at a local daycare, and attended parties where she danced into the night with two devoted admirers, the narrator sums up Mary's attitude toward life: "She frolicked on the knees of the gods."[36]

When Mary's best friend marries, family members comment that Mary is lovelier than the bride; and when Mary tells the narrator that the bride was somewhat fearful before the wedding, the narrator asks, "Do you think she was really afraid or just admitting to herself that there are bad spots in a good life, Mary?" "I'm not going to have bad spots in my good life," Mary replies idealistically, "not any at all."[37]

Like heroines Mary has read about in romance novels, when it is her turn to choose a bridegroom, she comes up with a test to determine which suitor is worthy of her affection. On her birthday, with three carloads of friends and family members serving as an audience, she challenges Taylor and Jim to ride the rapids with her. Taylor declines, but Jim agrees to accompany her on this dangerous adventure. Six weeks after Mary and Jim survive their plunge over the falls, they are married, and as the newlyweds depart for their honeymoon, Mary tells the narrator, "This is only the very beginning of my life."[38]

The turning point in this story occurs when the family receives a telegram alerting them that, while on their honeymoon, Mary and Jim have been involved in a serious automobile accident. Jim has sustained life-altering injuries and is paralyzed, but Mary is reported to be unharmed, which causes great rejoicing. "They didn't understand that something exceedingly precious had perished in that instant's happening," the narrator explains, "nor did they see what was born in that same instant to replace it."[39]

When the narrator and Mary meet several months later, Mary has undergone a major attitude adjustment:

> "No one ever told me," she cried, "how selfish I was! Oh, darling, the things I have learned!
> "Hard things," I said, for I cannot forgive life for hurting her.
> "Oh yes, but good things, too."[40]

Mary goes on to recount the hardships that she and Jim will have to endure, but she concludes that nothing matters so long as she has him. The narrator offers a ray of hope when she tells of hearing good reports about the possibility of a cure for injuries such as Jim's. The extent to which Mary's naïve optimism has been altered becomes even more apparent when she says, "If I only dared believe them."[41]

The story ends ironically when the narrator, who fails to see how the accident has changed Mary for the better, addresses the reader directly: "Oh don't you see what had happened to her? How life had failed its trust with her? Brave she was, yes, when I wanted her carefree; patient when I wanted her eager; good when I wanted her lovely."[42]

REGARDLESS OF THEIR DIFFERENT STYLES, all four of the short stories by Winifred Sanford that appeared in American magazines in 1925—"Blue Spruce" and

"Saved," published in the *Mercury*, and "The Monument" and "Mary," published in *Woman's Home Companion*—were listed in Edward J. O'Brien's *The Best Short Stories of 1926*. That a woman with two preschool-age children and no household help managed to produce four highly acclaimed short stories and complete a novel in a single year is remarkable. Unfortunately, Winifred's literary successes did not alleviate her anxiety about her writing, her frequent migraine headaches, or her occasional bouts of depression.

She appears to have been suffering just such a bout of depression when she wrote to her sister Helen Toulme on March 31, 1925.

> I liked the Constant Nymph [*sic*] [a new book by Margaret Kennedy that was labeled Bohemian and considered racy at the time it was written] *very* much. Had been anxious to read it but unable to obtain it in this wilderness. In fact, I am crazy about the Nymph [*sic*]. . . . Mother S[anford] sent me Straws and Prayer books [*sic*], and O'Brien's 1924 Short Stories [*sic*], and I am now about to purchase some books on my own account, because I have sold two more stories to the Mercury [*sic*] . . . .[43]

In this letter, Winifred reproduced a list of the "idiotic criticisms" she had received from relatives and acquaintances about "Wreck."

> 1. (De Groats)—"Life savers aren't like that—wouldn't be tolerated in the service."
> 2. Auntie Flo—"No ending irritates me."
> 3. Harriet S. S. (writing to Mildred Wamburn who liked "Wreck")—"Too bad she didn't add a touch of heroism."
> 4. Someone in F[ort] W[orth]—"Oh it's all right if you like that choppy northern style."
> etc. etc.

The following comments leave little doubt that Winifred was in a dismal mood when she wrote this letter:

> I had a note from mother yesterday, written from Hemet, but she doesn't say whether she is coming back here or not. It will be an awful comedown after high society. No excitement here except Mr. Mencken's letters.
>
> We are drilling a well but all wells are dry in my experience, so I can't get very much of a thrill out of it.
>
> I do hope you will invite me to visit you in the fall. Maybe I can save enough money by then. I am really homesick for NY—for the first time since I left, but I

suspect that two days of it with the children will be more than enough. Perhaps I had better wait until I sell a few novels and can stay at the Pennsylvania. Besides, I shall have to teach E[merett] table manners first. She won't do anything unless she is convinced that there is a good reason for it, and I can't find any for table manners [*sic*] that appeal to her.

She doesn't take a nap any more, and Helen doesn't either, except rarely.[44]

On October 28, 1925, Winifred sent H. L. Mencken another revision of "Sick for Home," along with a letter in which she wrote the following:

You remember [*sic*] that you suggested rewriting it, and you see I did, so thoroughly, indeed that practically nothing of the old story remains except the stage setting. Whether it is better or worse or just as bad, I don't know. But naturally, I hope you can use it.

I have written nothing else because of the vow I took to finish my novel before it finished me. I didn't know what backbreaking business a novel could be. But I think I see my way through it now. I hope it will be ready early in 1926 if not before. After that is out of the house, I intend to write a hundred things which are jumbled together in my head.[45]

Although there is no record that Mencken rejected this version of "Sick for Home," the story never appeared in the *Mercury*.

In fall 1925, after Mencken had urged Winifred repeatedly to submit her novel to the Knopf publishing company, the wife of Alfred A. Knopf Sr., Blanch Knopf, wrote to Winifred to inquire about the novel's progress. On December 2, 1925, Winifred thanked Mrs. Knopf, who, it appears, had asked on behalf of her husband and perhaps at the urging of Mencken. When Winifred replied to Mrs. Knopf's letter, she wrote:

I wish I could say that it is ready, but it is farther from the end than I was two months ago, when I decided to rewrite it from a different point of view. Before it was a straight story; now it is ironic. I think you will agree with me when you see it that the change was for the better. . . .

Your asking for it is by far the most complimentary thing anyone has said about my stories in the American Mercury [*sic*].[46]

On December 21, 1925, Mencken expressed his delight at hearing (probably from Mrs. Knopf) that Winifred was in the process of reworking the novel. He assured her that doing so was a good sign, and he advised her to take all the time she needed.

He expressed confidence that the novel would be a "first rate piece of work" when she finished it.[47]

Winifred thanked Mencken for his encouragement and wrote: "I suppose everyone goes through the same experience, and writes and throws away and writes again as cheerfully as I. I got so sick of the whole thing that I dropped it, six weeks ago, and decided to take a vacation. Now I am ready to start it again . . . Meanwhile I find it almost impossible to write anything else."[48]

In this letter, Winifred also indicated that Mencken had accepted a story entitled "The Blue Spruce" (see 36–37) and told him that originally she had intended for this story to be a "paean of a northern winter." However, as she was in the process of writing, two skiers competing in a ski-jumping tournament had become the story's focus, and a tragic character named Lena, who had appeared in an earlier draft that Mencken had read and liked, had been eliminated. Winifred promised that she would try to think of another story for Lena in the near future. Just five days after she wrote this letter, Mencken responded, "It is excellent news that your novel is giving you a hard tussle. Hard writing makes smooth and charming reading. Take your time."[49]

Despite her insistence that she was giving all her available writing time to the novel, Winfred managed to submit an additional story to the *Mercury* editors on February 9, 1926. Mencken rejected this story, entitled "The Aphrodite," and when Winifred wrote to him again on March 9, 1926, she told him that he had been right to reject it. "It was artificial, based upon a fallacy and all that," she wrote, "and although I confess to liking it at times for the type of story it tried to be but probably wasn't, I shall lay it aside."[50]

Winifred's progress on the novel and any short stories that she might have been in the process of writing in spring 1926 was unexpectedly halted by the sudden illness of her mother, who was visiting relatives in Maryland when she became sick. Apparently, Winifred had informed Mencken of her plan to visit her mother in Maryland and to make a side trip to New York City before returning to Texas, for in a letter dated June 7, 1926, Mencken told Winifred that it would be a "great pleasure" to see her in New York the following week. He also expressed the hope that her mother's health was improving.[51]

But Helen Mahon's health did not improve. She died during the latter part of July 1926. When Winifred next wrote to Mencken on August 28, 1926, she was in Duluth without her husband and children, presumably taking care of her mother's business affairs and recuperating from her sudden and unexpected loss. During the days that followed her mother's death, Winifred had resumed writing, probably as a means to recovery, and had produced another short story. And once again, she needed Mencken's reassurance about her writing:

I am sending you this story with a good many qualms. I gather from the rather hesitating criticism my friends make of my stories that I have failed to make them beautiful. But I don't for the life of me see how anyone could write prettily of a character like Callie. I suppose they would have me make her a soul starving for beauty,—something like that. And if a story is psychologically sound, (as I think this is) I don't care, personally, whether it is pretty or not. Indeed I think prettiness would spoil it. Yet when I read it over, I admit it sounds crude and jerky . . . a good deal like poor Callie. Am I right or wrong?[52]

"Black Child," published in the *Mercury* in January 1927, is a story set in rural West Texas that illuminates the plight of an African American family. Sanford relates the events of this story through the consciousness of a five-year-old preadolescent named Callie. Callie frequently has the responsibility of caring for her younger siblings while their mother works as a domestic servant for a white lady who Callie calls "Mis' Carpenter." Humor that is a direct result of Callie's innocent, and therefore unreliable, point of view makes this story a delightful read. The story is told in four separate vignettes. In the first, the attitude of upper-class white society toward African Americans is illuminated when Mis' Carpenter demands that Callie's mother help with a party shortly after giving birth.

In the second section of the story, both of Callie's parents are now working for Mis' Carpenter, and Callie, who has been left in charge of her younger siblings, is hanging the family's wash as her siblings play around her. While she works, her brother Washington says, "Let's have a baptizin', what do you say Callie?"[53] A conversation between Callie and Washington ensues about who will be baptized and where the play baptism will take place. Then, without Callie's permission, her brothers run away down the road to a water tank. By the time Callie, who is clutching baby Theodore and holding her little sister Bernice by the hand, reaches the tank, the baptizing has already begun. Washington dunks Leroy three times— once in the name of the Father, once in the name of the Son, and once in the name of the Holy Ghost. When Leroy goes limp after the second dunking, Callie administers the following lifesaving techniques:

Callie grabbed Leroy by the leg just as Washington was about to duck him the third time. . . . "Washington, you done drowned him!"

"Huh," said Washington. Suddenly he looked scared and ran away up the road. Beatrice began to cry.

"Shut up," said Callie. "I've got to find me a barrel. Leroy, he's drowned." She laid the baby carefully on the ground. . . .

Just a little way up the slope Callie found a barrel full of tin cans and broken bottles, and dragged it down to the tank. . . . Heaving and tugging and pulling, she got Leroy over the barrel. . . .

Leroy was sick. He choked and cried in the mud. Callie rolled and rolled and rolled him on the barrel.

"Leroy is you drowned?"

"I sure is!"

"You ain't dead yet Leroy!"

Yet all the way home Callie was scared. Suppose Leroy fell down dead in the road . . . drowned![54]

In the third section, a slightly older Callie, who is substituting as Mis' Carpenter's domestic while Mama recovers from childbirth, follows her mother's Cousin Bertha's lead and steals a gold pin from one of Mis' Carpenter's gowns. Mama discovers what Callie has done and marches her back to Mis' Carpenter's house to return the pin and apologize. As a dejected Callie follows her mother and siblings home, Washington threatens to tell the lawman what she's done, and when the family passes a barbecue café and Callie sees a lawman, she hides her face.

In the fourth section, Washington and Leroy report that Cousin Bertha has stolen a dress from one of her employers and the lawman is looking for her. When the lawman knocks on the door of their house, Callie orders the children to hide under the bed, and when he enters the house, Callie is so frightened that she fights with him until someone outside says Bertha has been apprehended at the barbershop. The story ends with the lawman saying, "You damn little fool! Why didn't you tell me in the first place she wasn't here, eh?"[55]

WHILE "BLACK CHILD" is politically incorrect by twenty-first-century standards and contains some stereotypical portrayals of African Americans who are minor characters in the story, Winifred treats Callie and her family with respect and compassion. She portrays the children as innocents and their mother as a woman who maintains high moral and ethical principles, even as she struggles against hardships imposed upon her family by white society.

Near the end of the letter that accompanied her submission of "Black Child," Winifred told Mencken about her mother's death, an event that had occurred since they last communicated:

This is the only thing I have written this summer. You remember that when I was in New York in June, my mother was very sick. She lived until the end of July, since when I have been here [in Duluth], trying to get back to a normal state of mind. I suppose it is all part of the orad [sic] to wisdom, but sometimes I don't think I care very much about being wise.[56]

She added, "I haven't touched the novel, and shan't for another month, when I expect to be back in Texas."

The speed with which Mencken read Winifred's story and responded to her letter indicates the high regard that he had for her writing. He answered the letter within five days of receiving it and declared "Black Child" to be one of the best stories she had sent him. "It goes into type at once," he wrote. Once again, he advised her to pay little attention to unfounded criticisms. Then, in the final paragraph of his letter, he addressed her comments about Helen Mahon's death with a personal revelation of his own: "I won't attempt to offer you any consolation on the death of your mother. My own mother is now dead nearly a year but it is still impossible for me to adjust myself to her absence."[57]

After completing "Black Child," Winifred remained in Duluth for some time and resumed work on her novel. In the following passage from an undated letter that she wrote to Mencken, she indicates that she felt she was making progress:

At least I have my mind free—again for the novel. I *think* it is going to be good. I have to fight everything from literary clubs to influenza germs in the rest of my family for my time, and though sometimes I envy the fellow who is sure of his straight eight hours, at other times I think I get ahead almost as fast as things are.

At present the book is crude and jerky . . . very . . . but the various threads are interweaving quite neatly and I have at last some sort of design, adaptable to chapters and books, so that all I need now is the time to fill it in. And rewrite and rewrite and rewrite what is already down. And there are, of course, a thousand facts to check, and heaven knows how many thousand words to copy.[58]

However, when she wrote to Mencken on September 20, 1927, to tell him that she had finished the novel and was sending a copy of the manuscript to Mrs. Knopf and a copy to him, she was far from satisfied with the outcome:

Please don't think that I am begging for mercy where the novel is concerned. I don't think it deserves any mercy. I think it is about the flattest thing I ever read in my life, and although I had some hopes for it until recently, I can see now that it is pretty bad.

Writers, however, can't afford to have any pride, and when you have worked on anything for so long, you feel that it is entitled to its chance in the world; and so I am sending it out, rather against my better judgment, but hoping that you or someone else may be able to give me some advice.

Of course my state of mind may be due to the pressure under which I have been writing, but I feel today as though there were no possibility of its passing muster in its present state. It has no style and no good title; it is horribly jerky; it is all conversation (I have suddenly realized that for the last six months I have been consistently crossing out all the descriptive and expository passages and leaving only the naked dialog [sic]); several of the characters are wooden; and many of the issues have lost any interest they may once have had for me. The last half is better than the first, but that is about all that can be said for it.

Now what shall I do? . . .

No matter what happens to it, I am not sorry I wrote it, because I have learned a great many things in the process, and unless you tell me I am wasting my time . . . and maybe even then . . . I shall soon be starting one of the other novels I have in mind, to say nothing of a few short stories I have been postponing until I finished the book.[59]

Winifred also shared the news that "Forest Fire," a story Mencken had previously published in the *Mercury*, was being translated into German. "One reason for my haste in finishing the novel and shipping it off just now," she wrote, "is this: If there were anything to be gained by it, I *could* come to New York about the first of October for a few days,—something I am not always able to do when I have my children in Texas."

Mencken attempted to reassure Winifred about the novel, newly entitled *Arrows of the Almighty*, when he wrote to her on September 24, 1927: "It is excellent news that you are full of doubts about your novel. The bad ones are all written by authors who are absolutely sure of them." He ended this letter with what had by then become a familiar question: "Have you done any short stories of late? If so, I surely hope you give me a chance at them for *The American Mercury*."[60]

*Letters exchanged between Mencken and Sanford are reprinted in Appendix A.

Plans, Pressures, and Expectations

ON NOVEMBER 10, 1927, WINIFRED
Sanford notified David Lloyd of Paget Literary Agency that she was interested in
having his agency represent her. She had chosen Paget from a list of agencies that
had contacted her about representing her work after Edward J. O'Brien listed four
of her stories in *The Best Short Stories of 1926*.

Nearly a year ago you wrote to me and asked for some of my work. At that time I
had nothing to offer, having temporarily abandoned short stories in order to finish
a novel. I believe I told you that Knopf had asked for the first reading of it. . . .

Six weeks ago I finished the book and immediately sent it to Knopf, and this
morning I heard as follows . . . "I am afraid that should we accept your novel
now, we should hardly be able to do it justice. If you have not placed it in several
months from now, we shall be glad to reconsider it. And of course we shall want
to see anything you may do in the meanwhile. . . .

You will probably want to know what else I have done. I have been writing
only a few years and since I am married and have small children, I have so far been
unable to give full professional time to my typewriter. But I have had six stories, I
believe it is, published in *The American Mercury*, and two (with a third purchased but
not yet published) in *Woman's Home Companion*. Except for perhaps a dozen stories

which I wrote while learning my technique, this is all I have written i.e. I have sold everything, and have been asked for more by both magazines. . . .

I realize that this isn't a very awe-inspiring list of work, but I do feel that it is a fairly good start, and that I am justified in going ahead.[1]

Knopf returned the manuscript of *Arrows of the Almighty* to Winifred on November 29, 1927, and she forwarded it to David Lloyd. In the letter to Lloyd that accompanied the manuscript, she agreed to allow Paget to handle all future work with the exception of any stories that she submitted to the *Mercury* or to *Woman's Home Companion*—publications where she had established a reputation and did not need representation. Concerning *Arrows of the Almighty*, she wrote:

> There are . . . a great many other things about it that do not suit me. Being a first novel, it is a little messy in technique and has been taken apart and put together again too many times to look quite natural. And yet I do think it has its good points. I only hope that you . . . can find them.
>
> As for the future, I am too much up in the air, just now to know just what to predict. I am thinking of beginning another novel with the scene laid, perhaps, in Texas . . . which would make it an altogether different type of story.[2]

Lloyd, who also served as a literary agent for Pearl S. Buck, acknowledged receipt of *Arrows of the Almighty* and congratulated Winifred on the novel's "interesting plot and effective characterization." While he agreed that the style was somewhat monotonous, he felt that the novel overall was impressive and should not be shelved.[3]

On February 9, 1928, Lloyd informed Winifred that the title she had given the manuscript had been used in 1901 by Owen Johnson. In comments that Winifred made on both the front and back of the envelope containing Lloyd's letter, she left a few clues as to the novel's content. She had chosen the title *Arrows of the Almighty* hoping it would give a key to the story's content and indicate the novel's ironic tone. She noted that the main character, Robert Hollister, would "doubtless consider himself in some heroic relation to the almighty." She referred to choosing titles as a "discouraging business" and indicated that she disliked both narrative and expository titles. Then she listed alternates "Take Morning," "The Empty Cup," and "Bridge of Time" and noted that none of these pleased her.[4]

Despite Lloyd's positive comments regarding this novel, his responses were slow in coming, and Winifred, who was accustomed to receiving almost instant feedback when she submitted a short story to the *Mercury* editors, was beginning to have serious doubts about the manuscript. In a letter to Lloyd dated April 6, 1928, she wrote:

The more I think about that novel I sent you . . . the less I think of it. I wish now I had never sent it out.

The main character is not so bad; neither I think are Olive and Faith, but I am very strongly opposed to the whole socialistic intrusion and Ralph's conscientious objection to the war. It sounds so reminiscent of Ernest Poole and Upton Sinclair. I'd like to out all of that.[5]

Once again, Lloyd acknowledged that Sanford's concerns were valid, but he assured her that the total effect was one of substance and reality. Although agents at Paget did not think the novel was Winifred's best work, they agreed that it should be shopped around. They would return it for revision only if they failed to receive an offer on the current draft. Lloyd reported that already he had sent the manuscript to Putnam, whose editors had returned it with a comment that, although the book was well written, it was neither profound enough nor moving enough to appeal to the general public.[6]

Winifred responded to Lloyd's letter on April 23, 1928:

It is quite evident that I didn't succeed with my original intention, which was . . . to give a rather ironic portrait of Robert as seen in the mirror of his own reaction to living and his own interpretation of his family . . . I realize that a successfully ironic novel appeals to only a limited number of people and if the irony wasn't apparent in this one, it must have seemed flat.

I really don't know whether it is worth working over or not. These things that try to be subtle are fearfully hard to write.[7]

In this letter, Winifred told Lloyd of her plans to write a second novel, with a college-bred girl from the Midwest as the protagonist, and after she finished that novel, she was planning to write one set in the oil-field towns of Texas.

Less than a month later, David Lloyd returned the manuscript of *Arrows of the Almighty* to Winifred and reported on the agency's efforts to place the book. After careful consideration, Boni and Liveright had rejected the manuscript because their editors did not believe the novel would produce a sufficient number of sales. However, their readers had commented favorably, noting the humanity and realism with which Sanford's characters were drawn. *Harper's* also had expressed interest, but the final vote of their editorial board was split. Therefore, they had returned the manuscript. Both Dial Press and Putnam had seriously considered publishing *Arrows of the Almighty* before eventually returning it to Lloyd. Although readers at each of these major publishing houses had made favorable comments about Winifred's writing, Paget had been unsuccessful in placing her first novel. Lloyd wrote that the book had just missed hitting the target, and he suggested that she now consider rewriting it.[8]

Winifred had expressed a willingness to rewrite *Arrows of the Almighty* several times in earlier correspondence with Mencken and with Lloyd, but Lloyd's suggestion that she now do so came at a bad time. Following her mother's death and the completion of the novel, she had experienced a case of writer's block and had not produced a single piece of writing that she deemed worthy of submission in almost two years. But just prior to receiving news that Paget had failed to place her novel, she had managed to complete a new short story entitled "Windfall" and had sent it to H. L. Mencken.

On April 11, 1928, Mencken indicated his pleasure at receiving "Windfall" and informed Winifred that he was accepting the story for immediate publication. He told her that a check and proofs would be in the mail to her soon and ended his letter with his now-to-be-expected "I hope there is something else on the way."[9]

The main character in "Windfall," Winifred's first story about oil drilling, is a shy West Texas farm wife named Cora Ponder. When the story begins, Cora is experiencing an internal conflict because she wants to see the oil well that was brought in on the Ponder family's farm the previous night, but she is reluctant to go down to the well site because she fears that her presence will attract attention. All day Cora has used her chores as a delaying tactic, but in the late afternoon, she washes herself, dresses in a clean gingham dress and sunbonnet, and leaves the house.

In the story's second section, Cora views the following scene as she approaches the well:

> Cars were standing everywhere, like shiny-backed beetles, in the sun. . . . When she came nearer, she saw the people—the city people, first, spreading rugs in the shade of their sedans, and drinking ice water from thermos jugs, and eating sandwiches and reading the Sunday paper. A little farther on she saw the country people—the men with their suspenders crossed on their backs, and the women with their flowered hats and their black shoes and stockings.[10]

Just as Cora, who is self-conscious about her missing teeth, feared, people try to engage her in conversation: "'Say,' they said, all of them looking her up and down, 'you won't be speaking to us, Mrs. Ponder, now you've got a well on your place. You and Luke will be too good for us poor folks.'"[11]

Cora cannot see the oil for all the men gathered around the rig. While she waits for them to disperse, her eyes search the crowd for her children. She sees her girls dancing to a phonograph "on Sunday afternoon!" She sees that her younger son,

Whitney, is helping the men with the pipe, but her oldest son is nowhere in sight. When the women ask what Cora and her husband, Luke, will do with all the money they will get from the well, Cora answers with her hand over her mouth. "'I don't rightly know what we'll do.' She did not like to speak of her teeth, and yet she could think of nothing else she particularly wanted."[12]

The women continue to talk, criticizing Cora's child-rearing techniques and making predictions about the ways sudden wealth will change her family's life forever. As the women talk, Cora becomes more and more uncomfortable, and to make matters worse, she witnesses firsthand how oil money has changed Jasper Gooley, the son of a former neighbor.

> He had a woman with him now, a large blonde woman in a red hat. Cora saw her squint in a little mirror while she dabbed powder on her nose. She saw Jasper's Panama hat, and his fat hands resting on the wheel, and his puffy cheeks; and when he climbed out of his car, backward, she saw his blue and white striped seersucker trousers, and his white silk shirt and his white shoes.[13]

In section three of the story, Cora's son Whitney leads his mother to the well and insists that she put her finger in the oil. She tastes it, then begins to feel uncomfortable in the presence of the men and backs away.

In the description of Cora's slow walk back to her house, Winifred demonstrates her masterful use of sensory detail.

> She saw part of a newspaper impaled on a mesquite thorn, beyond the well. She walked over to it, without attracting anyone's attention and picked it up. Then she saw a scrap of shiny brown paper and a wad of tinfoil, and beyond that, in a clump of cactus, a piece of sandwich wrapping, streaked with yellow salad dressing. There was an empty bottle lying under the wrapping, and the bits of broken glass shining here and there over the pasture. "Tomorrow," thought Cora, "after the washing is finished and on the line, I'll bring a bucket and gather it up before the cattle get into it."[14]

Cora stops at the top of a rise and looks back toward the well, where Jasper Gooley stands with one arm around the blond woman and one arm around Whitney's shoulder. The story ends with Cora wondering "with fear in her heart, what Jasper is saying to her son."[15]

IN "WINDFALL," the first of several stories that Winifred wrote about Texas oil drilling, she captures the historical moment when mechanization in the form of the oil industry came into conflict with long-held agrarian values that had been in place for centuries. Cora's fears regarding the changes that sudden wealth will bring about for her family reflect concerns that many Texas agrarians experienced during the Burkburnett and East Texas oil booms.

Winifred's comments to David Lloyd, shortly after she submitted "Windfall" to Mencken, indicate that she was not always the best judge of her own writing. "It isn't very good," she wrote of "Windfall," "but it is the first story I have been able to do about the oil fields."[16] Not long after this story came out in *The American Mercury*, Texas poet, journalist, and literary editor Hilton Greer included it an anthology entitled *Best Short Stories from the Southwest*. Two years after the story's publication, Southern Methodist University professors John Owen Beaty, Ernest Erwin Leisy, and Mary Lamar included "Windfall" in an early college textbook entitled *Facts and Ideas for Students of English Composition*. In this anthology, Winifred's story appears between selections by Kipling and Chesterton, a circumstance that, Winifred told S. Omar Barker, "ought to be glory enough for any author."[17]

Nevertheless, after the publication of "Windfall," another full year elapsed in which Winifred did not submit a single story to the editors of *The American Mercury* or to any other publication. Finally, in a letter dated May 14, 1929, Mencken inquired, "What are you up to? . . . It is now more than a year since we last printed you, and the time seems far too long."[18]

Winifred responded to Mencken's inquiry ten days later writing, "I wish I *did* have something worth printing." "I have a dozen things in mind, but nothing I have written for the last year or two has pleased me or anyone else. If I were only sure that the bird would rise from the ashes, I would light a big bonfire."[19] Once again, Mencken supplied Winifred with needed encouragement, telling her that it was excellent news that she was getting back to work and that he would be delighted to see more of her fiction in the *Mercury*.

As Winifred's comments to H. L. Mencken and David Lloyd indicate, she was a perfectionist about her writing and was rarely satisfied with the results of her efforts. In the 1936 feature article that Hilton Greer wrote about her, he described her writing process thus: "She composes slowly, tears up many a draft that does not suit her, rewrites and rewrites, working at the final drafts until they are done to suit her."[20]

This desire for perfection accounts, in part, for the limited number of published stories that bear Winifred Sanford's name. Her comment to Mencken about her temptation to "light a big bonfire" may also account for the disappearance of *Arrows of the Almighty* and other manuscripts that Winifred mentioned by title in her correspondence with various editors and literary agents.

Winifred's daughters were also aware of their mother's perfectionist tendencies toward her writing. All three witnessed her burn letters, literary reviews, and manuscripts that failed to meet her expectations and/or her high literary standards. In an undated letter that Emerett Sanford Miles wrote to her sister Helen sometime in the 1950s, Emerett told of receiving an undated Wichita Falls newspaper clipping that had appeared in the local newspaper sometime between 1925 and 1930 from a former Manuscript Club member who was a friend of Winifred's. Instead of forwarding the original article to Helen, Emerett copied passages into the body of her letter because she was afraid that Winifred might "get hold of it and throw it in the fire."[21]

Winifred's desire to control her public image, as well as the quality of her writing, was neither unusual nor peculiar. The practice of burning substandard manuscripts and personal correspondence has a long history among literary writers. Virgil left instructions for a draft of *The Aeneid* to be destroyed after his death; Franz Kafka instructed his literary executor to burn his diaries, letters, manuscripts, and sketches, unread; and Emily Dickinson left a directive that her sister was to burn all her papers and correspondence. Mikhail Bulgakov is said to have reconstructed *The Master and Margarita* from memory after he burned an earlier draft of this famous novel. (For more information about this practice, see Chapter Eight, footnote 6.)

No one was more aware of Winifred's inability to be objective about her writing than Mencken. He attempted to soothe her doubts and offer her reassurance in numerous letters: "I see nothing wrong at all" (August 3, 1924); "Don't let imbeciles annoy you!" (March 28, 1925); "Please pay no heed to such foolish advice" (September 3, 1926); "What are you up to?" (May 14, 1929); "Have you any new stories?" (August 20, 1927).

Mencken's words usually had the desired effect, but a full year elapsed before Winifred responded to his May 14, 1929, inquiry with a story submission. On May 8, 1930, Mencken wrote to thank her for giving him an opportunity to see "Luck," which he declared to be an excellent short story.[22]

According to Winifred's daughters, the title for this story was suggested to her by one of Wayland Sanford's favorite phrases. In conversations with friends and family members, he often attributed his success in oil and gas ventures to "Sanford luck," something he claimed to have inherited from his father, Wayland William Sanford. The incident at the center of this story is the blowout of an oil well located in one of the largest oil fields in South Texas. Although the central character is a speculator named Mr. Cox, the character through whose perspective the story is narrated is an oil-field worker named Roy.

When the story opens, Roy is in the local domino parlor hoping a job will turn up, when he hears that the derrick man on Mr. Cox's well has been injured so severely that Mr. Cox has brought the man into the hospital. Hoping to get a job as the man's replacement, Roy sits on the running board of Mr. Cox's Ford until he returns. Cox has the reputation of being unlucky, and although men in the pool hall have said Cox is close to bringing in a good well, Roy is wary. He is even more wary when he catches a glimpse of the injured man's burns through a hospital window. When Mr. Cox finally returns to his truck, Roy asks for a job, and Mr. Cox says, "Pile in if you want to."[23]

As Mr. Cox and Roy make their way down a muddy dirt road in the second section of the story, they have a conversation that demonstrates Winifred's ability to reveal character and dramatize a situation with a minimum of words:

> "Have any trouble bringing your man in from the lease?"
> "Yeah, I had a little trouble."
> "Didn't go in the ditch did you?"
> "No I didn't go in the ditch."
> "Hurt pretty bad was he?"
> "Yeah."
> "Think he'll get over it?"
> "Not hardly."[24]

As Roy rides along beside Mr. Cox, he thinks:

> Oil men were all the same. If they weren't making deals, or traveling back and
> forth to town, they were standing around on the derrick floor, smoking cigarettes
> and getting in the way of the crews. Maybe, when nothing much was happen-
> ing, they'd double up on the seats of their cars and go off to sleep for a while, but
> they'd be back before long . . . A man couldn't sleep very long at a time when he
> needed a well as bad as Mr. Cox needed this baby.[25]

When Mr. Cox meets a fuel truck and attempts to leave the ruts, his Ford skids off the road and the engine dies. He and Roy get the engine started again but the truck's tires are stuck in the mud. While they are trying to get the truck unstuck, it slides down an embankment and overturns.

In the third numbered section, rain has turned to snow, and Roy and Mr. Cox are making their way down the road after a farmer with a team of mules pulls the Ford truck out of the ditch. As they pass the oil lease of a Mr. Rouse, Roy is reminded of the owner's successes.

Some birds got all the *luck* . . . It didn't seem to make any difference where [Rouse] happened to drill: he always got a well. He could put down a hole ten miles from the nearest production and get a thousand-barrel well. He could take a lease which was spotted all over with dry holes, and find a new sand nobody had ever heard of before."[26]

Like Wayland Sanford, Mr. Rouse appeared to have "every damn thing he wanted."[27]

In the final scene of the story, Roy and Mr. Cox arrive at the lease, where the crew is gathered around a fire, trying to stay warm. Mr. Cox orders the men to drill deeper. When the driller asks if Cox wants them to dry drill, a method that is much riskier than filling the hole with mud, Cox says yes. Not wanting to risk hurting his crew, the driller calls for the fire on the derrick floor to be extinguished. Cox tells the driller to pull the tools and orders Roy to the top of the derrick. When the driller hollers again for the fire to be extinguished, Mr. Cox replies, "Didn't I say I'd look after the stove?"[28]

As soon as Roy sets the pipe and the driller releases the brake, a steam of oil spurts sideways from the joint. Roy hears a roar and sees a sheet of flames when the oil reaches the fire. He jumps from the derrick to the slush pit, and one of the men pulls him out unharmed. Roy is choking and spitting mud when he sees someone he doesn't recognize sitting on the ground. "He didn't have any hair or eyelashes or eyebrows or any skin on his face, and he was staring at his hands as if he didn't know what it meant." Only when the man looks up and grins does Roy recognize Mr. Cox, who is burned so badly that he doesn't feel pain. "It's your *luck*," Roy screams. "It's your goddamn *luck*."[29]

ON SEPTEMBER 26, 1930, Winifred wrote to H. L. Mencken concerning a review of "Luck" by Kathleen Norris that a member of the *Mercury* staff had forwarded to her:

I want to thank you . . . or whoever it was . . . who sent me the clipping which mentions that last story of mine. I do get provoked though, sometimes, at these people who make so much of "stark realism." I am not setting out to write stark realism or anything else in particular except what strikes me as a possibly interesting story.[30]

Mencken urged Winifred once again to pay no attention to newspaper discussions of her writing. He told her that Kathleen Norris was an enthusiastic admirer of Winifred's work. "It differs enormously, to be sure, from her own," he wrote, "but she is a very intelligent woman and knows a good story when she sees it."[31] Once again, Mencken's encouraging words had a positive effect, for in November 1930,

Winifred submitted another new short story—one entitled "Mr. Carmichael's Room"—to *The American Mercury*. "You wrote me some time ago that you would like to see another story," she wrote to Mencken in a letter that accompanied the manuscript. "Well, here it is,—and as doleful as usual . . . There are, I may add, a vast number of Mr. Carmichael's in our part of the country, now that the oil business has blown up."[32]

"Mr. Carmichael's Room" was the last story by Winifred Sanford ever to appear in *The American Mercury*. Like Mr. Cox in "Luck," the central character in this story is a down-on-his-*luck* oil prospector. Once again, the story's events are related through the consciousness of a minor character, this time a middle-aged woman in whose house Mr. Carmichael has been living for the last ten years.

When the story begins, the time is mid-morning in a West Texas oil town, and Mrs. Philips is wearing her overcoat and sitting outside in her porch swing. The weather is so cold that the water pipes inside her house have frozen, but she prefers sitting outside to being inside because of the unpleasant events that had taken place earlier that morning.

When Mrs. Philips went to Mr. Carmichael's room, she found him dead, and now she can't quit thinking about him. Mr. Carmichael was like most of the oil men she had seen come and go. During the boom, he had made money faster than he could spend it and was always "on the go," playing cards or placing bets on prize-fights and wrestling matches. Since the oil boom had waned, creditors had reclaimed his car and typewriter, and he had gotten into fights with his ex-wife, owners of the local hotel, and owners of the local country club. But always he had been kind to Mrs. Philips.

In the second section of the story, the undertaker arrives and inquires if Mr. Carmichael's daughter will be coming to the funeral. When Mrs. Philips tells him she doubts the girl's mother will allow it, he searches the room for any items he can take as payment for services rendered. Through the description of these items, Winifred Sanford reveals that Mr. Carmichael was a somewhat flawed character.

Mrs. Philips is not so much a naïve narrator as she is a woman in denial. In the story's third section, the undertaker uncovers a gold cigarette lighter and a revolver as he searches through Mr. Carmichael's closet. But when Mrs. Philips spies a silver cup that Mr. Carmichael won in a dog show, she prefers to remember how much he loved his dog rather than consider the lighter and revolver. She remembers how, because of unpaid bills, Mr. Carmichael couldn't afford to have his clothes laundered anymore and was forced to wash his things by hand and hang them on the back of a chair to dry. And when the undertaker turns up a box of shotgun shells, she remembers how much Mr. Carmichael liked to hunt.

In the story's fourth section, the undertaker focuses his attention on Mr. Carmichael's desk, where a picture of Mr. Carmichael's daughter reminds Mrs. Philips just how much he loved his child. When the undertaker uncovers a flask, she remembers how Mr. Carmichael shouted, "Here's to *luck!*" when he poured drinks.[33] And when the undertaker uncovers letters from investors who lost money in Mr. Carmichael's oil deals, Mrs. Philips assures herself that

> there was nothing crooked about Mr. Carmichael; she wouldn't believe that, no matter what anybody said, but it just seemed sometimes like he didn't know how to take care of himself. He was always getting mixed up in things without half knowing what they were about. . . . No, there might be mail-order operators who never expected to make any money for their stockholders, but Mr. Carmichael wasn't one of them.[34]

Finally, the undertaker finds something of value—Mr. Carmichael's "sucker list," and with Mrs. Philips watching, the undertaker folds the sheet of paper containing names of people who have invested in Mr. Carmichael's failed oil deals and slips it into his coat pocket.

In the final section, the dead man's daughter returns Mrs. Philips's telephone call, and just as Mrs. Philips predicted, the mother won't let the girl travel to West Texas to attend her father's funeral. When Mrs. Philips asks if the girl wants her father's things, the girl asks if there is any money. When Mrs. Philips asks if the girl or her mother can pay Mr. Carmichael's overdue rent, the girl hangs up the telephone.

In the story's last scene, Mrs. Philips follows the undertaker outside, where the weather suddenly has turned pleasant, and the story ends where it began, with Mrs. Philips on the front porch of her house. "Because she couldn't stand going back inside the house, just then, she sat down in the porch swing, with her coat wrapped more tightly than ever around her, and watched Mr. Haley drive away in the hearse."[35]

MENCKEN RESPONDED TO Winifred's letter immediately, telling her that "Mr. Carmichael's Room" was a story he would be delighted to publish. He closed this letter, dated November 21, 1930, with the last recorded words from the famous New York editor to the Texas housewife/short-story writer: "It is a pleasure, indeed, to see you writing again."[36]

When Mencken wrote these words, approximately one year after the New York stock market crash of October 29, 1929, signaled the start of the Great Depression, the *American Mercury* readership was dwindling. With economic conditions paramount in the minds of most Americans, and with political tensions in Europe escalating, subscribers were no longer as interested in Mencken's acerbic criticisms of American life as they once had been. A now-beleaguered public preferred literature that was upbeat, optimistic, and hopeful to stories that were starkly realistic and essays that were cynical and satirical. The sharp decline in the Mercury's readership that began with the New York stock market crash would continue unabated until 1932, when Samuel Knopf, the major stockholder in the magazine, died and financial advisors recommended that the magazine undergo reorganization.[37]

"Mr. Carmichael's Room" appeared in the April 1931 issue of The American Mercury, and shortly thereafter, Robert Innes Center, literary advisor for Bobbs-Merrill/Macmillan, one the most prestigious literary agencies in the world, wrote to the American Mercury staff to inquire about the author of "Mr. Carmichael's Room." At his request, they forwarded his letter to Winifred. In this letter, Center told her that he had been so impressed with her story that he was writing on the chance that she might have plans to write a novel. He felt that her style and material were suited to the novel genre, and that if she would put as much effort into writing one as she apparently had devoted to "Mr. Carmichael's Room," her efforts certainly would be rewarded.[38]

Winifred responded to Center's letter on April 27, 1931:

As for a novel, I am afraid I have nothing you want. Four years ago, I did complete a novel of sorts, which lingered for a time in Knopf's offices, and Harper's [sic], etc. and apparently just missed the mark,—a fate over which I have no regrets. Indeed I am glad it was never published as it stands, although I still feel it has possibilities for reworking. And that is what I intend to do if I ever see time enough ahead to devote to it.[39]

On the same day that Winifred wrote this letter to Center, she also addressed a letter to A. W. Barmby, a literary agent with Knopf who had made favorable comments about "Mr. Carmichael's Room" and had asked if she might have a novel to send him. She wrote that she had written one "unsatisfactory" novel that was rejected by Knopf in 1927 and added, "I am now more than glad that this novel was never published." She told Barmby that a number of people, including H. L. Mencken, had urged her to publish a volume of short stories, but that she, personally, had never cared for such collections and supposed they would be hard to sell.[40]

As Winifred had told Mencken when she wrote to him on November 18, 1930, the oil business in West Texas had "blown up." The average price of West Texas crude dropped from $1.27 a barrel in 1929 to $.65 a barrel in 1931.[41] With oil production in the Burkburnett field on the wane, the local economy had begun to experience the negative aspects of the Great Depression that had affected the rest of the country for months already.

About the same time that oil production in the West Texas fields was declining, a new discovery in East Texas attracted the attention of oil speculators to that region of the state. A wildcatter named Columbus Marion "Dad" Joiner drilled a well he named the Daisy Mae and brought in a gusher in a field near Kilgore, Texas. This well led to the discovery that a giant oil reservoir lay beneath the pine forests of East Texas, and oil exploration quickly shifted from West Texas to an East Texas field that was forty-three miles long and five miles wide. Like many other West Texas businessmen and speculators, Wayland Sanford decided to relocate his law office to Longview, Texas.

Once again, Winifred utilized her observations of life in an oil-boom town to record in fiction the upheaval that such an event precipitated on agrarian communities. She entitled this story "Fever in the South," and for some unknown reason, she did not submit the story to H. L. Mencken.

"Fever in the South" captures both the chaos and the excitement that accompanied a major oil boom. The story is divided into four sections, with each section narrated from the point of view of a different character. The first narrator is a retired oil prospector named Mr. Donovan who, when the story opens, is driving through East Texas in a rainstorm. As he tries to keep his vehicle in the ruts of the road, Donovan sees trucks carrying drilling pipe and drilling rigs and passes hitchhikers, hamburger stands on wheels, wagons loaded with household goods, and other signs that signal an oil boom is in progress. When he enters the town, he sees cars from Arkansas, Michigan, California, New York, and Pennsylvania. When he finally finds a parking place, he encounters friends that he has known in other oil drilling locations. Oilmen with maps are scribbling down descriptions and puzzling over abstracts, and Donovan begins to think about what he would need to bring in another oil strike. He wishes he could get in touch with a first-rate fortune-teller named Rita who had told him several times where to drill. When an old friend says, "I heard you was quitting," Donovan replies, "Me quitting? Hell no, I ain't quitting—not yet awhile."[42]

The central character in the second section of "Fever in the South" is the fortune-teller, Rita, who arrived with her husband, Tom, and the couple's portable hamburger stand the previous evening. While Tom finishes unloading their belongings, Rita goes in search of water and surveys the area:

Except for the pine trees, which gave her a kind of shut-in feeling, this was just like all the other oil fields she had seen. There were the same horses, sweating and straining at their loads; the same oilmen honking behind them, trying to get past; the same wagons, with bedsprings and washtubs and oil stoves and crates of chickens; the same hamburger stands, and as you came closer to the railroad tracks, the same signs—Townsite lots $50; Gas and electricity; high and dry . . . .

She liked all the excitement . . . the smell of coffee, and the rangers sitting on their horses with their guns in their holsters . . . the oil men sneaking into her tent to have their fortunes told . . . It was a racket . . . but she had made some lucky guesses, and her clients had a way of always coming back.[43]

While Rita is gone, Mr. Donovan recognizes Tom and asks for Rita. Rita returns, and as she winds her fortune-teller scarf around her head and prepares to tell Mr. Donovan's fortune, she thinks, "As for telling him where to drill, well, that ought to be easy, with all the oil there seemed to be in East Texas . . . ."[44]

An African American man, Moses Tatum, is the central character in the story's third section. He is patching the gate to his property when he hears a car approaching. He and his entire family are frightened when a white man appears on their land. The white man is Mr. Donovan, who is in search of mineral rights. The words he uses—words like "royalty," "wildcat well," "mineral rights," and "oil and gas lease" confuse Moses, and as Donovan drives away, Moses asks his wife, Lovie, "What he mean? A oil well . . . ."[45]

The main character in section four is a longtime East Texas resident named Miss Carrie, who has been talked into taking in boarders by a stream of people asking for lodging. One of her boarders is Mr. Donovan, and when this section of the story opens, Carrie is preparing to accompany Mr. Donovan to the site of a well that he has successfully completed on Moses Tatum's land. As Miss Carrie dresses, she thinks about all the changes that the oil boom has precipitated in her once quiet hometown. The streets are now packed with noisy strangers, her housemaid has quit working for her to take a better-paying job, the courthouse is crowded with girls transcribing records on typewriters, and the church she attended for years has been sold to make space for an office building.

On what turns out to be a rather unpleasant ride to the oil lease in Mr. Donovan's vehicle, Carrie observes

oil men . . . hundreds of them . . . and slovenly women carrying paper flowers from door to door, and boys selling sandwiches and pralines on the courthouse steps, and blind beggars, and old Negroes with guitars, but they were all strangers, all of them, who had drifted in with the boom.[46]

When she and Donovan arrive at the well, Miss Carrie sees the wooden derrick, the Christmas tree, the slush pit, the machinery, and the pipe running to a row of tanks, and she thinks, "So this is an oil well!" Then she looks at Moses's home and thinks, "And this is the Negro's cabin."[47]

While Donovan inspects his oil tanks, Miss Carrie observes Moses and his family packing their belongings into a ramshackle wagon. She wonders where they'll go and if they will find another house. Seeing that this family is moving out of their home troubles Carrie, and she wonders if everyone will leave, eventually, "like Esau of old, selling their birthright for a mess of pottage."[48]

IN THE SUMMER OF 1931, Paget Literary Agency placed "Fever in the South" with the *North American Review* for publication in its November 1931 issue. Paget also placed "Two Junes" with *Household Magazine* for publication in its November 1931 issue. That same summer, Winifred placed a short story entitled "The Wedding" with *Woman's Home Companion*,[49] but for some unknown reason this story never appeared in print under Winifred's name. A story by that same title, but attributed to Jay Gelzer, did appear in *Woman's Home Companion* in June 1934. The plot and structure of Gelzer's story is strikingly similar to Winifred's description of a novel she planned to base on "The Wedding." (She described this novel in a letter she wrote to David Lloyd on May 9, 1932.) While no evidence exists that Winifred ever published under a pen name, this possibility cannot be eliminated for the following reason: in a letter she wrote to Lloyd on March 1, 1938, regarding her detective novel, *You Asked for It*, she asked, "Since I still hope to write a serious novel, and already have a very small reputation under my own name, hadn't I better publish this one . . . if at all . . . under a nom de plume?"[50]

Sometime in the summer of 1931, Wayland Sanford moved his family from Wichita Falls to Dallas, where Emerett and Helen, now eleven and nine respectively, could be shielded from the rough characters and rowdy lifestyles that so often accompanied a major oil boom like the one in East Texas. The family's relocation occupied much of Winifred's time and energy throughout the latter months of 1931 and most of 1932, and by the time the family was settled enough that she could turn her attention back to writing short stories, H. L. Mencken was no longer editor of *The American Mercury*.

Menken did not resign from his editorship at the *Mercury* until the end of 1933, but his attention to daily operations of the magazine had begun to dwindle in 1929, when subscription rates that once numbered more than 77,000 decreased dramatically following the onset of the Great Depression. With the sharp decline in readership, the magazine's influence on American life had been greatly reduced, and Mencken had little interest in changing the magazine's format to accommodate the shifting interests of American readers. Little by little, he turned more and more of his editing duties over to his assistant editor, Charles Angoff. No doubt Mencken's neglect of these duties resulted in an increased workload for his young assistant and may have become a contributing factor to Angoff's growing resentment.

After Mencken resigned from his post as editor of the *Mercury*, he continued to write for the *The Baltimore Sun* and to devote a great deal of time to making his wife's remaining years the best years of her life. Sara Hardt had contracted tuberculosis during her seven-year courtship with Mencken. The Menckens married soon after doctors removed one of Hardt's kidneys and told H. L. Mencken that she would live, at the most, three more years.[51]

Mencken was in his fifties when he married Sara; and after their wedding, his priorities shifted from the public world outside their New York apartment to the private life they shared for a few short years. He wrote less, relaxed more, and took vacations—to the West Indies and the Mediterranean and to a variety of locations within the United States. But ill health was never far from Sara Hardt Mencken. She died, quite suddenly, of meningitis on June 1, 1935. She and H. L. Mencken were married for only five short years, but during that time he was a devoted husband. So devoted to her needs, in fact, that she exceeded her doctors' expectations by living two years longer than they had predicted.[52]

After Sara's death, Mencken continued to write, but his essays and articles lacked their former intensity, often taking the form of nostalgic memoirs or humorous, anecdotal essays. He had grown older, and the gap between his opinions and the opinions of a new generation of American citizens continued to increase. He had reservations about the U.S. entry into World War II, and he held contempt for Franklin D. Roosevelt and the New Deal—but he no longer had the energy or the desire to influence a rapidly changing American society.[53]

Unexpected Interruptions

DALLAS,

TEXAS,

1931–1938

WHEN THE SCHOOL YEAR BEGAN IN
September 1931, Winifred Sanford and her daughters, Emerett and Helen, were living in a house at 3601 Haynie Avenue, just a few blocks west of Southern Methodist University. Wayland, who lived in Longview during the week, traveled the two hundred and sixty miles from Longview to Dallas each weekend to be with his family. Although he was neither an uncaring mate nor an unloving father, Wayland was an ambitious oil and gas lawyer who devoted much time and energy to his business ventures. And in the spare time that being away from his family afforded him, he enjoyed hunting in the East Texas pine forest, fishing in the plentiful small lakes and ponds, and playing golf with business associates. After a time, he and his friend Ted Pitkin constructed a makeshift landing strip in an open field outside of Longview, where they took flying lessons.[1]

If Winifred resented these living arrangements, she left no record of her resentment, and neither Emerett Sanford Miles nor Helen J. Sanford indicated that they suffered any ill effects from their father's extended absences. However, they did say that they had a long-standing joke that Wayland was gone so much of the time when they were growing up that they met him for the first time when he attended their high school graduations.

Winifred Sanford in the front yard of her new home in Dallas, Texas, circa 1931.

When Winifred and her daughters relocated to Dallas in 1931, the girls were adolescents who no longer required their mother's constant attention, and they were old enough to provide her with lively companionship during Wayland's frequent absences. And with Wayland living in Longview during the week and both girls in school, Winifred was free once again to devote attention to her writing.

Her correspondence with various editors and literary agents during this time indicates that by 1932 she was working on a second novel. This novel, set in the oil fields of Texas, may have provided an outlet for any frustrations she may have felt about the family's living arrangements and Wayland's continued preoccupation with his business ventures. In a letter to David Lloyd, dated May 9, 1932, Winifred wrote, "I think I told you when I was in N.Y. last Nov., that I had some idea of trying another novel. I have been working on it all winter, and it is far from completed." She proceeded to describe a story line in which she would utilize the same characters that she had created in "The Wedding." Concerning this novel, Winifred wrote:

The novel is not a 'plot' novel, but a realistic account of oil field life, told from the view point [sic] of an oil field worker's wife . . . I have something like 80,000 words very roughly accounted for, in three books separated by several months or years, and I had planned a fourth book to bring the story down to "The Wedding," which would probably add another 20,000." . . .

The novel begins with Lila's own wedding and ends with the wedding of her little sister, the main theme being Lila's reluctance to see her sister set out on the hard road she had to travel herself . . . .[2]

Winifred was planning to reproduce "The Wedding" as the final chapter of the novel, and as she told Lloyd, she intended to write three additional novels utilizing the same set of characters. At the end of this letter, she wrote, "I have written no short stories at all since last summer but have spent all my available time on the novel."

Although Winifred was once again actively engaged in writing, she missed the companionship of her friends in the Manuscript Club of Wichita Falls. In an effort to fill the void that being separated from them had left in her life, she set about organizing what she hoped would become a similar writing club in Dallas. This club eventually became one of six study groups that met as a collective known as the College Club of Dallas.[3] Winifred also began to teach creative writing classes in the living room of the Sanford home, and she served as a consultant to less experienced writers who sought her advice on a variety of projects. Soon a steady stream of writers and would-be writers were coming and going from the house at 3601 Haynie Avenue. These activities became so commonplace that the Sanford children accepted them as everyday occurrences and paid the visitors little notice.

"Mother was not the kind of person who called attention to her accomplishments," Helen J. Sanford explained. "Her focus was always upon us and what we were doing. To us, she was just our mother." Helen recounted an amusing anecdote as a means of illustrating what she meant: A group of writers was gathered in the family's living room one day, and one of the writers asked Helen what she wanted to be when she grew up. Helen replied, "Just a plain mother—like my mother." The group laughed, and their laughter disturbed Helen for she had no idea what she had said that was funny.

In fall 1932, both the Sanford family's routine and Winifred's future writing plans were altered when she discovered that she was pregnant once again. On May 25, 1933, at the age of forty-two, she gave birth to the Sanfords' third daughter, Mary Mahon Sanford. When a former Manuscript Club friend visited Winifred and her new baby in the hospital, Winifred reportedly said, "I'll bet you thought I couldn't do this at my age."

With Mary's birth, Winifred's domestic responsibilities once again took precedence over her writing and her plans to finish her second novel. Now, in addition to caring for a new baby, she was parenting two teenage girls almost singlehandedly—but even with this added drain on her time and energies, she still made some time to write. In one of Mary Sanford Gordon's earliest memories, she lay in her baby bed, watching through the bars of her crib as Winifred sat at a nearby desk, pecking with two fingers on a manual typewriter.

Sometime after H. L. Mencken resigned from *The American Mercury*, Winifred sent "Wildcat" to the new editorial staff. In an undated rejection letter (probably written in 1934) Charles Angoff thanked Winifred for sending "Wildcat" and informed her that the editors were rejecting the story because they had a tremendous backlog of fiction. He encouraged her to submit a nonfiction essay instead. But if any subsequent letters or manuscripts were exchanged between Winifred Sanford and Charles Angoff or any other member of the *Mercury* staff after this time, proof of that correspondence has not been located.[4]

At the time that Angoff sent the rejection to Winifred, Harold Hazlitt was chief editor of the *Mercury*, but within six months of hiring Hazlitt, Alfred Knopf became dissatisfied with the new editor's performance. Knopf fired Hazlitt and promoted Angoff to the position of chief editor. However, less than six months after promoting Angoff, Knopf became dissatisfied with changes that Angoff was making to the *Mercury* and decided to sell the magazine. Frustrated and newly unemployed, Angoff focused his negative feelings upon Mencken, with whom he had an already strained relationship. Some scholars believe, as did Mencken, that Angoff began taking notes and making plans to write a book about his former boss during this time. In conversations with his brother, August Mencken, and with a few close friends, Mencken confided his suspicion that Angoff was gathering material to write a book that would cast him in an extremely unfavorable light. However, Angoff's book, *H. L. Mencken: A Portrait from Memory*, was not published until 1961, five years after Mencken's death.[5]

In 1934, Wayland Sanford moved his prosperous law practice from Longview to Dallas, and in 1935, when a majority of Americans were still recovering from the Great Depression, the Sanford family moved from their modest residence on Haynie Street to a larger home on Shenandoah Drive that could better accommodate their growing family. Now in addition to parenting two active teenagers and an infant, Winifred, who had never been fond of housework, had a larger residence to maintain, along with a husband who returned home each evening for dinner. Wayland's relocation of his law practice also meant an increase in social demands upon Winifred for, as the wife of a prominent attorney, she was expected to entertain and be entertained by his clients and associates. According to the Sanford daughters, Winifred was not fond of these social gatherings, but she dutifully fulfilled her obligations.

Wayland's reliance upon Winifred's social skills is evident in a letter he wrote to his mother on August 30, 1934, while he was attending a Bar Association meeting in Milwaukee, Wisconsin. "I'm somewhat lost without Winifred to keep me straight socially," he wrote. In this letter, Wayland also revealed that Winifred, who was by nature independent and perhaps more liberal in her thinking than her husband, was not always compliant with Wayland's wishes. Regarding his desire to have her accompany him on a trip to the Chicago World's Fair at the end of the meeting, Wayland wrote, "Winifred persists in her desire not to spend much time in Chicago and not to visit the fair."[6]

In separate interviews, the Sanfords' three daughters were reluctant to comment about whether or not their father supported their mother's writing endeavors. Emerett Sanford Miles called the matter "debatable" and explained that while Wayland was proud of Winifred's accomplishments and never prohibited her from writing, he did not assign any "real value" to her literary efforts. Helen J. Sanford recalled that Wayland was absent from the home so much during the years that Winifred was actively engaged in writing that his support or lack thereof was not an issue. Emerett, Helen, and Mary all agreed that while their mother's attention was directed toward her writing and the Sanford children's activities, their father's focus remained primarily on his business.

Members of the Sanford family who did not wish to be identified were reluctant to say outright that Wayland was a demanding spouse, but they told the following story: At one point, late in Winifred Sanford's life, when her health was declining and she lay in the hospital recovering from an operation, a hospital attendant

Wayland and Winifred with their youngest daughter, Mary, and
two unidentified friends (far left), circa 1934.

brought a tray that contained a bowl of Jell-O to her bedside. Winifred, who was
still groggy from anesthetic, raised her head, looked at the Jell-O, and said, "Your
father never liked Jello [*sic*]. He thought it was too easy for me to make."[7]

Clearly, Winifred's literary productivity declined after Wayland moved his office from Longview to Dallas, but his role in that decline remains unclear. Neither
Wayland's relocation to Dallas nor the birth of the couple's third child halted Winifred's writing entirely. In April 1934, "Derrick Jargon," an article coauthored by
Winifred and one of Wayland's business associates, Clyde Jackson, appeared in the
Southwest Review. The authors had begun work on the article two years before it was
published, for Winifred mentioned it in a letter to David Lloyd on May 17, 1932:

> Meanwhile I have been trying my hand at an article . . . on oil well technology . . .
> collaborating, in fact with a man who is in a better position than I to talk with
> drillers and roughnecks. While it isn't quite as dull as it sounds, still it is rather
> technical, and hardly the sort of thing editors fall all over themselves to buy. . . .
> We are calling it "Derrick Jargon," and writing in what we intend to be an
> informal, conversational style, as far removed as possible from a glossary.[8]

The amount of time that elapsed between Winifred's mention of this article in her letter to Lloyd and the article's actual publication date confirms her statements to Hilton Greer in the 1936 interview and to Robert Innes Center in a letter she wrote in 1931, in which she said that she was "an exceedingly slow writer."[9] "Derrick Jargon" demonstrates the knowledge of oil industry history and oil-field drilling procedures that Winifred had acquired during the years she lived in Texas.[10]

More than a year after "Derrick Jargon" was printed, another article by Winifred, "Writing the Short Story," appeared in *Southwester*, a magazine for and about regional writers of the Southwest. This article, as replete with vivid description as Winifred's short stories, is reprinted in full in Appendix C of this book with the permission of the Sanford family.

In summer 1936, both Winifred and her Manuscript Club friend Laura Faye Yauger received invitations to become charter members of the newly formed Texas Institute of Letters. The idea to establish an organization to honor Texas writers and to encourage Texas literature was first conceived in 1935 at the annual meeting of the English honor fraternity Sigma Tau Delta at the University of Mary Hardin-Baylor in Waco. In 1936, Texas Centennial Exposition authorities learned that Sigma Tau Delta had appointed a committee to form such an organization, and they encouraged this committee to hold the first meeting of the Texas Institute of Letters in conjunction with the Texas Centennial Exposition in Dallas in fall of that year.[11]

In Winifred's acceptance letter to TIL organizer and committee member William H. Vann, she expressed delight at having been selected for membership in the institute, but some other Texas writers who received invitations were not as enthusiastic.[12] J. Frank Dobie expressed doubts that a commission could do anything to advance the production of first-rate literature in the state or anywhere else. He wrote that the selection committee would do well to find two dozen outstanding writers in Texas, much less fifty. On September 14, 1936, after numerous attempts to dissuade TIL organizers from their task, Dobie reluctantly agreed to become a member of the institute.[13] In Donald Joseph's acceptance letter to Vann, Joseph wrote, "Not half a dozen people in Texas are doing nationally recognized creative writing, and most of these, if the truth were told, are jealous of each other's success."[14] John Lomax criticized the proposed list of charter members because too many were teaching English rather than writing it effectively.[15]

Such remarks were not without foundation, for in 1936, few Texans thought of themselves as professional writers. Of the institute's fifty charter members, only three, other than the nine journalists, listed their occupation as "writer." Seven listed "teacher," two "librarian," two "minister," and ten "housewife."[16] Winifred Sanford, along with noted poets Grace Noll Crowell and Karle Wilson Baker, wrote "housewife."[17]

Winifred had stated repeatedly throughout her career that she was not a professional writer. In his 1936 feature article in *The Dallas Journal*, Hilton Greer wrote:

> Mrs. Sanford, who is the wife of a prominent . . . attorney, the mother of three
> daughters and a homemaker who takes her responsibility as such seriously . . . is
> an occasional writer. . . . Mrs. Sanford admits . . . if she depended upon her stories
> for sustenance, she would often go hungry."[18]

Winifred's assessment of her earning power was probably accurate, for in *Magazines in the Twentieth Century*, Theodore Peterson states that it is unlikely that a significant number of American authors in the twentieth century ever managed to
earn a living from magazine writing unless they held staff positions.[19] Although
Winifred sold most of the short stories she submitted for publication, her yearly
income never exceeded $2,500. Fortunately, she did not have to depend upon the
income from her writing to sustain her family. Even when Winifred and Wayland
were living in Wichita Falls, the money that Winifred received from the publication of her work was only a supplement to Wayland's earnings. Later in their marriage, Wayland's business ventures became so prosperous that the sale of Winifred's stories had little or no effect on the family's economic circumstances.

When charter members of the Texas Institute of Letters gathered at the Hall of
State in Dallas on November 9, 1936, Winifred was one of seventeen writers in attendance. During the proceedings of the first business meeting, attendees became
extremely argumentative. Some complained about the snobbishness connected to
the word "institute," while others argued that membership in the Texas Institute of
Letters should be open rather than by invitation only. These discussions became
so heated that, in a letter Hilton Greer wrote to William H. Vann after the meeting,
Greer rationalized that the unpleasant crossfire assured that the Texas Institute of
Letters was in no immediate danger of becoming "a mutual admiration society."[20]

This was not the first time that some of these individuals had engaged in a public
debate with one another. In 1929, the editors of the newly christened *Southwest Review* had set off a lengthy and sometimes acrimonious exchange when they posed
the following question to members of their editorial board: "Do you think the
Southwestern and common traditions can (or should) develop a culture recogniz-
able as unique and more satisfying and profound than our present . . . culture and
art?"[21] This question inspired a flurry of articles, essays, and letters to the editors
that appeared periodically in the pages of the *Southwest Review* for well over a year.

In "The Culture Is Here," Stanley Vestal wrote, "To be conscientiously indigenous is as futile and fatal as to be consciously cosmopolitan. Delight in the native material, the native manner, must be spontaneous."[22] In "A Mosaic, Not a Synthesis," Albert Guerard argued, "You don't worry about creating a Texas brand of

mathematics, a Texas form of religion: don't worry about Texas art or Texas literature."[23] Dobie expressed his opinion in an essay entitled "True Culture is Eclectic, but Provincial":

If a distinctly Southwestern culture is developed it will employ cattle brands and not signs of the zodiac to ornament the facades of its buildings; . . . Its biographers will have to understand Sam Houston better than they understand John Quincy Adams . . . Its actors . . . will cultivate the drawl of old-time Texans rather than the broad a's of Boston; and . . . the sting of a dry northern; the lonely howl of the coyote . . . will appeal to the senses through the rhythms of its poets.[24]

"We are not ready to take stock," John William Rogers warned. "We have hardly begun; yet we are already beginning to be self-conscious—to foster self-consciousness in our young artists."[25] Jay B. Hubbell, who had been instrumental in transferring the journal formerly known as the *Texas Review* to Southern Methodist University and was now a professor at Duke University in North Carolina, offered the following admonition: "The New Regionalism . . . is a good movement, and it has great possibilities; but it may err by overrating the products of the region."[26]

Ernest E. Leisy, a professor of English at Southern Methodist University, wrote in a letter to the editors:

I do not like the hue and cry about Texas as the home of desperadoes, cowboys, and bold bad men. Such advertising, even when it is set back a few years, does the state a grave injustice elsewhere. . . . I want someone with ability to picture Texans as they really are, and in a way that shall gain as much currency in the East as has been given an overwrought period by our assiduous and capable antiquarians. It is time we were getting over our sentimental nostalgia for the past and realizing that there is as much romance, conflict, and tragedy in Texas life today as there ever was."[27]

Texas poet Karle Wilson Baker responded to Leisy's letter in the very next issue of the *Southwest Review*:

I don't share the kindly impatience that Dr. Leisy and some others feel for the cowboy, the bad-man and buried treasure. . . . I think I know exactly how Mr. Dobie and others feel who have it actually in their blood and bones. . . . But I agree that there is another Texas and that it is just as worthy of being transmuted into art as any other world where actual human beings actually live. That, in fact, is what some of us are trying to do.[28]

Winifred Sanford, whose realistic stories were set in modern-day Texas with characters that were modeled on contemporary people and current events, did not participate in the debate that would continue to resurface among Texas writers for many decades. The minutes of that first TIL business meeting give no indication that Winifred, who was quiet and reserved by nature, made a single comment during the rowdy exchange that took place at the Hall of State in Dallas on that rainy November day in 1936.[29] But Winifred's thoughts, as she sat surrounded by men in cowboy boots and bolo ties who were attempting to out-argue one another, are not difficult to imagine. As her daughter Mary Gordon said in an interview, Winifred "did not tolerate fools well." No doubt she, Karle Wilson Baker, and other writers in attendance that day were relieved when TIL president, Pat Moreland, adjourned the meeting.

The institute's evening session was probably more to Winifred's liking. The dinner meeting was better attended and less rancorous than the daytime gathering—that is, until J. Frank Dobie, who had been vocal at the earlier meeting, took center stage to deliver the main address. In a speech entitled "The Earth Remembers," Dobie addressed the subject of regional writing. "Great literature transcends its native land, but there is none that I know of that ignores its own soil," he told the assembled group. Then, with Winifred seated in the audience, Dobie took a jab at the kind of writing that was being produced by followers of H. L. Mencken.[30]

Although Winifred may have been incensed by Dobie's remarks and frustrated by the conduct of TIL members at the business meeting earlier in the day, these incidents were not the cause of her absence from the TIL meeting the following year. In a letter she wrote to William H. Vann in October 1937, Winifred explained that she would be unable to attend the fall meeting because she had a "bad lung" and was confined to her bed. A short time after the 1936 TIL meeting, she had contracted tuberculosis and spent the better part of the year in a sanatorium. Recently, she had returned to her home in Dallas, where a live-in nurse was now caring for Winifred and the toddler, Mary.[31]

Tuberculosis, once a leading cause of death in the United States, had declined steadily since 1900 due to improvements in nutrition and sanitation, but at the time that Winifred contracted the disease, complete cures were rare. Before 1946, when antibiotic treatment was popularly administered, bed rest and an improved diet were the most effective means of treatment. Patients were often confined to sanatoriums to ensure that they received proper care and that the contagious disease did not spread to others when it was in an active stage. In Winifred's case, an immune system that had been compromised by the stresses of pregnancy and childbirth may have contributed to her susceptibility to the disease.[32]

Whatever treatment Winifred received must have been effective, for by fall 1938, she had regained her health and was once again participating in community activities. With her oldest daughter, Emerett, returning to Louisiana State University and her middle daughter, Helen, entering Sweet Briar College, Winifred accepted the presidency of the College Club that she had helped to organize shortly after moving to Dallas.[33] Although she had never been fond of attending organized church services, in 1938, she became a member of the First Unitarian Church of Dallas, a congregation that she attended regularly until her death in 1983. Mary Sanford Gordon attributed her mother's association with the Unitarian religion to her independent nature and her lifelong admiration for "ideas that were unconventional."

When the Texas Institute of Letters reconvened in Dallas for the organization's third annual meeting, Winifred accepted a leadership role in the hastily arranged event. By summer 1938, when no plans had been made for a fall meeting, current TIL officers appealed to Hilton Greer for help in making arrangements. Greer in turn contacted personnel at Cokesbury Bookstore who then engaged Laura Krey, author of a new best-selling book entitled *And Tell of Time*, to be the institute's keynote speaker. In *The Texas Institute of Letters, 1936–1966*, Vann tells that the hurriedly organized 1938 meeting turned out to be one of the best in the institute's history and that this meeting may have saved the fledgling organization from becoming extinct due to a lack of leadership. Vann credits the meeting's success to the efforts of four female members: Karle Wilson Baker, who taught a symposium on fiction, and the three women who assisted her—Sigman Byrd, Helen Topping Miller, and Winifred Sanford.[34]

An article that appeared in the *Dallas Daily Times-Herald* prior to the meeting reads: "Membership in the institute comprises most of the accountable writers of the state."[35] Yet in a newspaper issue filled with columns of news about a variety of local social events and athletic contests at Texas A&M College, Texas University, and Southern Methodist University, the editors of the newspaper devoted only thirty-four lines of one column to the 1938 TIL meeting. As Lon Tinkle points out, via a quotation by Plato, in the introduction to William H. Vann's *The Texas Institute of Letters, 1936–1966*, "Whatever is honored in a society will be produced in that society." With the organization of the Texas Institute of Letters complete, the people of Texas had only initiated this process.[36]

Although Winifred was proud of her TIL membership, paying annual dues for many years and frequently attending the organization's annual meeting, her name does not appear on the roster of active members in 1966, when the Texas Institute of Letters celebrated its thirty-year anniversary. It is doubtful that an organization that provided so little opportunity for members to have contact with one another, except at yearly meetings, could ever have supplied the level of stimulation to Winifred's writing career that she had received from her participation in the Manuscript Club of Wichita Falls.[37]

Pieces of the Puzzle

DALLAS,

TEXAS,

1938–1962

WINIFRED SANFORD'S DAUGHTERS AND
her Manuscript Club friends have associated the end of her writing career with
one or more of the following events: the family's move to Dallas in 1931, Winifred's
unplanned pregnancy in 1932, and her illness with tuberculosis from 1937 to 1938.
Winifred herself gave the following reasons for the termination of her career when
she wrote to M. K. Singleton in 1962, "I had to stop writing after the birth of my
third child when I contracted Tuberculosis [sic] and was advised to cut down on
my activities."[1] However, her correspondence with magazine editors and literary
agents between 1936 and 1945 reveal a quite different story.

During the months that she was recuperating from tuberculosis, Winifred
wrote a detective novel that contained thirty chapters and 55,000 words. She sent
a manuscript of this novel to David Lloyd on March 1, 1938, along with a letter that
contained the following:

It has been so long since I have written or published anything that you may have
forgotten me, but I hope not because I am longing to get back to writing. Last May
I was sent to bed by my doctor and told to stay there for a year, and the result of
this enforced idleness has been . . . not a work of art, alas!—but a detective story.
. . . I have no illusions about it. It is lowbrow . . . and not particularly original . . .

the main character, much as I hate to admit it, is . . . the girl reporter. I . . . have handled her fairly well, and I believe the book . . . ought to sell . . . I want to call it "You Asked for It."[2]

And in a letter dated September 1, 1938, she asked for Lloyd's advice concerning another novel that she was planning to write:

I have long wanted to write a novel of the oil fields. Or would I do better to stick to the short story? . . . Are the writers' magazines correct in stating that the editors are less and less cordial to any story which is not standardized and written to formula? I cannot quite believe this since I find many stories in magazines which are anything but standardized.[3]

Lloyd sent the manuscript of *You Asked for It* to *American, Holland's, Chatelaine*, and *Lee Furman* before returning it to Winifred on November 11, 1938. In the letter that accompanied the manuscript, Lloyd informed Winifred that his attempts to place the detective novel had not met with success. He answered the question she had asked in her previous letter, telling her she had not been successful enough with the short story to limit her writing to that genre. He encouraged her to begin work on the novel that was to be set in the Texas oil fields.[4]

Winifred may have been ill-advised by Lloyd. For several years thereafter, she devoted her creative energies almost entirely to writing novels. Because the manuscripts of these novels have disappeared, it is impossible to assess their literary quality, but the reactions of readers, editors, and literary agents who read them indicate that Winifred's ironic literary style was better suited to the short story than to the novel. And by the time she quit working on these novels and returned to composing short fiction, all of the editors who had published her earlier stories, including H. L. Mencken, no longer occupied the same editorial positions.

Neither Winifred's friends nor her daughters connected Mencken's resignation from the *Mercury* with the end of her writing career, but the loss of such a knowledgeable and influential mentor cannot be discounted. The interest that Mencken took in promoting Winifred's writing, the honest criticism he provided, and the encouragement he supplied in almost every letter he wrote to her while he was editor of the *Mercury* served as a major stimulus during the years that she was most productive as a writer.

There is no evidence that Winifred Sanford and H. L. Mencken had any contact whatsoever after he resigned from his post at the *Mercury*. Sometime after Sara Mencken's death, Mencken vacated the New York apartment that he and Sara had shared and returned to his boyhood home in Baltimore, where he lived with his bachelor brother August Mencken. In July 1939, Mencken suffered a mild stroke and made a seemingly complete recovery. His mind remained acute, and he continued to compose articles and essays and to serve as an advisor for *The Baltimore Sun* until November 23, 1948. On that date, he suffered a massive stroke that left him partially paralyzed and largely incapacitated for the remainder of his life. He could no longer read or write, and he spoke haltingly and with great difficulty. Deprived as he now was of the activities that had made his life meaningful, Mencken considered suicide. He lived eight years in this condition, and when he referred to himself, he often did so in the past tense. Mencken died in his sleep at his boyhood home in Baltimore, Maryland, on January 29, 1956.[5]

WINIFRED SANFORD'S DAUGHTERS were surprised to learn that, in addition to short stories, their mother wrote two complete novels and produced 80,000 words of a third one. They thought she wrote only one novel, the one they watched her burn in the fireplace of the family's home. They conjectured that the manuscripts of these two novels probably ended up as ashes in the fireplace, as well.[6]

If this is what happened to Winifred's novels, her habit of destroying manuscripts that displeased her or failed to gain immediate publication may constitute a significant loss to southwestern literature. While it is true that her first novel, *Arrows of the Almighty*, was rejected, it was rejected by credible publishing houses, all of whom made positive comments about her writing. It is quite possible that, had she refrained from destroying these manuscripts, one or more of them might have been deemed worthy of publication after the release of her short story collection, *Windfall and Other Stories*.[7]

Another factor in the termination of Winifred's writing was her refusal to think of herself as a professional writer. Her identity was linked to her role as a housewife and mother who continually placed the needs of her family and community ahead of her desire to write fiction. However, doing this produced an internal conflict that may have contributed to the migraine headaches that often plagued her. "Mother could never devote full time to her writing," Emerett Sanford Miles said, "although I think she would have liked to do so." "There was always a conflict," Helen J. Sanford explained, "because she had a very strong sense of duty toward family and home. Intellectually, she was very keen, and I think—to some extent—she resented the lack of respect accorded women."

On September 7, 1939, Emerett, the Sanfords' oldest daughter, married Clyde Webb Railsback, a fellow student at Louisiana State University, in a wedding at the Sanfords' Highland Park home. Like many middle-aged Americans who had experienced the tensions of World War I when they were young adults and were now the parents of a new generation of young adults, Winifred and Wayland listened with grave concern to radio broadcasts about Hitler's army invading one European country after another. Shortly after Japanese forces bombed the American naval fleet in Pearl Harbor in December 1941, Helen joined the Marine Corps Women's Reserve. Because women were not assigned to combat duty in World War II, Helen served her tour of duty in Washington, D.C., and Paris Island, South Carolina. And nine months after Emerett and Clyde Railsback's first son, Paul Wayland Railsback, was born, Clyde volunteered for active military duty. With her two older daughters making life-altering sacrifices for the war effort, Winifred felt that she should make a contribution, as well. She purchased a knitting machine and set it up in the family's living room. Now, instead of hosting literary meetings of the College Club and teaching creative writing classes in the family's living room, she and her friends met there to knit balaclava helmets and wristlets for American soldiers on the war fronts.

When World War II ended in victory for the Allies, neither Emerett nor Helen returned to Dallas. Helen accepted a position as an advertising executive in New York, and Emerett and Clyde Railsback moved their rapidly expanding family (Emerett gave birth to six boys between 1942 and 1955) to Shreveport, Louisiana, where Clyde went to work for the Halliburton Company. With only her youngest daughter, Mary, still living at home, Winifred once again turned her attention to composing fiction.

In the foreword to *Windfall and Other Stories*, Emerett Sanford Miles states that her mother's writing career began in January 1925 with the publication of "Wreck" in *The American Mercury* and ended in 1931 with the publication of "Fever in the South" in *North American Review*.[8] However, letters that Winifred exchanged with magazine editors after 1931 tell a different story. In 1945, she submitted a story entitled "Deep C" to the editors of *Saturday Evening Post, McCall's Magazine, Good Housekeeping*, and *Today's Woman*. "Deep C" was not accepted by any of these magazines, but Winifred's letters to the editors offer irrefutable proof that she continued to seek publication of her work until at least 1945.[9]

According to Mary Sanford Gordon, her mother talked very little about the reasons she quit writing for publication. The only explanation that she ever offered her daughters was that her "style of writing had become dated." Gordon assumed that her mother was quoting the words of an editor or literary agent when she made this statement and that she found it painful to talk about a once promising literary career that was now in decline.

In the 1920s, when Winifred first submitted her short stories to the editors at *The American Mercury*, her realistic portrayals of present-day people and current events coincided with the style of writing that was popular at the time. But literary styles, like clothing fashions, change with the passage of time—and with the onset of the Great Depression, followed by World War II, American readers' taste in fiction shifted from starkly realistic stories with tragic endings to more optimistic and uplifting literature that offered relief from the troubling conditions that so many United States citizens were experiencing.[10]

Helen J. Sanford suggested other possible reasons for her mother's loss of interest in seeking publication. After the Sanford family moved from Wichita Falls to Dallas in 1931, Winifred had more opportunities for companionship with like-minded people than she had had in Wichita Falls. As a result, she may no longer have felt a pressing need to express herself through her writing. Helen noted that her mother labored long and hard over her compositions and as Wayland's business ventures became increasingly successful, she no longer had a financial incentive to work so hard.

In Emerett Sanford Miles's foreword to *Windfall and Other Stories*, she offers a rather simplistic explanation for the termination of her mother's career when she writes: "New interests grew to fill her days, and she went on to other things."[11] And indeed, as Winifred Sanford approached the age of sixty, her life was filled with many worthwhile activities. On May 4, 1947, her picture appeared in *The Dallas Morning News* along with an announcement that she had been named president-elect of the newly formed Auxiliary to Parkland Hospital, a volunteer position that must have consumed many hours and much energy. Also in 1947, Wayland, Winifred, and Mary moved from their home on Shenandoah Drive to one of the stateliest of residences on Beverly Drive in the Highland Park neighborhood.

Four years later, Mary left Dallas to attend Antioch College in Ohio. After she finished college, she relocated to Berkeley, California, and married Norman Schneider on December 28, 1957. Winifred, who might now have devoted her full attention to her writing, took on additional public service responsibilities instead. On February 18, 1962, her picture appeared in the the the *Dallas Daily Times-Herald* when Alpha Phi Sorority honored her for her outstanding contributions to the community. The article that accompanied this picture provided a list of the organizations in which Winifred had engaged: the YWCA, the Lawyers' Wives, the League of Women Voters, the Health and Science Museum Guild, and the Dallas Council of World Affairs. She had also been a board member of the American Association of University Women.[12] Clearly, at some point between 1945 and 1962, Winifred's efforts on behalf of her community supplanted her efforts to produce novels and first rate short stories that editors, agents, and book publishers were no longer interested in publishing.

Taken alone, none of the explanations that Winifred's friends and family offered for the demise of her writing career are entirely satisfactory. But the obstacles she encountered and the responsibilities she assumed did not occur singly.

When Winifred Sanford was in her late fifties, her sorority honored
her for her service to the community, circa 1947.

Eventually, like the proverbial straws that were piled higher and higher until they broke the camel's back, the impediments to Winifred's writing accumulated until one day she stopped sending work out to be published.

Winifred never quit writing entirely. Throughout the latter years of her life, she composed poems, short stories, and character sketches for the pleasure of her friends, her children, and her grandchildren. She prepared lectures and gave readings at meetings of the College Club of Dallas and the Shakespeare Followers. And she enjoyed traveling—to New York City to visit Helen, to Berkeley to be with Mary, and to Louisiana to visit Emerett and her family of rowdy boys. Winifred also traveled to Europe. When Wayland's business activities prevented him from accompanying her, Helen and Mary became Winifred's traveling companions.

In 1962, when Duke University Press released M. K. Singleton's book, *H. L. Mencken and the American Mercury*, Winifred, now in her seventies, obtained a copy. To her consternation, she discovered that in a footnote, Singleton identifies her as the mysterious unnamed woman whom Charles Angoff wrote about in *H. L. Mencken: A Portrait from Memory*.[13] In his memoir, reputed to be about the years he served as assistant editor of *The American Mercury*, Angoff wrote: "Another newcomer was a woman writer of short stories. . . . I cannot give her name for a reason that will be obvious later."[14]

Angoff claims that Sara Hardt, who later became Mencken's wife, brought the mystery woman's stories to Mencken's attention, and that Mencken was so pleased with them that he bought three immediately and seven or eight more at later dates. Angoff describes these stories as "superb" and tells how Mencken had pleaded with the woman to attempt a novel, but she refused, saying she was not interested in the form. Angoff relates an amusing incident that supposedly happened when Mencken offered to send the woman some good Scotch as an incentive to write more stories, only to learn, to his dismay, that she was a prohibitionist.

According to Angoff, the woman's submissions to the *Mercury* ceased abruptly after she sent Mencken one last letter. In this letter, the woman, who was now in California, promised that if she ever wrote another story she would submit it to *The American Mercury*, but she told Mencken that she doubted she would ever write again. Angoff quotes the following mysterious line from the letter: "I have gone through a tremendous emotional upheaval, and I beg of you to understand if you ever hear about it—only please don't ever think me silly." According to Angoff, Mencken never heard from the woman again and became convinced that she had "left her husband and run off with the local preacher or the piano player in the town movie house."[15] Angoff concludes his account of the woman with the following statement: "If somebody ever writes a history of the American Mercury [*sic*], he will have to take account of this woman's stories of life in an American oil town."[16]

After reading Singleton's footnote and looking up the passage in Angoff's book to which the footnote refers, Winifred addressed the following words to Singleton in a letter:

A few days ago, I saw your book on Mencken and the American Mercury [sic] in a local bookstore, and bought it for old time's sake. Somewhat to my surprise, I found my name—Winifred Sanford—in the index and enjoyed the kind remarks you made about my stories. I was, however, puzzled by your statement that "Nothing else is known of her." After all, stories of mine appeared in other magazines, and one, at least, had been reprinted in several anthologies, with biographical data, the latest being "21 Texas Stories," edited by William Peery and published by the University of Texas Press in 1954. I also had correspondence with *The Mercury* [sic] and the Knopfs, mostly in regard to a novel I was writing, long after I stopped sending them stories.

Your reference to Angoff's "Portrait" intrigued me, and I have just now come from the SMU library, where I studied pages 111–113, which you say in your footnote refer to me!

I must confess I am completely baffled. May I ask what makes you think these pages refer to me? Did you just make a wild guess, or has Mr. Angoff identified me as the strange creature he describes? . . .

Only two details in the whole description are applicable to me. I did write and sell eight or nine stories to the Mercury [sic], and eventually I did fade out of the picture. Nothing else he says is true of me.

My husband was not a junior bank official . . . and he is hardly the type to be amused by the conjecture that "she had left her husband and run off with the local preacher . . ."

My stories were not brought to Mencken's attention by Sara Haardt or anyone else. I simply mailed in the first one, "Wreck," on my own.

I was writing a novel (the woman in Angoff's book was not) and Mencken knew that and inquired about its progress in almost every letter.

I was not an authority on the language of oil men's "sweethearts" and cannot remember ever writing about one. In fact I didn't know any.

I was not in California at any time between 1915 and 1956, and did not have "an emotional upheaval" of any sort, nor would I have confided in Mencken if I had.

As for the story about the Prohibitionist [sic], no such correspondence passed between us. And I am not a prohibitionist.

I had many letters from Mencken over the years, and met him personally in New York in 1926, but the Mencken I knew was quite different from the one Angoff describes. To me, at least, he never displayed the flippant, wisecracking side of his nature.

I am, of course, impressed by the high tribute Angoff pays to the stories written by this woman, whoever she is. I should like to think that part of it really was about me, but I fear not. He must have had someone else in mind,—real or imaginary.

I know it is too late to make any corrections in your very interesting book. But I did want you to know that a mistake had been made, somewhere along the way. . . .

I have three daughters . . . They were all here in Dallas last week, and have dreamed up a writing project on which to collaborate . . . So sometime in the future, you may have occasion to write about another Sanford. If so, PLEASE DOUBLE CHECK your sources, will you![17]

Helen J. Sanford followed up her mother's letter with one that was even more indignant. In it she wrote:

I am appalled that a University professor would permit himself to make a published statement of conceivably damaging effect without apparently, even the slightest attempt to substantiate facts through research.

My mother is a highly respected member of her community, the wife of a successful attorney, and above all a gentlewoman. She has never in her life done anything to deserve the character defamation which you so casually inflicted.[18]

In a postscript to this letter, Helen added, "I might add that their [Winifred and Wayland's] three daughters were in Dallas last week to celebrate the 45th anniversary of their marriage."

Singleton, possibly fearing a lawsuit, wrote immediate letters of apology to both women. In his letter to Winifred, he promised to contact Charles Angoff and ask him to clarify his part of the misidentification. Singleton also promised to notify two other researchers, currently working on books about H. L. Mencken, of this mistake. In a postscript to his letter to Winifred, Singleton encouraged her to finish her abandoned novel, pointing out that another Texas woman writer, named Katherine Anne Porter, had recently finished her long-delayed novel, *Ship of Fools*."[19]

Winifred's response to Singleton's letter was probably more gracious than he deserved, given the damage to her reputation that this misidentification might have precipitated. In a letter dated September 26, 1962, she wrote:

Please do not feel too badly about the mistake in identification. I am by no means sure it was *your* mistake. I suspect that Angoff or someone else connected with the Mercury must have given you reason to call it as you did.

As you suggest, Angoff was evidently "yarning." I can easily imagine Mencken blowing off . . . telling Angoff he was going to write that letter about Prohibition, etc; and Angoff putting in "Yes, but suppose she turns out to be a Prohibitionist" . . . without any actual correspondence having take place except in Angoff's imagination. As to whether I was the writer under discussion, I have my doubts, but I'll admit I can't think of anyone else who wrote for the Mercury about the oil fields.

So far as my reputation is concerned, I don't think any harm has been done. As you know, few readers pay heed to footnotes and fewer still look up references to other books unless personally involved. But for the sake of my family, I will appreciate your correcting the error as far as you can.

I thought your book was very well done, and I wish you the best of success in the future.[20]

Winifred Sanford's two letters to Singleton make clear, as does earlier correspondence between Winifred and Mencken, that the information contained in Singleton's footnote is erroneous. Either Singleton wrongly identified Winifred as the unnamed woman in Angoff's book, or as scholars such as William Nolte, Charles Fecher, and Carl Bode have long suspected, Angoff's unflattering portrait of H. L. Mencken is an inaccurate representation of what took place during the years that Mencken was chief editor of The American Mercury.[21]

One Story Ends and Another Begins

DALLAS,

TEXAS,

1962–1983

IN THE 1960S, WHEN WAYLAND SAN-
ford's health began to decline, Winifred and Wayland moved from their spacious
home on Beverly Drive to a smaller residence on nearby Carruth Street that required less maintenance. With the help of hired caregivers and the Sanfords'
daughters, Winifred cared for Wayland at the couple's home as his dementia wors-
ened. In 1977, when his condition reached the point that he required around-the-
clock care and Winifred was diagnosed with a series of ailments, the couple moved
to an assisted living facility in North Dallas. Within their first year of residency at
Meadow Green Retirement Home, Wayland suffered a brief bout with cancer and
died on May 3, 1978, at the age of eighty-seven. Winifred, whose ailments included
a diseased gall bladder, a perforated stomach ulcer, and the formation of kidney
stones in the latter years of her life, continued to live at Meadow Green. Although
her physical health continued to decline, her mental faculties remained acute.

In 1979, when Winifred's ninetieth birthday was less than a year away, her
daughters began to arrange a special birthday present that would honor her life
and her writing on this occasion. Emerett Sanford Miles assembled her mother's
short stories into a collection that Helen J. Sanford then edited and arranged to
have printed. Along with their younger sister Mary Sanford Gordon, Emerett and
Helen distributed copies of this volume of short stories (all more than fifty years

old) to selected friends and family members. Emerett and Helen's purpose in assembling this privately printed edition of *Windfall and Other Stories* was twofold: to honor their mother's life, and to preserve her literary accomplishments for subsequent generations of her descendants.

Fourteen stories were included in this slim green volume in the order in which they were first published. Also included was an introduction by Emerett entitled "About the Author" and two previously unpublished nonfiction sketches that provided insight into Winifred Sanford's family heritage. Words on the front flap of the black, white, and green book jacket read:

> Winifred Sanford is best remembered for her classic story of the Texas oilfields, "Windfall," but she is equally adept at capturing the essence of the Minnesota people she knew as a girl.
>
> It is a tribute to her craftsmanship that her characters still live, as real today as when she first wrote about them over fifty years ago.[1]

Characters that come to life on the pages of this collection are, for the most part, ordinary people struggling to survive the difficulties they encounter in their rather ordinary lives. Margaret, the young widow in "The Monument," Hattie, the main character in "The Forest Fire," Mrs. Philips of "Mr. Carmichael's Room," and Miss Carrie of "Fever in the South" take in boarders in order to sustain themselves and/or to provide for their families. The main character in "Allie" clerks in a dry goods store, and Kate of "Fools" is a hard-working widow who has taken many odd jobs to survive. Rita of "Fever in the South" is a fortune-teller, and the mother in "Black Child" is a maid who takes in white women's washing. Mr. Donovan in "Fever in the South," Mr. Carmichael of "Mr. Carmichael's Room," and Mr. Cox of "Luck" are down-on-their-luck oil-field speculators, while Cora, the main character in "Windfall," and Moses, another major character in "Fever in the South," are farmers. Only Pauline in "Fools" and Mary in a story by the same name represent the privileged upper middle class.

Winifred's comments in letters to various editors indicate that characters in her stories were amalgams of people she had observed, either in Texas or in Minnesota. In an outline that she used when she taught writing classes to novice writers in the living room of her Dallas home, she instructs students to "model your characters on real people, and study these people for peculiarities and mannerisms." Additional proof that Winifred created characters from her observations of real people in specific locations appears in a letter that she wrote to Gertrude Lane in February 1926:

I am sending "Fools" with some misgivings. I am afraid you will find it roughly written . . . But I find that when I write of people like my Kate, I invariably fall into that style, and any attempt on my part to polish it off, spoils the story. What I want to bring out, of course is that very quality in Kate . . . her roughness, and also her power. Texas is full of Kate's . . . and Pauline's [sic].[2]

"Fools" first appeared in Woman's Home Companion in January 1928. This story is narrated from the point of view of Kate, a middle-aged widow who has recently suffered a stroke. Despite a number of misfortunes in her life, Kate has succeeded in raising a lovely daughter named Pauline and in putting money in the bank that will ensure that Pauline never has to endure hardships like the ones her mother has known.

Pauline's main concern, at the beginning of this story, is deciding which suitor to marry—Harry Hale, whose father owns the local bank, or another well-established local man, Hoke Weatherby. While Pauline is on a date with Hoke, Kate learns that the bank she entrusted with her money has failed. The banker, Ben Hale, has committed suicide, and his son Harry has promised to pay back all the money that his father owes. When Pauline returns and hears this news, she collapses into a chair beside her mother's bed.

"All my life, it's been like that. Hard luck, and hard luck and hard luck," Kate tells Pauline.[3] Kate's agony is increased by the knowledge that she is no longer in a physical condition that will allow her to overcome this most recent loss. Overwhelmed by grief and worry, Kate shares with Pauline a litany of difficulties that she has experienced in her lifetime.

When Pauline responds that marrying is one way out of such situations, Kate realizes that Pauline is talking about her present situation rather than about Kate's past and asks if Pauline intends to marry Hoke Weatherby. When Pauline responds, "Why not? He's very rich,"[4] Kate reveals that Pauline's father was murdered by Hoke's brother.

With Hoke Weatherby revealed to be an unsuitable mate, Pauline is left to assume the care of her ailing mother. When Kate offers to go to the "poor farm," Pauline responds, "Don't be a goose."[5] As Pauline's forehead puckers and her hands clench into fists, Kate recognizes, in her daughter, a younger version of herself. Kate asks Pauline what she is planning, and Pauline replies that she will make Harry Hale marry her and then she will open a dancing school. She assures Kate that there is money to be made in dancing if one goes about it the right way. By the story's end, Kate realizes that their financial crisis has provided Pauline with a necessary rite of passage. When Pauline says, "From now on I'll do the worrying . . . And listen Mama, I don't mind it a bit; I have an idea that it will be rather fun,"

Kate replies, "We're fools both of us." But Kate says these words in a voice that, according to the omniscient narrator, is "absurdly tender."[6]

REFERRING TO "FOOLS" and other stories that Winifred published in women's magazines, Don B. Graham wrote, "Even when she is not at her strongest, her clear forceful style and sharp eye for telling social observation make her always a writer to respect."[7]

As Winifred Sanford once pointed out to H. L. Mencken, a number of her short stories focus on a central incident in a specific location. Six of the stories in the Sanford family edition of *Windfall and Other Stories* are set in Texas during the time of two famous oil booms. "Saved," "Luck," "Windfall," "Black Child," and "Mr. Carmichael's Room" take place in West Texas during the Burkburnett oil boom of the 1920s, while "Fever in the South" is set during the East Texas oil boom of the 1930s. Events in three stories in the collection occur in Minnesota. "Wreck" takes place on the shores of Lake Superior, and "The Forest Fire" and "The Blue Spruce" are set in logging towns located in the Minnesota pine forests that surrounded Winifred's hometown. While the settings of three other stories in the collection, "Mary," "Fools," and "The Monument," are not clearly defined, Winifred indicated in her letter to Gertrude Lane that "Fools" was based upon her observations of individuals who lived in West Texas.

One of Winifred's favorite structuring devices was to divide a story into numbered sections, with each section representing a separate scene or time period. She employed this structure in ten of the thirteen stories in the collection. Her spare writing style and her use of irony are distinguishing features of narratives that are often told from the viewpoint of a character that has less understanding of the story's central event than do readers of the story.

"Fannie Baker" is one of two previously unpublished stories that Winifred's daughters included in the family edition of *Windfall and Other Stories* because these stories had special significance for them and for their children. "Fannie Baker" is about a china doll that, at the time Winifred wrote the story, had been handed down through four generations of Brooks females. Different parts of Fannie Baker have been replaced over time, including her clothes, arms, and the covering of her cloth body. And from time to time, her head has had to be reattached. Winifred traces this doll's journey from child to child, from generation to generation, and from one location to another. As Winifred relates the doll's journey, she also provides information about her own maternal ancestors who once lived in New England.[8]

The second previously unpublished story in the Sanford family edition of the collection is a character sketch of Winifred's paternal grandmother, Sarah Mahon, entitled "A Victorian Grandmother." Sarah was an Irish immigrant who, according to family tradition, was the first woman in the United States to be issued naturalization papers. In this piece, Sanford portrays her grandmother's strong, opinionated personality and illuminates character traits that family and friends of Winifred have indicated were passed down from grandmother to granddaughter.[9]

In addition to preserving a sketch of the author's paternal grandmother, this story supplies information about the Mahon family's immigration experience. For this reason, SMU Press included the sketch in the publicly offered edition of *Windfall and Other Stories*. About Sarah Mahon, Winifred wrote:

> She never quite trusted this new country where the standards she knew to be right were so often reversed or ignored . . . Had she not seen my grandfather convert all his possessions in Ireland to cash, which he packed in a trunk for the journey, lest he be cheated by the bank? Had she not walked the pavements of New York seeking a hotel where the meats were roasted on a spit, as at home? Had not a young lady in a house where they stayed gone into ecstasies about a very inferior ballad called "Dixie" which grandmother had been kind enough to pick out for her on the piano, but which had no musical merit whatever? Was not the whole country for which she had left everything that was dear to her in the past . . . engaged in a foolish civil war of which she could make neither head nor tail?[10]

Among the people who received copies of the Sanford family edition of *Windfall and Other Stories* were three former members of the Manuscript Club—poets Laura Faye Yauger and Fania Kruger and novelist Anne Pence Davis. In a congratulatory letter, Yauger wrote, "I have seen your little book of short stories and in my opinion it is truly a literary masterpiece." She added, "I am glad I knew you then and proud to be able to say now, 'Oh, yes, I knew Winifred when she was writing these stories.'"[11] Referring to the poem "Invocation" that appears on the dedication page of the Sanford family edition, Davis wrote, "This volume proves that each year of Manuscript was and is 'acceptable.'"[12] Such favorable comments from old friends and from recent acquaintances, who had been unaware that these stories even existed until they received a copy of the book, must have been a great source of pleasure for Winifred in the final three years of her life.

She died on March 24, 1983, just eight days after her ninety-third birthday. The official cause of her death was septicemia, a blood infection that resulted from a recurring kidney ailment. Winifred's remains were placed in a crypt in the Sparkman Hillcrest garden mausoleum in North Dallas where Wayland Sanford's remains had been interred five years earlier. Her survivors, whose names appeared in her obituary, included her three daughters, Emerett Sanford Miles, Helen J.

Sanford, and Mary Sanford Gordon; her sister, Helen Toulme; six grandsons; two granddaughters; and three great-grandsons.[13]

Reverend John Buehrens, minister of the First Unitarian Church of Dallas, officiated at a memorial service at the Sparkman Hillcrest chapel on Saturday, March 26, 1983. Reverend Buehrens recalled visiting with Winifred in the latter years of her life. He told the audience that despite a variety of health problems, Winifred bore herself with dignity and "kept her hands occupied with knitting and her mind sharp with word games and crossword puzzles." He described her as a woman who did not "waste words" or "worry about death," and he thanked the "eternal source of all being" for the "works of her hands . . . the thoughts of her mind . . . the aspirations of her spirit . . . the affections of her heart." After reading Psalm 90, he read "Invocation," a poem that Winifred had composed in January 1925, when she was a charter member of the Manuscript Club.[14]

Invocation

Within the clean white book of this new year
Help me to write my days.
Make sharp the pencil of my mood
That I may trace in letters good
Each syllable and phrase.

Give me a steady hand to write my years
As life bids me compose,
In comedy or tragedy,
In romance or in rhapsody,
In poetry or prose.

And when my volume is complete
Be this my only plea:
That I have proved myself equipped
To write a year of manuscript
Acceptable to Thee.

Reverend Buehrens exhorted mourners to remember Winifred Sanford with a spirit of gratitude for all that was "honest, unpretentious, and courageous" about her and for the spirit of tenderness that she displayed toward "every human frailty." He quoted a passage from her short story "The Monument": "Oh, but dying takes such a minute, Julia. It's living that takes the time and the courage." And he told the audience that Winifred revealed much of herself in the following passage from "A Victorian Grandmother":

> She was the last person in the world, of course, to preach any sort of cant. Knowing right from wrong as she did, she was not averse to passing judgment, but it was never with any thought of self-righteousness or any sentimentality. The insipid or sugary in religion disgusted her. And yet, matter of fact as she was, plain spoken and frugal with verbal embroidery, she had her emotions, which were, for that reason perhaps, the deeper. When the occasion demanded it, she was not ashamed of tears. And she had, for all her scorn of individuals, an immense pity for life.[15]

A REVIVAL OF INTEREST IN Winifred Sanford's short stories actually began in 1982, a year before her death, when Lou Rodenberger included "Mr. Carmichael's Room" in an anthology entitled *Her Work: Stories by Texas Women*. In 1986, Don B. Graham mentioned Winifred's writing favorably in the introduction to an anthology of short fiction entitled *South by Southwest: 24 Stories from Modern Texas*, and in 1987, four years after Winifred's death and eight years after her family collected her short stories, William T. Pilkington told Suzanne Comer about the existence of the Sanford family edition of *Windfall and Other Stories*. When Comer became fiction editor at Southern Methodist University Press a short time later, she located a copy of this collection at the library of Midwestern University in Wichita Falls.

At that time, editors at SMU Press had begun a series entitled Southwest Life and Letters with the intent of publishing reprints of novels about Texas and the Southwest. The first three publications in this series were *The Staked Plains* by Frank X. Tolbert, *Sam Chance* by Benjamin Capps, and *Dallas Stories* by Marshall Terry, and Ms. Comer was concerned by the fact that all these authors were men. She felt that the series needed to be balanced by the addition of a book by a Texas woman writer. Comer made two photocopies of the Sanford family edition of Winifred Sanford's short story collection and returned the borrowed book to the Midwestern University Library. Then she sent these copies out to designated readers to be evaluated for possible publication.[16]

William T. Pilkington, a professor of literature at Tarleton State University in Stephenville, was one of the readers. In his report he wrote:

> It seems a real loss not only to Texas literature, but to American literature generally, that Mrs. Sanford chose to give up her literary career so early in life . . . The book is, to be sure, uneven in quality. Some of the tales . . . appear to be—well, they appear to be exactly what they are: stories from a woman's magazine of the

1920s. Still, they are pretty good, and I don't think they should be dropped . . . In general, the tales set in Texas are better than those set in the upper Midwest, perhaps because the Texas tales were written last, after Mrs. Sanford had had a chance to hone her craft.[17]

Don B. Graham, who holds the J. Frank Dobie chair in literature at the University of Texas, served as second reader. He wrote:

> I read this volume with great interest and believe the collection is worthy of being reprinted and made available to a larger audience . . . . The collection, as you know, is extremely rare. Most of the stories were placed originally in quite good magazines . . . and I was struck once again by Mencken's importance in American literature and his willingness to publish unknown regional writers when not too many others would. . . .
>
> In terms of Texas literature, Sanford fills a definite gap in the literature of the 1930s. Next to Katherine Anne Porter, she seems to be the best woman short story writer of that era, but more than that, she seems the best short story writer next to Porter, gender aside. I can think of no one in Texas letters at that time who was doing work to match hers or Porter's. Certainly not G. S. Perry or J. Frank Dobie, for example. Also, her stories of oil from the woman's perspective, seen beautifully in "Windfall" and "Fever in the South," afford a unique critique of oil's impact on culture, landscape, values, and human relationships.
>
> The Michigan stories are also lean, unsentimental glimpses into the lives of working women and are therefore of interest as well. . . .
>
> Sanford is a strong regionalist from the Thirties, and though she's no Tillie Olsen, (of whom I am not, I have to admit, that big a fan), she is a real writer, not a hack.[18]

On the basis of these reports, the staff of SMU Press decided to reprint *Windfall and Other Stories* as part of their Southwest Life and Letters series. Suzanne Comer included all the stories that had appeared in the Sanford family edition with the exception of "Fannie Baker," a story both readers felt should be eliminated. She also included Emerett Sanford Miles's foreword and engaged Lou Rodenberger to write an afterword. And in 1988, approximately fifty years after Winifred Sanford's last short story appeared in print, the first commercial edition of *Windfall and Other Stories* was released by SMU Press.

Reviewers' responses to the collection were mainly positive. Most of the critics who reviewed the book had never heard of Winifred Sanford, and they wrote about these fifty-year-old stories as if they had just been written. More than one reviewer lamented the fact that the thirteen stories in the collection were the sum total of the talented author's literary production. In *Booklist*, Brad Hooper wrote, "These trim but meaty pieces deserve a better fate than obscurity and their collection here is laudable. Sanford utilized a direct, unadorned style; writing of rough, resilient, but still bruisable characters . . . ."[19] In "Books of the Southwest: A Critical Checklist of Current Southwestern Americana," a writer identified only by the initials JPS wrote, "These wonderful short stories . . . deal with life in the Southwest during that time, and a rare portrait of an era emerges from the whole."[20] In S. S. Moorty's full-page review for *Texas Books in Review*, he compared Winifred Sanford's stories to the writings of F. Scott Fitzgerald and wrote,

> Unlike Fitzgerald's short stories that focus on the "flappers" and the rich, Sanford's stories are about ordinary folk—their lives, their privations, their self-delusions, their failures, and their sadnesses. . . . Winifred Sanford is a remarkable and talented storyteller who painfully recognizes conflicts in and traumas of the human spirit."[21]

For Judith Rigler, Winifred's stories exemplified the best kind of short fiction, "evoking a time and place with an economy of words." Writing for the *Fort Worth Star-Telegram*, Rigler said: "Knowing that they are our only record of the literary life of a very talented woman makes them all the more special."[22] In *Review of Texas Books*, Clay Reynolds wrote: "Although few have heard of Winifred M. Sanford, one of the founding members of the Texas Institute of Letters, readers are in for a delightful sampling of one brilliant writer's imagination. . . . The book is also the story of one woman's struggle toward literary identity as she wrote and participated in Texas letters."[23] Bob J. Frye made the following comment in *Western American Literature*: "She demonstrated that the woman writer can produce quality work even when its quantity is limited by life's circumstances,"[24] and in *Legacies: A History Journal for Dallas and North Central Texas*, Dan Baldwin wrote:

> Sanford's publishing career . . . produced some startling stories. . . . "Windfall" offers the clearest example of Ms. Sanford's ability to show the dark side of obsession, luck, and apparent good fortune. "Wealth at what cost?" Her stories ask. . . . What stands out the most about these stories is the prose employed in the telling, the sheer writing ability. No matter the character or tone . . . the dialogue and description evoke marvelous images of people, time and place.[25]

Only Diana David Olien from the University of Texas of the Permian Basin gave a negative assessment of the collection. In *Southwestern Historical Quarterly*, she wrote:

Far from the flapper, Sanford's typical heroine offers us submissiveness, domestic-
ity and maternity as paramount values.... Though evocative of boomtimes in
North and East Texas, Sanford's stories relating to oil ... fall back on stock figures
of oil-field folklore.... Sanford's perspective on petroleum is emphatically negative: oil causes littering and pollution; oil ruins people economically, morally,
physically, and emotionally. Oil is, in short, destructive—a time-worn theme in
American culture worth more attention from scholars.[26]

In their responses to Olien's review, Winifred Sanford's daughters acknowledged
that their mother's stories reflect the views of the society in which she lived. But
they insisted that, although Winifred was generally supportive of oil drilling and
traditional family values, she was an independent thinker who did not always
adhere to societal restrictions. As proof, Helen J. Sanford produced a letter from
Emerett that contained a feature article that had appeared in a Wichita Falls newspaper sometime after 1924. An excerpt from this undated article by Dorah McClin-
nico Wade appears below.

Mrs. Sanford is a careful mother as the well-kept ... children attested, but [she]
refused to say she gave them all her time, or to have her picture made with one
or both of them twined 'round her ... An insistent hunger, engendered by the
absence of lunch, suggested the idea to ask her to go out to the kitchen and make
a pie with her own fair hands ... But no! ... She was as obdurate about that as she
was about her writing.[27]

Such conflicts were not uncommon to women of Winifred's generation. In the afterword to *Windfall and Other Stories*, Lou Rodenberger wrote: "Most of the women
writers who were publishing at the time that Winifred Sanford's stories appeared
struggled to structure a compromise in roles so that they could both manage a
home and create fiction."[28]

Several years after SMU Press released the public edition of *Windfall and Other
Stories*, three additional short stories by Winifred were discovered—one that had
appeared in the November 1931 issue of *Household Magazine* and two others that
had never been published. The receipt for the sale of "Two Junes" was among Winifred's papers, and a microfilm copy of the story was also located. (A précis of this
story appears at the end of Chapter Two.)

Sometime after the death of Winifred's sister, Helen Mahon Toulme, in 1986,
one of Winifred's nieces discovered a mimeographed copy of another unpublished story, "Star in the East," among Helen Toulme's possessions and returned
it to Helen J. Sanford. The title of this story had appeared in correspondence that

Winifred exchanged with Maxwell Aley, fiction editor for *Woman's Home Companion*, in 1925.[29] The date of this correspondence establishes that an early version of "Star in the East" was one of the first stories, if not the very first story, that Winifred submitted for publication. She sent a later draft to her agent, David Lloyd, in 1931, and in all probability, it was this later version of the story, with the image of a Christmas wreath encircling a winter landscape on the cover page, that Helen Toulme's daughter returned to Helen J. Sanford.[30]

The setting of "Star in the East" is a private home where the main character, an elderly woman known only as Grandmother, is living and being cared for by a nurse and relatives. The narrative begins when Grandmother, through whose confused consciousness the story is related, awakens before dawn on Christmas Eve morning. As she lies in her bed and watches the light on the ceiling of her room grow brighter, she ponders what she has heard "them" say about her—that she is "very very old" and "hardly herself now." But Grandmother concludes that what "they" are saying about her is wrong. All she has left is "herself, her memories, and her visions."

In a narrative that collapses time and confuses present and past events and current caregivers with people who are deceased, Grandmother struggles to remember the significance of Christmas. She sees a table "piled high with strange and lovely things" and remembers that gifts are part of Christmas. She recalls a Christmas tree surrounded by presents when her daughter, Amy, was a child. She knows that Santa Claus and decorated trees are part of the celebration, but there is something about Christmas that eludes her. When Millie, the nurse, takes Grandmother into the decorated main room, Grandmother is reminded of a church where her husband Rom was once the minister. She knows that snow and white are somehow associated with Christmas, as are the sounds of sleigh bells and Christmas carols, but there is a deeper meaning that she can't quite recall. She remembers teaching a Sunday school class of young children, and when her granddaughter, Ruth, who Grandmother now mistakenly thinks is her deceased daughter, Amy, shows grandmother the baby that was born during the night, Grandmother recalls that a baby is somehow associated with the deeper significance of Christmas.

Long after Millie has put Grandmother to bed, she awakens and sees a bright light shining through her window. She mistakenly concludes that the streetlight that is shining into her room is a bright star. When Millie enters Grandmother's room the next morning, Grandmother reaches for Millie's hand and says, "Last night, from the window I saw the Star in the East . . . the Star of Bethlehem!"

In the last scene of the story, it is Christmas morning, and Grandmother is at peace and enjoying another visitation from her long-dead husband, who is reading the following passage from the Bible to her: "And it came to pass in those days, that there went forth a decree from Caesar Augusta ..." (For a complete draft of "Star in the East," see Appendix B.)

A SECOND UNPUBLISHED short story, entitled "Deep C," was discovered at the bottom of a cardboard box that contained Winifred's papers and correspondence. In 1945, she submitted "Deep C" to editors of *Good Housekeeping, McCall's Magazine, Saturday Evening Post*, and *Today's Woman*. The dates on letters that accompanied her submissions of this story indicate that "Deep C" was the last short story that Winifred ever submitted for publication.[31]

In her letter to Margaret Cousins, managing editor of *Good Housekeeping*, she indicated that her inspiration for this story was a true event that she read about in a newspaper article.

> I am afraid you brought this story on yourself by including my name in your com-
> ments on the short story writers of Texas in last Sunday's Times Herald [*sic*]. Ill-
> ness ... and the war ... have kept me from writing for publication for some time,
> but I am starting again, and this story, "Deep C," is the first effort. I confess that I
> hardly expect you to like it. Because of the rattler. But ever since I read of that years
> ago, I have been haunted by it. Even toned down, however, (the real life affair was
> more tragic), you may think it is too strong meat for your readers.[32]

In "Deep C," Winifred framed the "real life affair" that had haunted her for so many years with a coming-of-age story in which a nine-year-old girl named Judy Graham travels to West Texas to spend the summer with her paternal grandparents and learns the meaning of the word "courage." When this story opens, Judy, who is traveling alone on a train for the first time from Fort Worth to her grandparent's ranch, has just bitten down on a hard mint candy and broken a tooth.

Just a week earlier, Judy's mother, who had concerns about Judy's welfare on the Lazy G, took Judy to the family dentist for a checkup. "You know she's going to spend the summer down by the forks of the creek, with Tom's folks," her mother told the dentist, "and I don't suppose there's a dentist within a thousand miles." The dentist laughingly replied, "They don't need dentists out there, Mrs. Graham ... When a cowboy gets a toothache ... he gets the boss to jerk ..."

Remembering the dentist's words, Judy becomes fearful and decides to remain quiet about her broken tooth for the duration of her visit. She occupies herself on the lengthy train ride with watching the landscape change as she travels further west and by making up stories about life on the Lazy G. These stories include bandits attacking a stagecoach and her grandfather galloping up on horseback with a "Hi Ho, Silver" to defeat the bandits and rescue the passengers.

When Judy reaches her destination, where the train makes a brief stop, the porter deposits her and her bags on the platform and the train departs. Judy experiences a moment of panic as she stands alone on the platform. Her grandparents soon emerge from the darkness, and Judy reacts to them as if they are little more than strangers. She recognizes Grandfather because he looks like a stereotypical cowboy, with his cowboy hat, weathered face, droopy mustache, khaki clothes, and high heel cowboy boots. When Grandmother, who is stooped, wears her gray hair pulled back into a knot, and walks with a limp, greets Judy, she says, "So it's Tom's baby."

On the way to the car, Judy asks Grandmother how she hurt her foot, and Grandmother answers, "Well hon, if you must know,—a snake bit me." Judy forgets all about the promise she made to herself on the train not to tell her grandparents about her broken tooth and says, "I hurt myself, too. I bit down on a piece of candy, Grandmother, and I broke my tooth off."

When Judy awakens the following morning, her tooth is aching, but she remembers that the dentist said if cowboys got a toothache, their boss jerked the sore tooth out with pliers. And when Grandfather appears with a horse for Judy to ride and asks, "How's the toothache," she tells him her tooth isn't really broken and doesn't hurt a bit. She mounts a horse that is nothing like the horse she had imagined riding, and she and Grandfather go out to survey the ranch, a western landscape complete with jackrabbits, mesquite trees, a canyon with red rock cliffs, and a stream in the valley. When Judy asks if she can get off her horse and take a closer look, Grandfather tells her there are rattlers hiding in the rocks.

Judy asks him about the time the rattlesnake bit her grandmother. She asks why he didn't get a hoe and kill it, and he replies, "I wasn't there . . . . I'd done a mighty foolish thing. . . . leaving her alone on the place, her and Tom." Then he turns his horse and starts back toward the house. When Judy reaches the house, she continues to ask questions about the incident, but Grandmother doesn't want to talk about it anymore than Grandfather does. Finally, Grandmother agrees to tell Judy the story and show her the scar, but only if Judy promises never to mention the incident again.

The story that Grandmother tells is the same incident that haunted Winifred when she first read about it in an unidentified West Texas newspaper. In Grandmother's story, she and Grandfather were a young married couple with a small boy when Grandfather started off to Junction to get food and supplies. "You won't be afraid now?" he said to Grandmother as he departed on his journey. "I'll be gone a week, likely."

A short while later, Grandmother left Judy's father, a two-year-old toddler, inside the house while she went into the backyard to empty a pan of dishwater. She didn't see the snake until she heard it rattle, and by then she had already started to put her foot down on top of it.

When the snake bit her, she knew she had to tie a tourniquet around her leg and slash the wound to get the poison out as quickly as possible. But she didn't have a knife and knew that she couldn't make it back to the house to get one. Then she saw a rag that she had left hanging on the fence and found a piece of wire with a barb on it nearby in the dirt. She tied the rag around her leg and shut her eyes so she wouldn't have to see the damage she was causing when she cut her leg with the wire. In the middle of doing this, she remembered that her son Tom was alone in the house. In the midst of the swelling and burning in her leg, her struggle to breathe, and the pains in her stomach, she thought about the dangers that her little boy would encounter if she died—the fire in the stove, the rattler in the yard, the water in the cattle trough. She tried to remember if there was any water in the house for Tom to drink, if she had left cornbread where he could get to it, and she thought about him afraid and crying for her all night in a dark house. While she slashed the flesh around the snakebite, a memory from her childhood came back to her, something the black workers on the plantation where she was raised had said: "Deep C ain't but a few notes down."

When Grandmother pauses, Judy adds the part of the story that Grandfather told her. When he arrived at the river, the rising water was too high to cross, so he turned around and went back to the house. He found Grandmother in the yard, picked her up in his arms, and carried her inside. With the story finished, Grandmother grips Judy by the shoulders and delivers the message that is the crux of the story: "Things are mighty dark, sometimes, Judy. They were so dark for me that I was praying for the waters to close over my head . . . I was ready to give up fighting it off . . . All the time I was lying there on the ground, crazy with pain and the fever, help was coming up the trail!"

Long after Judy has climbed into bed, she lies awake, thinking about something Grandmother said—"I had it to do, Judy. I had it to do!" Judy's tongue slides over the jagged splinters of her broken tooth and the sore place that her ragged tooth has scraped on the inside of her cheek. In the darkness of night, she smells the sweet scent of the plains, hears the bark of a dog and the howl of a coyote, and remembers what her father told her mother before Judy left home—"Danger calls for courage." Finally, Judy understands why her father wanted her to spend the summer on her grandparents' ranch.

By the time morning comes, Judy has made her decision. "I want you to pull my tooth," she tells her grandfather soon after she enters the kitchen. "Will you, Grandfather? Will you, please?" (For a complete draft of "Deep C," see Appendix B.)

IN A LETTER TO MARGARET COUSINS that accompanied the manuscript of "Deep C," Winifred reminded Cousins, a Texas native living and working as an editor in New York, that the two women had met once at a meeting of the College Club of Dallas that took place at the farm of Goldie Capers Smith. Winifred wrote that the College Club was still holding meetings all these years later. She also told Cousins that the mother of Frank X. Tolbert, a writer and journalist that Cousins had mentioned favorably in a recent newspaper article in *The Dallas Morning News*, was a member of the Manuscript Club of Wichita Falls when Winifred was a member.

Margaret Cousins acknowledged her Texas roots in her reply to Sanford's letter. She told Winifred that "Deep C" appealed to her like "a chapter out of my past," but unfortunately, the current editor of *Good Housekeeping* did not favor regional material. Although he recognized that "Deep C" was smoothly written, he felt that it was not right for *Good Housekeeping*.[33]

While "Deep C" was no more regional in subject matter than Winifred's stories set in the East and West Texas oil fields, it lacked the minimalist style and ironic viewpoint that had proved so successful for her in these earlier stories. In "Deep C," she reverted to a more romantic style of writing, one that she had abandoned soon after composing "The Monument." In "Deep C," Sanford utilized a main character who, despite her young age, was a stereotypical figure in western films and literature—the stranger from a metropolitan area who goes West, learns an important lesson, and returns home a changed individual. Perhaps in employing a romantic style of writing and a western stereotype, Winifred was attempting to adapt to a current trend in literature. For as she once told her daughter Mary, the starkly realistic style that had proved so successful at the beginning of Winifred's writing career had eventually become "dated."

Reviews that followed SMU Press's 1988 release of *Windfall and Other Stories* precipitated a flurry of interest in Winifred Sanford's short stories. In 1995, a screenplay based upon "Luck" and written by Winifred's grandson Philip Railsback was made into a movie by Clint Eastwood's production company. The movie, *Stars Fell on Henrietta*, was directed by James Keach and coproduced by another of Sanford's grandsons, Steven Railsback. It stars Robert Duvall as Mr. Cox and Billy Bob Thornton as Roy and also features Aidan Quinn and Frances Fisher. The movie appeared in a number of film festivals before it was released for general distribution in major theaters.

In 1996, an entry for Winifred Sanford, written by Lou Rodenberger, appeared in the revised, six-volume edition of *The Handbook of Texas*, and in 1997, Rodenberger and her co-editor, Sylvia Anne Grider, included a synopsis of Sanford's writing in *Texas Women Writers*. Also in 1997, "Windfall" was selected for inclusion in "Arts & Letters Live: Texas Bound," a popular program of literary readings produced by

Kay Cattarulla and cosponsored by the Dallas Museum of Art and the Friends of the Dallas Public Library. In 2003, Sanford's short story "Luck," along with an overview of her writing, were reprinted in an anthology edited by Sylvia Ann Grider and Lou Rodenberger. This anthology, entitled *Let's Hear It: Stories by Texas Women Writers*, features short stories by twenty-one Texas women writers who produced work between 1865 and 2003.

Finally, almost sixty years after Winifred Sanford stopped submitting stories for publication, her excellent short fiction was recognized by scholars and restored to the canon of southwestern literature.

Conclusion

ONE IMPORTANT QUESTION REMAINS
to be answered. Why, in a region that has often been maligned for the inferiority of its literature, sometimes by its own authors and scholars, was the work of
one accomplished woman writer overlooked for more than fifty years?[1] Although
fourteen published short stories and a few nonfiction articles are not a large body
of work, Winifred Sanford's excellent short fiction certainly deserved more attention than her stories were accorded before SMU Press published *Windfall and Other
Stories* in 1988.

The story of Winifred Sanford's abbreviated career and the circumstances that
contributed to her limited literary output deserve additional attention, as well.
In summary, various accidental circumstances acted as catalysts that ignited her
most intense period of creativity. For a brief time in the 1920s, social conditions
in the West Texas town of Wichita Falls were ripe for the production of literature.
The discovery of large oil deposits beneath the sandy red soil attracted individuals from a variety of cultural backgrounds into a previously conservative agrarian
community that had been a frontier only thirty years earlier. The cultural diversity
within this suddenly burgeoning population produced the kinds of internal and
external conflicts that often inspire great fiction.[2]

In Wichita Falls, Winifred became associated with a group of intelligent women who shared her somewhat liberal views as well as her interest in writing. Like Winifred, these women felt isolated in the conservative agrarian community. Many of them were strangers when they first came together to form the Manuscript Club, a group of mainly novice writers who were interested in literature and wanted to try their hand at composition. They soon became a mutually supportive group of serious writers whose friendship, competitive spirit, and superior critical skills aided Winifred's development as a writer.

Because Winifred was not a Texas native, the stories she wrote were neither inspired nor limited by the state's mythical past. Her midwestern background and her preference for realism over romanticism prevented her from becoming entrapped in romantic expressions of sectional pride that afflicted the writing of so many Texas writers. Her realistic portrayals of current events and modern-day characters in contemporary settings coincided with the literary style that was popular in the United States in the 1920s. Consequently, Winifred's fictional stories captured the attention of H. L. Mencken and George Jean Nathan, coeditors of *The American Mercury*.

Once H. L. Mencken took an interest in Winifred's work, she became increasingly successful in terms of publication, and her desire to write full time increased accordingly. Unfortunately, she was never able to realize the fulfillment of this desire. As the wife of an ambitious and increasingly successful oil and gas lawyer, and the mother of three lively children, her focus was continually bifurcated. Whenever a conflict between her duty to her family and her desire to write fiction arose, as it often did, duty always took precedence over desire. In addition, the high value placed upon the domestic role of women by the society in which Winifred lived and the small amount of money that she earned in comparison to her husband's income prevented her from placing her writing in a position of primary importance.

Winifred's perfectionist tendencies and her sensitivity to criticism also contributed to her limited literary output. She spent countless hours writing and then rewriting short stories and novels, only to set them ablaze in the fireplace of the family's home. Early on, her correspondence with H. L. Mencken supplied her with encouragement and reassurance during her most productive period of writing. But when Mencken resigned as editor of *The American Mercury* and Winifred no longer had contact with her mentor, both her confidence and her literary output declined.

Other factors contributed to the demise of Winifred Sanford's writing career, as well. When the Sanford family moved from Wichita Falls to Dallas, Winifred was deprived of the rich cultural mix that had served as inspiration for her earlier stories. In the affluent Highland Park neighborhood, she was surrounded by a homogeneous, upper-middle-class society. And although she helped to organize a writing club in Dallas and later became a charter member of the Texas Institute of Letters, these organizations never inspired her to write in quite the same way that her friends in the Manuscript Club of Wichita Falls had. In fact, records of early TIL meetings indicate that charter members of the organization were often more interested in bickering with one another than in pursuing fine writing.

An unplanned pregnancy, the birth of a third child when Winifred was forty-two years old, and the contraction of tuberculosis were major impediments to her literary production as she approached middle age. Although she continued to write even as she was recovering from tuberculosis, she devoted a majority of her effort and writing time to composing novels--a form that never proved as successful for her as the short story.

Finally, Winifred's letters to M. K. Singleton indicate that the mystery regarding the unnamed woman writer who Charles Angoff wrote about in *H. L. Mencken: A Portrait from Memory*--a woman that Singleton identifies as Winifred Sanford in a footnote in *H. L. Mencken and the American Mercury Adventure*--was either a case of mistaken identity on M. K. Singleton's part or a fabrication on Charles Angoff's. Winifred Sanford did not suddenly and mysteriously stop writing during the time that H. L. Mencken served as chief editor of *The American Mercury*. In fact, she submitted a short story to Charles Angoff approximately one year after Mencken resigned from the magazine. And she continued to write sporadically and to seek publication of her fiction for at least fourteen years after her last short story appeared in print.

The factors that contributed to the brevity of Winifred's career were many and varied. Some were circumstantial; some were inherent in her personality; and some were cultural. Many of the same circumstances that prevented her writing career from flourishing have been operational in the lives of other women writers as well. Perhaps the inferiority of Texas literature, which many critics and writers have noted, is not so much due to a lack in the quality of the literature produced by Texas writers as it is to a flaw in historical record keeping. The possibility exists that at least some fault lies with scholars who have overlooked the work of writers like Winifred Sanford, women whose literary output has been limited by personal and cultural circumstances to a single novel, a slim volume of poems, or a few excellent short stories.

A LIST OF
WINIFRED
SANFORD'S
PUBLICATIONS

"England and the Home-Rule Question," October 1913, *South Atlantic Quarterly*
"Wreck," January 1925, *The American Mercury*
"The Forest Fire," April 1925, *The American Mercury*
"Allie," June 1925, *The American Mercury*
"Saved," January 1926, *The American Mercury*
"The Monument," January 1926, *Woman's Home Companion*
"The Method of Irony," March 1926, *The Editor*
"Mary," May 1926, *Woman's Home Companion*
"The Blue Spruce," May 1926, *The American Mercury*
"Black Child," January 1927, *The American Mercury*
"Fools," June 1928, *Woman's Home Companion*
"Windfall," June 1928, *The American Mercury*
"Luck," September 1930, *The American Mercury*
"Mr. Carmichael's Room," April 1931, *The American Mercury*
"Fever in the South," November 1931, *North American Review*
"Two Junes," November 1931, *Household Magazine*
"Derrick Jargon," April 1934, *Southwest Review*
"Writing the Short Story," October 1935, *Southwester*
"Fannie Baker," January 1988, *Windfall and Other Stories*
"A Victorian Grandmother," January 1988, *Windfall and Other Stories*

A LIST OF
WINIFRED
SANFORD'S
UNPUBLISHED
STORIES
AND
NOVELS

"APHRODITE"

Winifred sent this short story to H. L. Mencken on March 9, 1926, but he did not accept it for publication in *The American Mercury*.

ARROWS OF THE ALMIGHTY

This was the first novel that Winifred Sanford attempted. She completed it in the latter part of September 1927 and, as Mencken requested, sent one copy to him and another to Mrs. Knopf. When Knopf returned the manuscript to Winifred, she sent it David Lloyd of Paget Literary Agency. Unable to place the novel, Lloyd returned the manuscript to Winifred on May 18, 1928, along with a letter in which he told her, "It would appear that your target shot just not quite at the bull's eye."

YOU ASKED FOR IT

This was a 55,000-word popular detective novel. Winifred wrote the novel while she was recovering from tuberculosis. She sent the manuscript to David Lloyd on March 1, 1938. Unable to place it with a publisher, Lloyd returned the manuscript.

"DEEP C"

Winifred submitted this story, probably the last that she ever tried to publish, to the editors of several magazines in 1945.

"SICK FOR HOME"

Winifred submitted a short story by this name to H. L. Mencken twice, first on July 25, 1924, and again on August 6, 1925. Mencken rejected the story, set in "logging country," and returned both drafts to Winifred.

"STAR IN THE EAST"

Winifred submitted a draft of this story to *Woman's Home Companion* in 1925 and another to David Lloyd in 1931. Most probably, this was the first story that she submitted for publication.

"THE WEDDING"

This story was accepted for publication by *Household Magazine* in July 14, 1931, but for some reason, the story never appeared in that magazine under Winifred Sanford's name.

"WILDCAT"

Winifred sent this story to *The American Mercury* ca. 1934, when Charles Angoff was chief editor, but it was not accepted for publication.

UNTITLED NOVEL

In a letter to David Lloyd dated May 9, 1932, Winifred told that she had completed 88,000 words of a novel set in the oil fields of Texas that utilized the same characters as the short story "The Wedding." She was planning to use the story, after it appeared in *Household Magazine*, as the final chapter of this novel.

LETTERS
EXCHANGED
BETWEEN
WINIFRED
SANFORD
AND THE
EDITORS OF
THE AMERICAN
MERCURY

LETTERS WRITTEN TO WINIFRED SANFORD
by H. L. Mencken are published by permission of the Enoch Pratt Free Library in Baltimore, Maryland, in accordance with the terms of Mr. Mencken's will and his bequest to the library and by permission of the Southwestern Writers Collection at Texas State University in San Marcos, Texas, where they are housed. These letters are published in full, as they were written, with the original formatting retained.

Letters written to Winifred Sanford by George Jean Nathan are published by permission of Patricia Angelin, Literary Executrix of the George Jean Nathan Estate.

Letters written to H. L. Mencken and George Jean Nathan by Winifred Sanford are published by permission of Paul Railsback, Executor of the Winifred M. Sanford Estate, and The New York Public Library.

July 25, 1924

1301 Filmore St.
Wichita Falls, Texas

Mr. H. L. Mencken
Editor of the American Mercury
730 Fifth Avenue
New York City

My dear Mr. Mencken:
   The note you enclosed with my last story had me guessing. I couldn't make out whether my offering had been the laughing stock of the editorial staff or whether you were frantically anxious to see another. You didn't say you liked it; neither did you order me back to the

dishpan and the kitchen mop. If you decide, after reading "Sick for Home," that I belong in the kitchen, please be good enough to tell me so. I am in that miserable state of doubt that seems to be the lot of the incipient writer. One story out of a dozen or so—and that among the least worthy to my mind—finds its market in the Woman's Home Companion,—and oh! the things I have said against the ladies' magazines;—the others flit back and forth between Texas and New York, drawing occasional kind comments but nothing more. Something is obviously wrong, and with me, (I do not blame the editors), but how under the sun does one find out where the trouble is?

Most cordially yours,
Winifred Sanford
(Mrs. W H Sanford)

. . . . .

August 3rd [1924]

Dear Mrs. Sanford:—
If this story didn't deal with the logging country we'd probably take it. At the moment we have no more than three articles in type, all relating to that region.

I see nothing wrong at all. You are writing very good stuff. I'll be glad to see it, and soon or late I'll buy some of it. Maybe you are selecting markets unwisely. Every magazine has a long list of prohibitions, some of them irrational.

Sincerely yours,
H. L. Mencken

. . . . .

October 21st, 1924

Dear Mrs. Sanford:
I like your short story, "The Wreck," very much indeed and am accepting it for the American Mercury.

Sincerely yours,
George Jean Nathan

. . . . .

October 30th, 1924

Dear Mrs. Sanford:
Will you be good enough to send us at once some information about yourself for use on our American Mercury Authors' page?

Is the "Wreck" your first short story?

Sincerely Yours,
George Jean Nathan

. . . . .

March 18, 1925

Dear Miss Sanford,
Have you anything in hand or in mind that would fit into The American Mercury? It seems a long, long while since I last heard from you.

Sincerely yours,
H. L. Mencken

. . . . .

March 23, 1925

1301 Filmore Street
Wichita Falls, Texas

My dear Mr. Mencken:
Well, if you will have some samples, here you are. *Allie* is, I suspect, too much of a bad thing. *The Forest Fire* I have just this minute concocted, and I don't know how it will taste when the brew settles.

I haven't forgotten the American Mercury, nor what has seemed to me your unparalleled generosity in actually paying for and publishing *Wreck*. I wonder what, if anything, has been said to you about it. My own acquaintances are divided into two wings: the left write to me as to a major prophet; the right say to the left that is too bad I didn't put in a little heroism or self sacrifice, and besides lifesavers are not the least bit like Charlie—they wouldn't be tolerated in the service. To me they write that they have always known I can write, but what a mountebank this man Mencken is! And Mr. somebody or other, reviewing *Wreck* in the Bookman, evidently belongs to the right wing.

I haven't written many short stories lately because I am at work on a novel, my first, I need hardly say. It is going to be much more conventional in its method than my second, but it is well under way, and I can't drop it, though what will become of it when finished is more than I can imagine.

If you don't like either of these works of art I am sending you, I'll try something else. I have dozens in my mind, but it is a long way from my mind to my fingers.

Most sincerely yours,
Winifred M. Sanford

. . . . .

March 28th (1925)

Dear Mrs. Sanford:—
I like the two stories so much that I am taking both of them. My best thanks.

The best of luck with the novel! When you finish it, it might be a good plan to let Knopf see it. He handles first novels very effectively.

Everyone I respect thought "The Wreck" was excellent stuff. And it undoubtedly was! Don't let imbeciles annoy you!

Sincerely yours,
H. L. Mencken

P.S. Will you please send me materials for our writers' notes about yourself, longer than the one we printed in January? *postscript written in longhand

. . . . .

April 5, 1925

1301 Filmore Street
Wichita Falls, Texas

My dear Mr. Mencken:
You are the most astonishing editor! I am not used to finding editors who are guilty of considering even one story, let alone two. The thanks, I am sure, should come from me.

Yes, if the novel is ever finished, it will go first to Knopf, but it is a much more personal,—subjective,—intimate,—whatever you want to call it—affair than the stories, and I may decide that is a mistake.

As for my autobiography, there is little of interest. I was born in Duluth, Minnesota, was educated at Mount Holyoke and the University of Michigan, taught school for a while, and am now the wife of a lawyer, and the mother of two small and omnipresent daughters.

Most sincerely and gratefully yours,

Winifred Sanford

. . . . .

April 10, 1925

Dear Mrs. Sanford:

I certainly hope you let me see the novel when it is finished. Your three stories have interested me enormously. It seems to me that there is genuinely distinguished work in them. Needless to say, if you do anything else suitable for *The American Mercury*, whether a story or an article, I'll be very glad to see it.

Sincerely yours,

H. L. Mencken, Editor

. . . . .

July 19, 1925

Dear Mr. Mencken:

I have just finished "Saved by Grace", a story inspired by a recent revival in our town. Will it do at all?

I hope you won't mind my sending you at the same time a story you have seen before. You wrote nearly a year ago that you would probably have taken it, if . . . Perhaps the conditional mode is now past. I admit cheerfully enough that it has been the rounds,—was even accepted once by the Midland and returned after several months because Mr. Frederick thought the title misleading. What I dislike about the story is the artificiality of the beginning and end,—which could, of course, be worked over if necessary.

I am still at work on the novel I spoke of some time ago. It goes slowly when the thermometer is at 110, but in time I hope to reach the end.

With many thanks for all your courtesies in the past, I am

Very cordially yours,

Winifred Sanford

. . . . .

July 29th (1925)

Dear Mrs. Sanford:—

I have a feeling, as you have, that "Sick for Home" is damaged by its machinery—that it would be more effective without the present opening. Why not lay it aside for a month or two, and then rewrite it.

Thanks very much for "Saved by Grace". I like it very much, and am putting it into type at once. I incline to think that the title could be improved. Why not make it simply "Saved"?

The best of luck with the novel. Mr. Knopf is very eager to see it.

Sincerely yours,
H. L. Mencken

.....

August 6, 1925

My dear Mr. Mencken:
I am glad you liked the revival story. As for the title, I don't like it any better than you do. Saved is preferable to Saved by Grace, but I wonder what you would think of The Tent Meeting . . . or The Revival. Not that either is distinctive, but because it carries on the tradition of Wreck and The Forest Fire. In all three, at least, there have been the two elements: the story, and the more or less typical incident. Or am I talking in my old and forsaken role of school teacher?

The same thing may be said of Sick for Home, which you sent back. I'm going to rewrite it and see what happens.

Most cordially yours,
[Winifred Sanford]

.....

October 28, 1925

Mr. H. L. Mencken,
Editor of the American Mercury
730 Fifth Avenue
New York City

My dear Mr. Mencken:
Here is the latest version of "Sick for Home." You remember you suggested rewriting it, and you see I did, so thoroughly, indeed, that practically nothing of the old story remains except the stage setting. Whether it is better or worse or just as bad, I don't know. But naturally, I hope you can use it.

I have written nothing else because of the vow I took to finish my novel before it finished me. I didn't know what back-breaking business a novel could be. But I think I see my way through it now. I hope it will be ready early in 1926 if not before. After that is out of the house, I intend to write a hundred things which are jumbled together in my head.

Most sincerely yours,
Winifred Sanford

.....

December 21, 1925

Dear Mrs. Sanford:
I am delighted to hear that you are rewriting your novel. It is a good sign. Take all the time you want on it. I am thoroughly convinced that it will be a first rate piece of work when you finish it at last.

Sincerely yours,
H. L. Mencken

.....

January 14, 1926

1301 Filmore Street
Wichita Falls, Texas

My dear Mr. Mencken:
You are very kind to encourage me about the novel. I suppose everyone goes through the same experience, and writes and throws away and writes again as cheerfully as I. I got so sick of the whole thing that I dropped it, six weeks ago, and decided to take a vacation. Now I am ready to start in again, and it looks promising. I know at last exactly what I want to do ... *if* I can do it.

Meanwhile I find it almost impossible to write anything else. I am glad you liked "The Blue Spruce", and I am also glad that you missed Lena. I couldn't work her in. You see I started out to write a sort of paean of a northern winter, and then I thought of Lena, who was tragic, and didn't fit in at all well with the other idea. Some time I shall think of a story for her.

Most sincerely yours,
Winifred Sanford.

. . . . .

January 19, 1926.

Dear Mrs. Sanford:
It is excellent news that your novel is giving you a hard tussle. Hard writing makes smooth and charming reading. Take your time with it. And the best of luck to you.

Sincerely yours,
H. L. Mencken

. . . . .

February 9, 1926

1301 Filmore Street
Wichita Falls, Texas

H. L. Mencken
Editor, The American Mercury,
730 Fifth Avenue
New York City

My dear Mr. Mencken:
When I finished this story a month ago, I said to myself, "Well, I won't send this one to Mr. Mencken; it's too light, and too flippant, and too smarty." And then I got my statement from the bank on the first, and then I got desperate, and here I go. My feelings will not be hurt in the least if you ship it back in the next mail. I know exactly what it is.

What I want to know is this: Who *will* publish such stuff? Or won't anybody? They seem to want them light enough, but not subtle.

I'm going back to work on the novel tomorrow, and I shall stop for nothing from now on until I finish it. Up to the fated first of the month it was going along nicely.

Most sincerely yours,
Winifred Sanford

.....

March 9, 1926

My dear Mr. Mencken:
You were right in sending back "The Aphrodite". It *was* artificial, based on a fallacy and all that, and although I confess to liking [it] at times for the type of story it tried to be but probably wasn't, I shall lay it aside. You know I said I didn't think you would like it, but I have held back stories before for the same reason, only to find that you *did* like them. I thought that maybe the critics knew what they were talking about when they said that writers are no judges of their own work.

Now I shall put it away with an easy conscience.

In the same mail, I sent another story to the Woman's Home Companion. You remember they had the doubtful honor of being the first magazine to buy from me, though they waited until you had published three before turning it loose on the world. Now they have accepted this other, their third, and again I suspect that my appearance in the Mercury has something to do with it. I read the other day that E. W. Howe claims the distinction of being the only man praised by both H. L. Mencken and Dr. Frank Crane, and it may be that I am almost as rare a bird.

At least I have my mind free for the novel. I *think* it is going to be good. I have to fight everything from literary clubs to influenza germs in the rest of the family for my time, and though sometimes I envy the fellow who is sure of his straight eight hours, at other times I think I get ahead almost as fast as things are.

At present the book is crude and jerky ... very ... but the various threads are interweaving quite neatly and I have at last some sort of design, adaptable to chapters and books, so that all I need now is the time to fill it in. And rewrite and rewrite and rewrite what is already down. And there are, of course, a thousand facts to check, and heaven knows how many thousand words to copy.

But it is the best fun in the world.

Most sincerely yours,
Winifred Sanford

.....

June 7th, [1926]

Dear Mrs. Sanford:—
I surely hope that your mother is much better. I'll be in New York tomorrow (Tuesday) and also Wednesday and Thursday. It will be a great pleasure to see you at the office at your convenience. Will you please call me up in the morning? Mr. Knopf, unfortunately, is sailing for Europe on Wednesday.

Sincerely yours,
H. L. Mencken

.....

August 28, 1926

2432 East First Street
Duluth, Minnesota

My dear Mr. Mencken:
I am sending you this story with a good many qualms. I gather from the rather hesitating criticism my friends make of my stories that I have failed to make them beautiful. But I don't for the life of me see how anyone could write prettily of a character like Callie. I suppose they would have me make her a soul starving for beauty,—or something like that. And if a story is psychologically sound, (as I think this is) I don't care, personally, whether it is pretty or not. Indeed I think prettiness would spoil it. Yet when I read it over, I admit it sounds crude and jerky . . . a good deal like poor Callie. Am I right or wrong?

You will probably think it too long. It is, as you will see, four related episodes, rather than a normal short story. I have considered leaving out the last one, but I don't like it that way, either, because the others are all leading up to it. If you see anything that can be cut, please tell me.

This is the only thing I have written this summer. You remember that when I was in New York in June, my mother was very sick. She lived until the end of July, since when I have been here, trying to get back into a normal state of mind. I suppose it is all part of the orad to wisdom, but sometimes I don't think I care very much about being wise.

I haven't touched the novel, and shan't for another month when I expect to be back in Texas.

I am
Most sincerely yours,
Mrs. Winifred Sanford

.....

September 3rd, 1926

Dear Mrs. Sanford:
Please pay no heed to such foolish advice. "Black Child" is one of the best stories you have ever done and I am delighted to have it for the magazine. It goes into type at once.

I won't attempt to offer you any consolation on the death of your mother. My own mother is now dead nearly a year but it is still impossible for me to adjust myself to her absence.

Sincerely yours,
H. L. Mencken

.....

August 30th [1927]

Dear Mrs. Sanford:
It seems ages since we last printed anything of yours. Have you any new stories? If so, I certainly hope you will give me a chance at them.

How are you coming on with the novel?
Sincerely yours,
H. L. Mencken

.....

September 20, 1927

2432 East 1st Street
Duluth, Minnesota

My dear Mr. Mencken:

About two weeks ago, I wrote to the Knopfs that my novel was all but ready. They wrote back, of course, that Mrs. Knopf was still away, but asked me to send it along . . . as I am doing.

I have no idea whether you are in the East just now or whether if you are, the manuscript will ever find its way to you, but since you are the only one I have talked with about it, I'd like to blow off a little steam, if I may.

Please don't think that I am begging for mercy where the novel is concerned. I don't think it deserves any mercy. I think it is about the flattest thing I ever read in my life, and although I had some hopes for it until recently, I can see now that it is pretty bad.

Writers, however, can't afford to have any pride, and when you have worked on anything for so long, you feel that it is entitled to its chance in the world; and so I am sending it out, rather against my better judgment, but hoping that you or someone else may be able to give me some advice.

Of course my state of mind may be due to the pressure under which I have been writing, but I feel today as though there were no possibility of its passing muster in its present state. It has no style and no good title; it is horribly jerky; it is all conversation. (I have suddenly realized that for the last six months I have been consistently crossing out all the descriptive and expository passages and leaving only the naked dialog); several of the characters are wooden; and many of the issues have lost any interest they may once have had for me. The last half is better than the first, but that is about all that can be said for it.

Now what shall I do? Nobody has read it, and I have reached the point where I need someone else's opinion. I don't react to it any more myself. Is it worth working over or if the Knopfs scorn it, would anyone else take it? Or would I be foolish to try to publish it? Or is it merely because I am tired that it looks so impossible to me?

No matter what happens to it, I am not sorry I wrote it, because I have learned a great many things in the process, and unless you tell me I am wasting my time . . . and maybe even then . . . I shall soon be starting one of the other novels I have in mind, to say nothing of a few short stories I have been postponing until I finished the book.

Incidentally, you will be interested to know that "The Forest Fire", one of those stories of mine you published in the Mercury, was translated into German and accepted by some German magazine whose name I have forgotten. It was supposed to appear in one of the spring issues, but I have never heard whether it did or not.

One reason for my haste in finishing the novel and shipping it off just now is this: If there were anything to be gained by it, I *could* come to New York about the first of October for a few days,—something I am not able to do when I have my children in Texas. Otherwise I shall be going back to Texas about that time.

Most sincerely yours,
Winifred Sanford

. . . . .

September 24th [1927]

Dear Mrs. Sanford:—

It is excellent news that you are full of doubts about your novel. The bad ones are all written by authors who are absolutely sure of them. I have nothing whatever to do with the Knopf book business, and so the MS. will not come to me. Nor would my judgment of it have any weight there if it were offered. So I shall leave it to Mr. Block, who is very competent. As for coming to New York, I don't know. It might be well to ask Mr. Block (Harry A.) or Mr. Knopf.

Have you done any short stories of late? If so, I surely hope you give me a chance at them for The American Mercury.

Sincerely yours,

H. L. Mencken

. . . . .

February 28th [1928]

Dear Mrs. Sanford:

What are you up to? I'd certainly like to see you in *The American Mercury* again. Have you any ideas for short stories? I certainly hope that the novel is finished and that you are in good spirits.

Sincerely yours,

H. L. Mencken

. . . . .

April 11th [1928]

Dear Mrs. Sanford:—

Thanks for "Windfall". I like it very much, and am putting it into type at once. The usual check and proof will reach you in a week. I hope there is something else on the way.

Yours,

H. L. Mencken

. . . . .

May 14th [1929]

Dear Mrs. Sanford:

What are you up to? Haven't you any stories in hand or in mind that would fit in to *The American Mercury*? I surely hope so. It is now more than a year since we last printed you, and the time seems far too long.

I may add that the magazine is now a shade more prosperous than it was, and can pay better prices.

Sincerely yours,

H. L. Mencken

. . . . .

May 24, 1929

My dear Mr. Mencken:

I wish I *did* have something worth printing. I have a dozen things in mind, but nothing I have written for the last year or two has pleased me or anyone else. If I were only sure that the bird would rise from the ashes, I would light a big bonfire.

However, I'll get out some of those abandoned stories within the next few days and try to finish them for you. I have even tried articles, having several things I should like to say, but they are just like everyone's else [sic] articles, and I don't like them.

Have you seen "Best American Short Stories of the Southwest", edited by Hilton Greer and published by the Southwest Press? It is nothing to lose one's head about, but it included that story of mine called "Windfall", which you published in the Mercury last year.

Sincerely yours,

[Winifred Sanford]

. . . . .

May 29, 1929

Dear Mrs. Sanford:

It is excellent news that you are getting back to work. I'd certainly be delighted to see you in The American Mercury [sic] again. Will you let me see whatever you do?

Sincerely yours,

H. L. Mencken

. . . . .

May 8th 1930

Dear Mrs. Sanford:—

Thanks very much for the chance to see "Luck". I think it is an excellent story. As it stands, it is obviously somewhat longish, and I shall try to make a few discreet cuts, but probably there won't be many. The usual check and proof will reach you in about a week.

It was good to hear from you again. I surely hope another story is on the stocks. It is far too long since the last time you were in the American Mercury.

Sincerely yours,

H. L. Mencken

. . . . .

September 26, 1930

2006 Garfield Street
Wichita Falls, Texas
My dear Mr. Mencken:

I want to thank you . . . or your staff . . . or whoever it was . . . who sent me the clipping which mentions that last story of mine. I do get provoked, though, sometimes, at these people who make so much of "stark realism". I am not setting out to write stark realism or anything else in particular except what strikes me as a possibly interesting story. Oh well . . . .

May I also congratulate you upon your marriage. I have been married all of thirteen years and still I think highly of my husband although I shall have to confess that children and housekeeping have seriously interfered with what was known in my youth as a career. Not that I think it makes any great difference.

Most cordially yours,

Mrs. Winifred Sanford

. . . . .

September 30, 1930

Dear Mrs. Sanford:

Thanks very much for your pleasant note. Please don't pay any attention to newspaper discussions of your writings. Nine times out of ten they are completely idiotic. I detest all labeling. A good story is a good story. I surely hope that another is on its way. As I wrote you some time ago, Kathleen Norris is a very enthusiastic admirer of your work. It differs enormously, to be sure, from her own, but she is a very intelligent woman and knows a good story when she sees it.

Sincerely yours,

H. L. Mencken

. . . . .

November 18, 1930

2006 Garfield Street
Wichita Falls, Texas

H. L. Mencken
The American Mercury
730 Fifth Avenue
New York City

Dear Mr. Mencken:

You wrote me some time ago that you would like to see another story. Well, here it is,— And as doleful as usual, I am afraid.

Stark realism in the middle west, or the south west, if you prefer, although Texas is as middle as Iowa on the map. There are, I may add, a vast number of Mr. Carmichael's in our part of the country, now that the oil business has blown up.

I am in doubt as to the title. Would plain "Mr. Carmichael" be better?

Most cordially yours,

Winifred Sanford

. . . . .

November 21, [1930]

Dear Mrs. Sanford:—

Thanks very much for "Mr. Carmichael's Room". It is a very good story and I'll be delighted to print it. The title, it seems to me, is all right as it stands. The usual check and proof will reach you in a week.

It is a pleasure, indeed, to see you writing again.

Sincerely yours,

H. L. Mencken

LAGNIAPPE:
TWO
UNPUBLISHED
STORIES BY
WINIFRED
SANFORD

TWO MORE STORIES BY WINIFRED SANFORD
were discovered after the SMU Press edition of *Windfall and Other Stories* was published in 1988. They appear in this appendix by permission of Paul Railsback, Executor of the Winifred M. Sanford Estate, and the Southwestern Writers Collection at Texas State University in San Marcos.

All the ellipses that appear in these stories are present in the original texts, but some spelling and punctuation has been altered for clarity.

"STAR IN THE EAST"

Although Grandmother heard them say, sometimes, that she was very, very old, she had never felt so light and free. She heard them say, too, that she was hardly herself now. She pondered over that when she awoke early in the morning and watched for the first long finger of dawn to touch the ceiling, because she knew it was not true. Not herself? They were wrong. She had nothing now *but* herself, her memories, and her visions.

Grandmother used to look back down the steep road of her life, and it seemed to her now that she understood it for the first time. She realized, for one thing, that the shadows were made by the trees. She had trudged through her time of shadows without knowing that. Now she saw that they were nightmares and nothing more, mere shadows of her blessings.

For instance, Rom. Only vaguely could she recall the Sunday morning when Rom lay so late and so still in his bed, with glazed eyes and hands folded on his chest, not half so clearly as she could remember that first Sunday after their marriage, when she took her proud place in the front pew and looked up into Rom's face as he preached.

She had worn a white muslin, with pink sprigs scattered over it, and a pink sash which tied behind, and a white poke bonnet, with pink roses set demurely under the brim. The black velvet streamers which hung down behind were too worldly, Rom had told her, so she had ripped them off for his sake, reluctantly. Rom had chanted a verse about the beauty of holiness, but she had long suspected, and now she was sure, that the devil within him had loved those black velvet streamers. Rom said it was the devil . . . she used to wonder why her heart leaped up so often in sympathy with that angel fallen from grace.

Lately, though she had not dared tell anybody, Rom had come back to her, usually at twilight, and they had sat together in contentment, reviewing the old years. Yet, strangely, the Rom who came back was not old; he was the Rom she had married at twenty, when his hair was thick and brown. He sat very straight in the chair across from her, with the Scripture on his knees, reading to her as of old, in his sober Scotch voice . . . "Oh give thanks unto the Lord, for He is good; for his mercy endureth forever . . . ."

Amy came too; though they told her that Amy had died long ago, and that this was Amy's daughter, Ruth. But she was a woman grown, and Grandmother knew well enough that Ruth was a tiny thing with curls on her shoulders. She always called her Amy, and Amy would smile and say, "Yes, mother." There was a man, too, who came often, but who didn't belong in her memories. She was always silent with him, wondering how he came there. And Millie, who always wore white, and who came and went without a sound, carrying the tender breast of a chicken or a cup of mutton broth. She couldn't place Millie, either, but she liked to have her near. She felt sometimes that she might have drifted out through the open window into space if Millie hadn't been there to draw the scarf about her shoulders and lead her safely from the bed to the chair.

One winter night, at dusk, when she and Rom were dozing in their chairs, Amy came in. She knelt on the floor by Grandmother's chair and laid her head against Grandmother's thin breast. Even an old, old woman could see the trouble in her face. "My little girl," whispered Grandmother to her baby. "My sweet . . . my darling," as she patted her cheek and her hair.

After a time Amy said, "Tomorrow will be Christmas. Do you know that?"

Grandmother said nothing, but she rocked back and forth just a little bit. She didn't want Amy to know that she had forgotten what Christmas was.

Someone called, "Ruth, where are you?"

"You're not Ruth," said Grandmother, holding her close, "You're Amy." But Amy folded the old hands on the black dress and went away.

"Rom," asked Grandmother, "Can you remember about Christmas?" But Rom had fallen asleep with his steel-rimmed spectacles pushed up on his forehead, as he used to do of an evening. The white stock she had ironed so smoothly was rumpled under his chin. She imagined she could hear him snoring.

"It's time for us to go to bed," she told Millie.

"What!" said Millie, "So early on Christmas Eve?"

Usually Grandmother paid no attention to Millie, but tonight she couldn't help it. Christmas Eve, and she had forgotten! She lay in the dark, trying to get it back. Under the door, she could see a line of light from the hall outside, and sometimes steps passed back and forth, hurriedly. Like another universe, she thought, with its milky way, and its sun and moon and stars. She knew nothing of that universe beyond the door.

Christmas! Well, she had a few memories. Something about a tree, not like the trees that had cast shadows upon the road of her life, but a small fir tree in the sitting room of the old parsonage. There were bright things and little flames on its branches. That must be a dream, thought Grandmother; I know trees don't grow like that. Yet its image persisted and pretty soon she could see little Amy reaching up to it from the floor. Amy's eyes were afire like the tree, and she wore the little dress that Rom's sister had made for her, with tiny strings of coral to hold the puffed sleeves from the bare arms.

Grandmother was almost asleep when she saw another tree, even brighter than the first, and much, much larger. It touched the parsonage ceiling. And here was Amy again, with her hair in long curls, made with loving care over her forefinger, tying a broad and beaming Santa Clause to a high branch. Santa Clause—she could remember that, but there was something else she couldn't yet reach. Santa Clause wasn't Christmas, nor the tree, nor Amy . . .

Every detail of the old sitting room was clear to her sight . . . the red carpet which bulged at the edges between the tacks, the stove, with the fire shining through the little glass windows, the organ, brown with red felt glued behind the openwork carving, the walnut chairs, upholstered in shiny black horsehair, the wreath of wax flowers under glass, the steel engraving, allegorical of the voyage of life, and another showing a maiden clinging to the Rock of Ages . . . a black rock in a bitter sea.

Grandmother fell asleep, not deeply, as she used to, not completely. She slept with one eye open, nowadays, half conscious, simply resting. But when she was awakened, she found it very hard to get back to sleep. Perhaps that was why she got out of bed in the middle of the night, for someone had been talking, more loudly than usual, in the hall. "Is this the Doctor? Well, I think you had better come . . . Ruth's pretty sick . . . and bring the nurse." It was like a foreign language to Grandmother; she didn't even try to translate it. She found a chair by the window, and a quilt which she pulled around her. She lifted the corner of the shade to discover if she had really heard this snow driving against the windo pane. She remembered now that Christmas was cold and white, with sleigh bells. Yes, the fine, white flakes were piling up against the glass.

But . . . Grandmother was startled. She hadn't been out of bed at nights for years. She had forgotten the stars! Surely no star had ever been so bright as this one. It dazzled her, hurt her eyes. "Star in the East," she said, but she couldn't remember what it meant, and that troubled her. Star in the East! She thought of a great gold star, gilt paper on the paste board back, that she had helped Amy make for the Sunday school, long ago . . . but why a star? What did it mean?

She could see the eager faces in that Sunday school room. Very decorous those children were, but their eyes seemed deeper and brighter than the eyes of the children who came afterwards. They didn't run about the room, or laugh, or shout; they sat in rows, with shining faces, watching the great gold star.

She left the shade up when she went back to bed, cold, and so tired that she was asleep again before she had half arranged the blankets.

Now Grandmother always woke in the morning before anyone else. Yet this morning, which was Christmas, there were people passing her door long before daylight. There was talking, gruff at first, worried,—and later there was laughter, low laughter, but happy. Grandmother called Millie, as always when she wanted to get up, but Millie didn't come.

Then she remembered her star in the East; still shining it was, though dimly against the dawn. She did wish she could be sure what it was all about.

It was full daylight, and the star had vanished when Millie brought her the glass of warm milk and the slice of softened toast. "Merry Christmas," Millie sang out, "And let me tell you it *is* a Merry Christmas in this house."

When she had finished her milk and toast, Millie said an astonishing thing: "How would you like to take a little walk around this morning, and see what old Santy has brought?"

It hadn't occurred to Grandmother for a great many years that she could step across the threshold into that other universe. As a matter of fact, she didn't want to go; she was afraid. For a moment she wondered if this could be the call to cross the black river to the City of God . . . but Millie's arm, when she touched it, was firm and warm and living. Millie didn't seem to see her shake her head. Instead she wrapped Grandmother in her best white shawl, and put her strong arm around her waist. "We'll go very slowly," she said, "Just a little bit at a time."

They crossed the hall and stepped into a vast room. It looked to Grandmother like the big church Rom had preached in when they lived in the city. Millie made her sit down in a chair big enough to smother her. There was so much furniture that she was confused. Her own room contained so little, the bed, the dresser, the table, and two chairs. But here were many chairs, eight or ten, shelves full of books, a piano, tall pedestals with tops like umbrellas. A large table, at her elbow, was piled high with strange and lovely things: she put out her trembling hand to caress a translucent blue vase . . . a tiny box of carved ivory, with a hinged cover, a scarf of flam-colored silk. Millie picked up a bottle of pale green liquid, drew out the glass stopper, and held it under Grandmother's nose . . . It reached her like a revelation . . . "They presented unto him gifts," she said, in her Bible voice, "Gold and Frankincense and myrrh . . ." Very faintly she was beginning to remember.

Gifts? Yes, they were a part of Christmas. She thought of the rag doll she had made for Amy—with what sweet labor she had painted the features on the muslin . . . One eye was always a shade higher than the other . . . Amy used to go to sleep with that doll against her cheek. She thought, too, of Amy's first gifts to her—a button bag, of printed red calico.

Suddenly Grandmother pointed at the opposite corner. "That is a Christmas tree," she said, confidently. Not so beautiful as the trees she had thought of in the night, but unmistakably a Christmas tree. Millie exchanged looks of surprise with the mysterious young man who didn't belong. "But I don't see Amy!"

"You will in a minute," the young man told her, stooping down and picking her up in his arms. He carried her a long way, it seemed, into a room whose curtains were drawn, where Amy lay on a broad white bed. Amy's troubles were gone; she was happy now.

"I saw your Christmas tree, Amy," said Grandmother. "But I didn't see you," and she began to remind Amy of those other trees so long ago. Amy smiled and said, "Yes dear, I remember; I'm sure I do."

"I don't know whether Rom remembers or not," Grandmother said. "He was asleep when I asked him. I shall ask him tonight about the star in the East."

Amy patted her hand. "Yes, dear, be sure you ask him."

Suddenly they all looked toward the window, as if listening. Grandmother listened too, and heard voices, very far away, it must be, very sweet:

Hark, the herald angels sing [. . .]

She leaned forward in her chair, and it seemed to her that a great light shone all around. She was beginning to remember something . . . a bed in a stable . . . a manger . . . the kindly cattle looking on . . . the wise men bringing gifts, gold and frankincense and myrrh . . . the voices of the heavenly host . . . she clasped her hands. The young man was saying, "It's the choir from the church . . ." He didn't know . . . In just a minute she would have the whole vision . . . "For unto you is born this day, in the City of David, a Savior, which is Christ the Lord."

She smiled. "Amy," she said, and the tears were on her cheeks, "I have seen the star in the East, I have heard the multitude of the heavenly hosts, I have seen the gifts of the three wise men . . . where is the Christ Child?"

Amy beckoned to the young man, who brought something in a blanket, which he laid on the bed. Amy folded back the blanket, corner by corner, until Grandmother saw the little newborn Christ child lying there, with the light of Heaven on his face. Grandmother got out of her chair to kneel by the bedside. She captured one of the tiny feet in her stiff, twisted fingers, and pressed the sole of it to her lips in adoration. She knew now; she remembered the whole of Christmas.

She began to tell them, still kneeling there, the very words she had heard as a little girl, the very words she had told Amy when Amy was a little girl, and Ruth, perhaps, though she couldn't remember much about Ruth. "And there were, in the same country, shepherds abiding in the field, keeping watch over their flock by night" . . . through to the end. There was no forgetting now. Her voice was clear and sweet and firm.

She could hardly wait for Rom to come at twilight. "Rom," she said, as soon as he had opened the Bible on his knees, "I have seen the little Christ Child . . ."

"Yes," interrupted Millie, going between them to pull down the shade, "I guess you did, all right. I'm going to tie that shade down tonight. It was half way up when I came in this morning, and when it's like that, the street light shines in your eyes."

Grandmother reached out for Millie's hand. "Millie," she said, and her voice was tense with the wonder and the mystery, "Last night, from that window I saw the Star in the East . . . the Star of Bethlehem!"

Millie, who had never done such a thing before, bent over and kissed her cheek.

Hush, Rom was reading: "And it came to pass in those days, that there went forth a decree from Caesar Augusta . . ."

"DEEP C"

It was nobody's fault but Judy's, of course.

Mother had warned her, back in the station at Fort Worth, when Judy was picking out the candy to take with her on the train. "You're sure that's the kind you want, are you?"

"Yes ma'am."

"And you'll remember to suck it? And not bite down on it? You could break a tooth without half trying, you know."

Father had stood up for Judy. "Leave her alone, Grace. She's old enough to look after herself. Why, when I was nine . . ."

"Oh I know, Tom; when you were nine you were practically running the ranch single-handed."

"No use keeping the kid in diapers, is there?"

"Don't be silly, Tom; but when I think of her way out there on that old ranch, with no doctor or anything, it scares me to death."

"Forget it," Father had said. "Forget it."

So they had bought Judy her mints, and put her on the train, and kissed her, and gone, and for the first few minutes, Judy had all she could do to keep the tears back behind her eyes where they belonged. That was when she began on the mints, peeling the wrapper down until the disk on top was exposed, prying it off with her thumbnail, and sucking it against the roof of her mouth.

By the time she had sucked three of them, the train had left the city behind and was in the country, and Judy could begin the game she liked best to play. Of course, it wasn't exactly a game; it was just the way she had of amusing herself when she didn't have anyone to play with. It was a game of imagining. Of telling herself stories.

So now, as the train flashed past the fields, Judy wondered if the ranch was like that—if there was green stuff growing in the rows, if it was cotton, or what. She saw a man working with a hoe in the middle of a field, breaking up the hard red earth, stopping to wipe his face with his sleeve, and she said to herself, "That's Grandfather. He's out hoeing his cotton. He got up early, before the sun was up, and he's been standing there all day, hoeing his cotton . . ."

But no; that was all wrong. Grandfather didn't have that kind of a ranch. He had a cattle ranch. Instead of cotton or whatever it was, there were cows. And cowboys. And jackrabbits. And coyotes. And rattlesnakes . . . .

Judy pried the fourth mint from the roll in her hand and popped it into her mouth. But this time, she wasn't thinking about what she was doing, and she forgot her Mother's warning. Instead, she was remembering last night. They were sitting out in the back yard, at home, after dinner. Father was leaning back in his chair, with his legs crossed, puffing at his pipe; and Mother was slapping at the mosquitoes that kept settling on her face and arms.

"Too bad she's waited so long to go to the ranch," Father had said.

Mother had laughed. "Your Father's a regular country boy, Judy. I don't believe he ever owned a pair of shoes until he went away to school."

"Why what are you talking about! Why I learned to walk in a pair of little cowboy boots Dad had made for me a purpose."

"With high heels, I bet!"

"Well, what of it?"

"Nothing. Only I wish I knew what was so wonderful about that ranch. No running water. No electricity. No neighbors. No nothing. I don't for the life of me understand why your folks want to stay out there with the coyotes and rattlesnakes."

"Because they know when they're well off," Father had said. And then he had waited a long time before he went on. "Yes . . . even with the coyotes and rattlesnakes, they're better off, Grace. In some ways. Coyotes and rattlesnakes spell danger, all right; but danger has its uses, Grace. Danger calls for courage. That's a lesson I had to learn young," he had said. "And it's a lesson a city child doesn't always get."

At that point in her thoughts, Judy came back to the present with a start. Something had happened. She had bitten down on the mint . . . and bitten hard, because she was so busy thinking about Father; and she had done what Mother had told her she should not do: she had broken her tooth.

For a second or two, after she felt it crack, she held perfectly still, hardly daring to breathe. Perhaps if she held still enough, why, it wouldn't be true. Then, very cautiously, she began to explore with her tongue, and oh dear: one whole side of her back tooth was gone, and there was nothing to be felt but sharp splinters that scratched her tongue.

And what was that, now? Judy reached up and took something out of her mouth between her thumb and finger . . . something that wouldn't dissolve, something that wasn't sticky, something very small but hard and sharp . . . .

Well, Mother had warned her. She had told her not to bite down on the candy. And it wouldn't do any good to tell Mother how it had happened because Mother didn't have any patience with Judy's games. She thought it was silly to waste your time imaging things.

Judy leaned forward and dropped the bit of tooth in the bright cuspidor by the seat, hearing the tiny tinkle as it struck the metal. Then she leaned back and shut her eyes and tried to concentrate on what had happened.

Only last week Mother had taken her to the dentist. "Just to make sure she won't have any trouble," Mother had told him. "You know she's going to spend the summer down by the forks of the creek, with Tom's folks, and I don't suppose there's a dentist within a thousand miles."

The dentist had laughed. "They don't need dentists out there, Mrs. Graham," he had said. "When a cowboy gets the boss to jerk his tooth out with a pair of pliers."

At the time, Judy had thought it was funny. She had imagined the big old cowboy with his cheek all swelled up under his cowboy hat. It had seemed funny then. But now that it was Judy's tooth . . . now that she was on her way to the ranch, where there wasn't a dentist within a thousand miles . . . well, it wasn't quite so funny. The tears she had been holding back came crowding up into Judy's eyes. She felt very homesick and very miserable.

To comfort herself, after a while, she sucked another mint. That was a mistake, though: it was so sweet that it made her tooth ache. And when she went down to the end of the car for a drink of ice water, that was even worse. Judy had to grab her jaw with both hands, it hurt so badly, and dance up and down in the aisle.

It was after she was back in her seat again that she had another thought. She didn't have to tell Grandfather she had broken her tooth. She would get off the train at Landers Junction, and when they came to meet her, to drive her out to the ranch, she would be very polite, just as Mother had told her to be, but she wouldn't say one single word about breaking her tooth. All summer, no matter how it hurt, even if it kept her awake all night every night, she wouldn't say one single word . . . .

Judy sat up, after a minute, and looked out of the window again. By now the country had changed. Instead of ploughed fields with rows of cotton, she saw cow country. That was what Father called it when they rode out of Fort Worth, sometimes, in the car. "Now this looks like cow country," he would say, and he would point out the mesquite and the cactus and the Spanish bayonet . . . and the cows. "The prettiest sight in the world to my eyes," he would say. "Is a nice fat Hereford steer."

Judy began her game again. That ranch they were flying past was Grandfather's ranch. The Lazy G. Every morning Grandfather jumped out of bed and climbed up on his horse and thundered down the trail. *Hi-ho, Silver!* If Grandfather rode fast enough he could save the stagecoach from the bandits. But Grandfather didn't know one of the bandits was waiting for him around the bend . . . .

It was fun to make up stories like that, even if there wasn't a stagecoach, really, or any bandits. Anyway, there would be a horse for Judy. Father had promised her that. His name would be . . . well, not Flicks . . . not Lassie . . . not Black Beauty or Beautiful Joe . . . Prairie Flower, that would be it! Prairie Flower would be waiting for Judy at Landers Junction with his saddle on . . . pawing the ground and snorting and shaking his mane and his tail. Oh, it would be wonderful! Judy would leap into the saddle, and they would dash away across the plains until they came at last to the Lazy G.

Of course, though, as it really turned out, it wasn't quite like that. For one thing, they didn't come to Landers Junction until very late at night, when Judy was too tired to want to ride Prairie Flower, even. As a matter of fact, she didn't know where she was when the porter shook her.

"Here's where you get out, Miss . . . You'll have to hurry, Miss; we don't stop but a minute . . . ."

It was a very short minute, too. Judy had just barely time enough to jump to the platform when she heard the train shudder and snort and clang its bell and begin to roll down the track. All Judy could think of to do was to run after it. "Wait for me! Wait for me!" Surely it didn't mean to go off and leave her on the station platform all alone . . . .

Then someone whistled. Someone called, "That you, Judy?" And it was Grandfather. Judy knew it was Grandfather as soon as she had swung around. He came out of the dark into the bright circle of light from the station lantern. She could see him plainly now . . . his cowboy hat . . . his eyes, with the wrinkles around them, his big old nose, his droopy whiskers that scratched her face and smelled of tobacco . . . his khaki clothes . . . his high heeled cowboy boots . . . .

And behind him, limping a little as if it hurt her to walk, came Grandmother. Grandmother wasn't so tall as Grandfather, but she was taller than Mother and stooped over more. She had gray hair, parted in the middle and drawn straight back to a knot at her neck.

"So it's Tom's baby!" Her dress had a nice clean starchy smell, as she held Judy against it.

"Grandmother?" Judy couldn't wait to ask about the limp. She simply couldn't wait. "Did you hurt your foot, Grandmother?"

"No, hon; that's just a limp I have, from an old hurt, a long time ago."

"But how did you hurt it? Did you fall down and break it?"

"Mercy, no."

"Well how *did* you hurt it then?"

"Well, hon, if you must know,—a snake bit me. Thirty year and more ago, it was . . . ."

Judy took Grandmother's hand in hers and held it very tightly as they walked to the car. "Listen, Grandmother," she said, forgetting all about the promise she had made to herself on the train. "I hurt myself, too. I bit down on a piece of candy, Grandmother, and I broke my tooth off." It was the tooth that woke Judy that first morning on the ranch. She didn't know how it happened, exactly. Maybe she rolled over on that side of her face. Anyway, the first thing she knew, the sharp corner of her broken tooth was digging into her cheek.

She lay there for a time, remembering. "They don't need dentists out there, Mrs. Graham. When a cowboy gets a toothache, he don't waste his money on dentists; he gets the boss to jerk his tooth out with a pair of pliers."

If only she hadn't gone and told them!

Oh well, she thought, after a minute, Maybe, if she didn't mention it again, they would forget it. Or maybe she could pretend she had only been fooling.

Yes but suppose they looked in her mouth!

"I won't let him, that's all," Judy told herself miserably. And she remembered how she used to knock Mother's hand away when it came toward her with the nose drops . . . .

The tooth stopped hurting, and Judy dozed off for a while, until she heard a horse whinny, not very far away. She sat straight up in her bed. Maybe that was Prairie Flower! She jumped onto the floor, ran across to the screen door that opened onto the long gallery, and saw him standing there . . . a big gray horse, guzzling water out of a trough under the windmill. For just a second she thought it was Prairie Flower speaking to her; then she saw Grandfather, cowboy hat and boots and all just like the night before.

"Top of the morning!" she answered.

"How's that broken tooth, this morning?"

Judy drew back. "It isn't really broken, Grandfather; it just felt like it was. And it doesn't hurt a bit."

Grandfather stared at Judy until she dropped her eyes. "Of course now," he said, "if it's really broken, it'll have to be taken care of; you understand that."

"Yes sir."

"I'll take a look at it after breakfast," he said. "And then I'll give you a ride on Old Gray here. How would you like that?"

Judy dressed quickly in a white shirt and the blue jeans Father had bought for her in the boys department at the Fair. "It's important to look right on a ranch," he had told her. "You can't ride 'round a ranch in frills and furbelows. You'd frighten the living daylights out of the cows."

In the kitchen, after breakfast, Grandfather tipped her head back and looked at her tooth.

"Hmm!" he grunted.

"It doesn't hurt, though. It doesn't hurt at all."

"It's playing the devil with your cheek, child. No . . . No, there isn't but one cure for a tooth like that."

"Please, Grandfather, please don't pull it."

She thought for one bad minute that he was going to take out his pliers and pull it then and there, but Grandmother kept him from it. "I don't know as I'd hurry her, John," said Grandmother. "Let her think about it a bit. She knows she has it to do. You've told her that; now give her time to make up her mind to it. She'll tell you when she's ready, John. She'll tell you yourself, or I miss my guess . . . ."

GRANDFATHER HELPED JUDY mount her horse. "Foot in the stirrup, now . . . other one over . . . that's the girl!"

"Will he run away?"

"No, he couldn't run if he wanted to. He's much too old and lazy. No, you'll have to kick him to keep him going, Judy . . . that's the way . . . ."

Judy felt very high, up on Prairie Flower. She clucked at him and flapped the reins, and kicked him with her heels every time he stopped. "Get up!" she would say. "Get up!"

Grandfather, on his horse, would ride on ahead, and then he would turn and wait for Judy to catch up with him.

"All right, Judy?"

"Yes sir."

The jolting made her tooth hurt again, but Judy didn't tell him that. She just bit her lip and kept still.

They were riding through cow country such as Judy had seen on the train . . . grass and mesquite and cactus and now and then a clump of Spanish bayonet, with raveling's hanging to the leaves.

"You'll see a jackrabbit, likely, if you watch," said Grandfather. And sure enough, after a while, Grandfather pointed, and Judy caught a glimpse of a gray thing with long ears, hopping in the grass.

"Will we see a coyote, too?"

"It isn't likely. Though you can hear them at night, sometimes, if you listen."

Presently a very strange thing happened. They had been riding along in perfectly level country. No hills and no valleys. Nothing but level grass and clump after clump of mesquite as far as they could see. And then suddenly, the ground fell away in front of them, and they were standing on the very edge of a great deep gully . . . all red earth and rock . . . with a tiny little stream twinkling down at the bottom, no bigger than a thread.

"That's what I brought you to see," said Grandfather. "That's my canyon. Where we're standing today is where I stood when I first happened on it, forty years ago. I didn't know it was here anymore than you did just now. I was just jogging along, hunting a bunch of cows that belonged to the outfit I was with, and I stumbled on my canyon. I told myself then I was going to have it, someday, for my own. And when I got it, I married your Grandmother and brought her here to see it, like I brought you just now."

"Grandfather?"

"Well?"

"Can I get down off my horse?"

Grandfather thought before he answered. "Don't think I would," he said. "There's too many rattlers in these rocks."

"Grandfather?"

"Well?"

"Was it a rattle that bit Grandmother?"

"She tell you about that, did she?"

"Yes sir. Was it a rattler?"

"Yes, it was a rattler. Funny she told you, though. She's hardly spoken of it from that day to this."

"Why didn't you get the hoe out and kill it?"

Grandfather took his hat off and wiped his face with a big red and yellow handkerchief. "I wasn't there, Judy; that's why. I'd done a mighty foolish thing,—a mighty foolish thing. I don't know now how I came to do it . . . leaving her alone on the place, her and Tom. I never thought too much about it, as a matter of fact. Somebody had to go to the Junction for supplies, was the way I figured it; and somebody had to stay to look after things at the ranch. 'You won't be afraid now?' I asked her. 'I'll be gone a week, likely,' I told her, 'Unless when I get to the river crossing, the water's up and I have to come back . . . .'"

"How old was Father?" asked Judy.

"Tom? He was two ... two and a half, I forget."

"Grandfather?"

"Well?"

"Can you die if a rattler bites you?"

"Yes, you can die ...."

Suddenly, Grandfather wheeled his horse around and started back, trotting briskly between the clumps of mesquite.

"Wait for me!" cried Judy. But Prairie Flower wouldn't trot. He would only plunk slowly along, stopping every few feet to taste the grass or the soft green leaves on the mesquite. Judy kicked and kicked and hit him with the ends of the reins, but still he wouldn't hurry.

He brought her home, though, as Grandfather had known, of course, that he would. He brought her home, and Grandfather was standing there by the windmill to lift her down.

"Did you like the canyon, Judy?"

"Yes sir."

"I thought you would," said Grandfather.

ALL THE REST OF THE DAY, when she wasn't thinking about her broken tooth, Judy was thinking about the rattlesnake. She made up a story around him. Maybe he came gliding across the floor of the ranch house, and shook his rattle as he came ....

"Grandmother?" Grandmother was in the kitchen, and Judy was on the gallery, playing hopscotch on a board she had made with chalk.

"What is it, hon?"

"Were you in the house when the rattler bit you?"

"No, hon, I was outside. I'd come out with the dish water, to empty it, and he was coiled up by the step ..."

"He rattled, though, didn't he?"

"Yes, hon, he rattled. I heard him rattle, but I'd started to set my foot down and it was too late to stop."

"Did he stick out his tongue?"

"Hon, I don't know. I couldn't see his tongue. You go on and play your game, now, and you forget about that old rattler."

Judy went on with her hopscotch, throwing the little piece of rock into the squares, and hopping on one foot to pick it up.

"Grandmother?"

"Well?"

"Do coyotes and rattlers spell danger?"

"Do they spell danger?" Yes, hon, I reckon they do. And she told Judy about the little baby coyote Grandfather had found, once, on the ranch, and had brought home to raise. He looked just like a police pup, she said. He was smart and cute, and they kept him tied to a stake by the kitchen door. He was like a pet dog, Grandmother said, and she was fond of him until one day he turned on Tom and bit his finger nearly off ....

"What did you do then, Grandmother?"

"Oh, we shot him, hon; we had to. It hurt me might bad ... him jumping up on me and licking my hand and all, but we had it to do."

"Which is worse, Grandmother, a coyote or a rattler?"

Grandmother thought for a minute. "They're both bad," she said. "There's nothing good about either one, but when it comes to which is worse,—well, I'd say the rattler, hon. I never was fond of a rattler."

And so it went, all day long. Whenever she wasn't busy, helping Grandmother with the work . . . feeding the chickens, carrying in the wood, stirring the beans . . . she was thinking about the old rattler, coiled by the steps, waiting for Grandmother to come out with the dishwater.

"Grandmother?" It was late in the afternoon, now, nearly suppertime, and Grandmother was putting the buttermilk on the table. "Grandmother, can I see your ankle? The one the snake bit? Can I, Grandmother?"

"Judy," said Grandmother after a minute. "I'll make a bargain with you. After supper, after the dishes are dried and put away, if you will promise me not to talk about my ankle, or the rattler, either one, as long as you're here, why, I'll let you look at it."

"I promise," cried Judy. "I promise."

THE LAST DISH WAS DRIED and put away in the cupboard,—the dishpan emptied in the yard, the dishcloth stretched across it to dry.

"Can I see it now?"

"Yes." Grandmother limped out to the gallery and sat down in the rocking chair. She leaned over and rolled down her stocking.

"It's not a pretty sight," she said, a second time.

Grandmother was right. It was a dreadful sight. It was enough to make a person sick. Judy bent down to look at it, and then she drew back. She couldn't help it. Why, Grandmother's ankle looked as if someone had chopped at it with an ax. It was all out of shape, somehow, and covered all over with ridges and scars.

"How could the snake do that!"

Grandmother stretched out her foot, so that she could see it herself. Then, very carefully, as if it still hurt her after thirty years, she drew up her stocking and rolled it over her garter at the top. "Most of that I did myself, hon," she said. "Trying to get rid of the poison, like I'd been told. That's what you have to do if the snake bites you, Judy: you have to tie something, as quick as you can, above the wound, and then you have to slash all around it with a knife."

"I couldn't ever do that!" cried Judy.

"Oh yes you could child. You'd do it, because you'd know you had it to do. You'd know there wasn't any other way."

Very slowly, she began to rock back and forth, looking way off into the distance somewhere, as if she had forgotten all about Judy. "It all comes back to me," said Grandmother, softly. "The feel of the creature under my foot, and the sound of its rattle, and before I had time to think what it was, even, the burning and the pain . . . ."

"Did you cry, Grandmother?"

"I cried for my Mother, like I was a child again, and in trouble . . . I remember I took my ankle in both my hands and rocked back and forth with the pain and cried for my Mother."

Grandmother went on with the story. Her ankle began to swell, she said, and that brought her back to her senses, and she began to hunt around her for something to tie above the wound,—a piece of rope or something. And then on the barbed wire fence that ran along not far from the house . . . where she could reach it if she dragged herself a little way along the ground, she could see an old rag, fluttering in the wind. She had left it there when she took her washing down the night before. "And there it hung, ready to my hand, Judy, like it had been put there a purpose."

Grandmother tied the rag around her leg, she said, and then she remembered that she must slash it with a knife. But there wasn't any knife out there by the fence. There wasn't any knife nearer than the house, and the house seemed a thousand miles away, she said, and Grandmother herself no bigger than an ant, crawling toward it.

And then she looked down, and lying in the grass, almost under her hand, was what she needed. Not a knife, no, but a loose strand of the wire, with the barb twisted in it.

"Didn't it hurt, Grandmother?"

Grandmother looked at Judy as if she had forgotten all about her. "Well now," she said, "I suppose it hurt, but I don't know as I cared much, or noticed. I was too scared and too sick to pay it any heed. I just remember I shut my eyes so I wouldn't have to watch, and I tore the flesh with the barb. And then, in the middle of it, I thought of Tom. It's a strange thing, Judy, but as crazy as I was about Tom, and all, I never once thought of him 'til that minute when I was sawing on my ankle with that barb. I hadn't even wondered where he was or what he was up to. All that time, Judy, I'd been thinking of myself. I'm ashamed to say it, but it's the truth. And then it came to me all at once that it was worse for Tom than it was for me, because when I was dead, there wouldn't be one living soul to care for him . . . ."

"Why couldn't he take care of himself, Grandmother?"

"Why hon, he was too little. And there was the fire burning in the stove, and the rattler, and the water in the trough . . . seemed like all at once I thought of every way a child could hurt himself. And there wouldn't be anyone to wash him or feed him, or put him to bed. Oh, many's the night since then I've dreamed it over. Many's the night I've waked in a cold sweat, thinking he was there in the dark, alone, crying for me . . . .

"It was mighty hard to think what to do," said Grandmother. "Even when you're well and strong, you don't always know what's best to do, and when you're as near dead as I was,— when you can't hardly get your breath, when your whole side is swelling and burning and the pains start in your stomach, why it's harder to think than it is to bear the suffering. I'd try to remember if there was water for him to drink, and if I'd left the cornbread where he could get it. And then the time came when I couldn't think at all. I didn't know if Tom was with me or if he wasn't. And a saying I knew when I was a child came back to me. 'Deep C ain't but a few notes down.' The negroes said it on the plantation where I was raised. 'Deep C ain't but a few notes down.'"

"Grandmother!"

It took Grandmother a long time to remember where she was. "Queer how it all comes back to me!" she said.

"Let me tell the rest, Grandmother," cried Judy, beating her hands together. "I know what happened. He told me this morning when he was showing me the canyon. Let me tell the rest . . . ."

"Well . . . ."

"Grandfather came back, didn't he? He got to the river and the water was high and he couldn't get across and he came home . . . ."

Grandmother took Judy by the shoulders and looked into her eyes. "Things are mighty dark, sometimes, Judy. They have been for me, and they will be for you. They were so dark for me that day that I was praying for the waters to close over my head, Judy; I was ready to give up fighting it off. But, Judy . . . listen to me, because this is what I want you to remember: All the time I was lying there on the ground, crazy with pain and the fever, help was coming up the trail! Help for me and help for Tom. I couldn't believe it at first, Judy, when I heard the wagon come in the yard. I couldn't believe it was true. I thought it was the fever in my head. And then he came to me, Judy, and found me, and picked me up in his arms and carried me to my bed. I'll never forget the wonder of it, Judy . . . ."

JUDY WAS CRYING WHEN Grandmother limped in to kiss her goodnight. "I should have known better, hon," said Grandmother. "I shouldn't ever have told you. I don't know but Tom was right never to speak of it . . . never to want me to speak of it, either . . . ."

Judy put her arms around Grandmother's neck and pulled her down against her cheek where the tooth was throbbing. "I love you," she sobbed. "I love you!"

"Then you remember what I've been telling you, Judy. Forget the bad part, and remember the good part . . . ."

"Yes ma'am."

But it was a hard promise to keep. For a long time after Grandmother was gone, Judy lay quietly, trying not to think. The story began to act itself out again in her mind. She could see Grandmother come through the doorway with the dishpan in her hand; she could see the snake coiled by the step, and Grandmother's foot . . . Judy sat up in bed and clutched her ankle and rocked back and forth . . . .

"I had it to do, Judy; I had it to do!"

It was her tooth, of course. Judy's tongue slid around to the broken tooth and passed, cautiously, over the jagged splinters and the roughened lining of her cheek. She felt very small. The night was big and dark, and the strong, sweet smell of the plains blew in through the open door to the gallery. Away in the distance, a dog barked, or maybe it was a coyote. Judy didn't know.

"Coyotes and rattlers spell danger, all right; but danger has its uses, Grace."

"Danger calls for courage." That was what Father meant. That was what he wanted her to learn on the ranch.

"She knows she has it to do."

Oddly, Judy began to grow. She stood up on the floor and stretched to her full height. Without stopping for her robe or her slippers, without lighting the lamp, she felt her way across the room to the door and across the gallery to the other bedroom.

"Grandfather!" she called. She had meant to whisper, but her voice sounded like thunder in her ears.

"What's that?"

"It's me . . . Judy." She felt as tall as the room, now.

"What is it, Judy? What do you want?"

"I want you to pull my tooth," said Judy, firmly. "Will you, Grandfather? Will you, please?"

APPENDIX C

TWO
NONFICTION
ARTICLES
FOR
WRITERS

IN ADDITION TO SHORT STORIES AND NOV-
els, Winifred Sanford wrote two articles about the craft of writing that illuminate her own writing process. These articles appear below by permission of Paul Railsback, Executor of the Winifred M. Sanford Estate. The first, "Method of Irony," appeared in the March 6, 1926, issue of *The Editor*.

"THE METHOD OF IRONY"

Unfortunately, I remember very little about the writing of "The Monument," which was published in *The Woman's Home Companion* for January. I wrote it two years and a half ago, and it had been buried in the files of the *Companion* for two years before they published it. I do remember, however, that it began as must be obvious, with my own observation of the differences in people's acceptance of bereavement. Naturally, I wanted a contrast and created two women, one on either side of the fence. But the actual writing of the story, as I remember it, was extremely simple. I scarcely revised it at all. I know I was tempted at one time to convert Julia at the end, or at least to bring her to see Margaret's point of view, but I wisely forbore.

Although "The Monument" was the first story I ever sold, the first to be published was "Wreck" which came out in *The American Mercury* for January 1925. It was written long after the other, and I remember every step of its development because it marked for me a new point of view and a new style—the ironic. In everything I had written up to that time the story was told sympathetically: I was so to speak, press agent from my hero. Since then I have either kept out of the picture altogether, or I have purposely taken the unsympathetic side, hoping that the wise will read between the lines. Thus in "Wreck," which is the story of a ship foundering at a harbor entrance, and of men freezing to death on her deck, I started out to overwhelm the reader with the tragedy of it by direct methods, tragic detail on tragic detail. I made two separate attempts to do it before I had another idea: to tell it indirectly through two good for nothing characters who were almost entirely insensible of the tragedy they were witnessing. Whether I improved it or not I don't know, but it is much more fun to write that way.

You may be interested to know that *The American Mercury* has published three other stories of mine, "Allie" in July, 1925; "The Forest Fire" in September, 1925; and "Saved" in January, 1926. Both the *Mercury* and *Woman's Home Companion* have others waiting for publication. For the last year, also, I have been working on a novel.

THE SECOND ARTICLE, "Writing the Short Story," appeared in the October 1935 issue of a magazine for and about regional writers of the Southwest entitled *Southwester*. This article is reproduced here with the permission of the Sanford family.

"WRITING THE SHORT STORY"

First capture your idea. Perhaps you will find it lurking in a newspaper item. Perhaps it will be suggested by a scrap of conversation overheard on a bus, or by an experience of your own or of somebody you know. Perhaps it will spring from the most unexpected sources . . . a telephone directory . . . an item in Popular Mechanics . . . an old man asking for work. The important thing is to be ready and on the lookout.

It is best, however, not to force these ideas. Don't, for mercy's sake, sit down at a typewriter and determine to invent a plot by sheer mental effort, unless you want an artificial-sounding tale as a result. Be patient and wait until it comes of itself.

Your idea, when you find it, may be a clear-cut plot or it may be something vaguer and more difficult and more intriguing. It may be a new angle from which you suddenly perceive the meaning in a situation as old as the hills. It may be a frame by means of which you isolate a part of life for purposes of your own. You may, for instance, make a story out of a day in the hospital or a hotel. It may be of the nature of a *tour de force*, it may be the working out of some technical problem . . . a story, for example, in which emotion is to supplant action . . . or a story with only one character or a story entirely in dialogue. But be sure to take an idea which appeals to you personally and which you are fitted to handle.

You will not be in too much of a hurry to begin your writing, if you want a good story. You will hold your idea in the back of your mind while you do other things, and let it sprout. Surprisingly it will take shape of itself, and at the most unexpected times you will suddenly become aware of a leaf budding here and a stem growing taller until at last the thing is ready to bloom.

Somewhere in this growing process, you will know how you want to present your tale. Perhaps you will know of two or three possible presentations and you will have to decide by the method of trial and error. You may prefer straightforward, chronological narration; you may want to tell your story in retrospect; you may want to jump around; you may want to use the diary form or the letter form or some other form.

You will also have to decide on your characters and your point of departure and your climax and, most important of all, your point of view. Shall the story be told in the first person or the third? Shall it be told by the principal character or by a secondary character, or by you as the author, or by some imaginary, omniscient being you assume for the purpose? Or do you prefer to shift from character to character, presenting each in turn? Your taste and your instinct must tell you which of these can best turn the trick. Some stories are more effective told one way and some are more effective told another way. But having selected your point of view, hold to it through thick and thin and avoid that all-too-common mistake of changing it suddenly for your own convenience, thus breaking into the reader's sense of illusion.

Now you are ready for your attack, and an attack it is in a double sense, for not only do you have to execute the complicated maneuvers of getting the story underway, but you must also take into consideration your reader and his psychology and manage everything so that his interest will be caught and held from the first sentence on.

Almost all writers find the introduction the hardest part of a story to get down on paper. Almost simultaneously you must identify . . . and characterize . . . the people of your story, give the time and the setting, and set the tone . . . whether tragic or comic or ironic or what. More often than not, you start a bit of action while you are doing this; and as if this juggling of half a dozen balls were not enough, you must be a showman, catching the eye of the audience with a laugh, or a wink or a little footwork so that your labors will appear easy and natural and pleasing. Every writer learns these little tricks of the trade . . . the vivid word . . . the appeal to color and sight and sound, the snapshot . . . the use of dialogue, the rhetorical question, the startling or unexpected remark. Such devices are not peculiar to the introduction: they are of value throughout the story; but they are doubly important at the beginning, where you must work fast and where you never for an instant dare lose the reader's eye.

Once you are under way, the story generally writes itself. How much dialogue you use . . . how much explanation . . . how much description . . . you must decide for yourself, remembering always that the average reader is partial to dialogue and detests the other two, unless they are sprinkled through the action so that he doesn't recognize them. He will forgive a great deal, however, if the tone is sustained so that he is never in doubt as to what sort of story he is reading; if the point of view is adhered to so that he loses himself in the characters; if the suspense is skillfully managed . . . if it mounts, that is, by progressive steps toward the grand climax without which no story is a success. This climax need not be of plot; it may quite as well be a climax of emotion; but since the mind by its very nature tends to lose interest as time goes on . . . since the period of attention is generally shorter than the story . . . there must be, for psychological reasons, a mounting of interest and a climax of some sort to compensate.

And, of course, the story must eventually end. Sometimes, as in a short short story, your climax and conclusion are one and the same; more often you add a denouement of some sort to tone down the abruptness of the climax, to unite any tangled threads which may remain, and, often, to polish off your point. And happy indeed is the writer when he adds the word *Finis* to a bit of wisdom or nonsense he has succeeded in capturing from the puzzle of life, and perpetuating, for his own satisfaction if for no one else's, in the form of a story.

*The ellipses in this article appeared in the original.

INTRODUCTION

1. See Don B. Graham, Second Reader's Report for *Windfall and Other Stories*, March 31, 1987, and William T. Pilkington, First Reader's Report for *Windfall and Other Stories*, n.d. Both Graham and Pilkington compare Sanford's short stories favorably to Porter's short stories. See also Don B. Graham, "The Short Story in Texas," *South by Southwest: 24 Stories from Modern Texas*, xiv. In the introduction to this collection, Graham makes an even stronger statement when he says that Winifred Sanford and Katherine Anne Porter were the only Texas writers who were writing first-rate short stories in the 1920s.

2. James Ward Lee, *Adventures with a Texas Humanist*, 3–32. In a chapter entitled "The Age of Dobie," Lee comments about J. Frank Dobie's dominant role in Texas letters between 1920 and 1960. On page twenty, Lee refers to Texas writing in the "age of Dobie" as being written in an "un-ironic mode."

3. Sylvia Ann Grider and Lou Halsell Rodenberger, *Let's Hear It: Stories by Texas Women Writers*, 138.

4. Ibid., 4–5.

5. Sara Ragland Jackson, *Texas Woman of Letters: Karle Wilson Baker*, 76.

6. Katherine Anne Porter, interview with Barbara Thompson Davis, *The Paris Review* (1963).

7. For more information about Mencken's relationship with Angoff, see Carl Bode, *Mencken*, 234–240. On 237, Bode tells that, from time to time, in conversations with his brother August Mencken, H. L. Mencken said that he suspected Angoff was composing a book about him that would be "derogatory in the extreme."

CHAPTER ONE

1. Arthur W. Baum, "The Cities of America: Duluth," *Saturday Evening Post*, April 16, 1949. Details about Duluth, Minnesota, in the early decades of the twentieth century were taken from this article.

2. Hilton Greer, "Prose Writers of Texas: xxxx Winifred Sanford Distinguished Realist," *The Dallas Journal*, July 8, 1936. In an interview, Sanford told Greer that she had attended a Sinclair Lewis reading in Duluth with her high school classmate and (future) popular novelist Marguerite Banning, née Culkin. While Banning mentions her lifelong friendship with Lewis in several interviews, there is no evidence that Sanford and Lewis ever became close friends. However, it is possible that they had some contact during the years that Winifred lived in New York City and worked at the New York Public Library.

3. Susan E. Meyer, *America's Great Illustrators*, 217.

4. Much of the information that appears in this chapter was supplied by Winifred Sanford's daughters, Emerett Sanford Miles, Helen J. Sanford, and Mary Sanford Gordon, in personal interviews. Helen J. Sanford also shared privately held papers and documents, including Max A. Pulford's letter to Wayland Hall Sanford. This letter also appears in Emerett Sanford Miles's foreword in both the privately published edition and the smu Press edition of *Windfall and Other Stories*.

5. *Duluth Central High School Yearbook*, 1907, 30.

6. Ibid., 42.

7. Winifred Sanford, "Fannie Baker," *Windfall and Other Stories*, Sanford family edition, 122–128.

8. Winifred Sanford, "A Victorian Grandmother," *Windfall and Other Stories*, smu Press, 165–172. Quote appears on 166.

9. Winifred Mahon, "Memories." This unpublished manuscript, along with other documents originally made available exclusively to me, now reside with Winifred's papers in the Southwestern Writers Collection at Texas State University in San Marcos.

10. Ibid. The Pulford couple mentioned in this manuscript may have been the parents of Max A. Pulford, the youth that Wayland later challenged to a duel for fourteen-year-old Winifred's affections.

11. "H. S. Mahon is Called," *Duluth Herald*, June 29, 1908. See also "Henry S. Mahon Dies Suddenly: Well Known Attorney Is Victim of Heart Trouble—Funeral Tomorrow," *Duluth News Tribune*, June, 20, 1908.

12. Winifred Sanford, "A Victorian Grandmother," *Windfall and Other Stories*, smu Press, 171. Winifred uses words to describe her grandmother Sarah Mahon that are almost identical to words that her daughter Mary Sanford Gordon used to describe Winifred.

13. On her 1911–1913 enrollment cards at the University of Michigan, Winifred listed her address as 4 Cutting Apartments. On a form entitled "University of Michigan Class Record," which she filled out on May 19, 1938, she named the following relatives who also attended the University of Michigan: uncles W. L. Mahon (1882) and Ross L. Mahon (?); cousins Ross Mahon (1911), John M. Stanley (1913), W. L. Mahon (1913), Sarah Stanley Tranty (1915); and sister, Helen Mahon Toulme (1914).

14. *Michiganensian Nineteen Thirteen*. Pictures of Winifred when she was a college student appear on 71, 299, and 337.

15. Information about Winifred's teaching career was provided by her daughters in personal interviews.

CHAPTER TWO

1. Emerett Sanford Miles, Foreword, *Windfall and Other Stories*, Sanford family edition, vii–xi.

2. For information about the Bronx neighborhood during the period that Winifred lived there, see Lloyd Ultan and Gary Hermalyn, "Introduction," *The Bronx in the Innocent Years 1890–1925*, xi–xxvii. See also Lloyd Ultan and Barbara Unger, *Bronx Accent: A Literary and Pictorial History of the Borough*, 46–77.

3. Ibid.

4. Ibid.

5. Wayland Hall Sanford, *Letters of Wayland Hall Sanford*. This privately printed collection was compiled and edited by Helen J. Sanford in 1999. Wayland's first letter to Winifred is dated October 15, 1916, but evidence within the letter indicates that this was not the first time the couple had communicated. See 37–38, 52–53, 65. Unfortunately, Winifred's side of this correspondence has been lost.

6. Ibid., 38–40, 51–53, 61–62.

7. Ibid., 38–39, 51–53.

8. Ibid., 51–53, 61–63.

9. Ibid., 52.

10. Ibid., 40.

11. Ibid., 53.

12. Ibid., 54–61.

13. Ibid., 62.

14. Ibid., 54–61.

15. Ibid., 65. Wayland's comment clearly indicates that his communication with Winifred was not limited to an exchange of letters. Perhaps they spent time together when they returned to Duluth for holidays, or perhaps Wayland visited Winifred in New York when law school was not in session.

16. Ibid., 63–65.

17. Ibid., 92. In a letter dated July, 3, 1917, Wayland indicated that Winifred's mother was no longer in the city. On July 4, 1917, he asked if Mrs. Mahon was going to go to Michigan or to Duluth and mentioned that Winifred now had a roommate whose name was Dorothy (102–104).

18. Ibid., 71.

19. Ibid., 75–76.

20. Ibid., 93.

21. Ibid., 96.

22. Ibid., 96–99. Quote appears on 98.

23. Ibid., 98.

24. Ibid., 97.

25. Ibid., 105–106. In this letter to his mother, Wayland indicated that only once did he consider asking someone other than Winifred to marry him, and that was when Winifred was romantically involved with a man named Russell McLean.

26. Ibid., 100–105. Quote appears on 103.

27. Ibid., 116–118. Quote appears on 118.

28. Ibid., 119–120.

29. Ibid., 121–124.

30. Ibid., 130–131.

31. Ibid., 132–133.

32. Ibid., 135–138.

33. Ibid., 140–143.

34. Ibid., 143–144. See also littlechurch.org

35. Ibid., 143–144. Quote appears on 143.

36. Ibid., 145–183. Information was compiled from letters that Wayland wrote to Winifred between September 17, 1917, and March 19, 1918.

37. Ibid., 185–194. Information was taken from letters that Wayland wrote to Winifred between July 17, 1918, and August 21, 1918.

38. Ibid., 200–201.

39. Ibid., 200–202.

40. Ibid., 203–206.

41. Ibid., 207.

42. Winifred Sanford, "The Forest Fire," *Windfall and Other Stories*, SMU Press, 17.

43. Ibid., 15.

44. Ibid., 18.

45. Ibid., 23.

46. Ibid., 24.

47. Wayland Hall Sanford, *Letters of Wayland Hall Sanford*, 211–213.

48. Proof that Paget placed "Two Junes" with *Household Magazine* appears in David Lloyd, letter to Winifred Sanford, August 12, 1931.

49. "Two Junes," *Household Magazine*, November 1931, 4–5.

CHAPTER THREE

1. Wayland Hall Sanford, *Letters of Wayland Hall Sanford*, 214.

2. Ibid., 215.

3. Ibid., 216–217.

4. Ibid., 218–220. Quote appears on 220.

5. Winifred Sanford, letter to Mrs. M. L. Toulme, February 1, 1920.

6. Daniel Yergan, *The Prize: The Epic Quest for Oil, Money, and Power*, 167–172. See also Walter Rundell Jr., *Early Texas Oil: A Photographic History 1836–1936*, 94–96. Other details about the city of Wichita Falls during the time of the Burkburnett oil boom were supplied by Mrs. Margaret Dvorken in a personal interview, Wichita Falls, February 16, 1991.

7. Wayland Hall Sanford, *Letters of Wayland Hall Sanford*, 224. See also Winifred Sanford, letter to Mrs. M. L. Toulme, March 31, 1925.

8. Wayland Hall Sanford, *Letters of Wayland Hall Sanford*, 225–226.

9. Ibid., 226–227.

10. Ibid., 227–228.

11. Ibid., 228–230.

12. Ibid., 230–231.

13. Ibid., 231–232.

14. Ibid., 232–233. When Winifred submitted "Wreck" to *The American Mercury* in 1924, she gave her return address as 1301 Filmore Street, the probable location of the house mentioned in Wayland's letter. When she submitted "Windfall" to the *Mercury* in May 1928, she was living at 2006 Garfield Street.

15. Ibid., 234–235.

16. Winifred Sanford, "The Blue Spruce," *Windfall and Other Stories*, SMU Press, 68–69.

17. Ibid., 69.

18. Ibid., 71.

19. Ibid., 73.

20. Ibid., 74.

CHAPTER FOUR

1. Information about Wayland and Winifred's move from Duluth to Wichita Falls came from personal interviews with the Sanford daughters.

2. Winifred Sanford and Clyde Jackson, "Derrick Jargon," *Southwest Review*, April 1934, 335–345.

3. Many of the details about Wichita Falls during the oil boom of the 1920s came from a personal interview with West Texas resident and former Manuscript Club member Margaret Dvorken. See also Walter Rundell Jr., *Early Texas Oil: A Photographic History*, 94–110, and Daniel Yergan, *The Prize: The Epic Quest for Oil, Money, and Power*, 167–173.

4. Winifred Sanford, letter to Mrs. M. L. Toulme, March 31, 1925.

5. Information about Wayland Sanford's law practice was compiled from listings in the Wichita Falls telephone directories between 1920 and 1929 and from interviews with the Sanford daughters.

6. Manuscript Club Proves Methods by Successes," *Wichita Falls Daily Times*, n.d. Many details about the Manuscript Club came from this undated newspaper clipping located in a scrapbook belonging to former Manuscript Club member Peggy Schachter. See also John A. Buehrens, "The Service in Memory of Winifred Sanford: March 16, 1890 to March 24, 1983." At Winifred's funeral service, Buehrens told that Winifred helped to organize the Manuscript Club.

7. Ibid.

8. In personal interviews, the Sanford daughters told that their mother held a cynical attitude toward organized religion. However, her poem "Invocation," featured in the first issue of a club publication entitled *The Manuscript: Published By and For the Wichita Falls Penwomen's Club* (January 22, 1925), leaves little doubt about Winifred's belief in a supreme creator.

9. Louise Hindman, personal interview, Wichita Falls, February 6, 1991. Much information about the Manuscript Club that appears in this chapter and throughout this book comes from personal interviews with former Manuscript Club members and/or daughters of former members: Margaret Dvorken, Mary Sanford Gordon, Jenny Louise Hindman, Emerett Sanford Miles, Helen Sanford, Peggy Schachter, Bert Kruger Smith, and Laura Faye Yauger.

10. "Manuscript Club Proves Methods by Successes," *Wichita Falls Daily Times*, n.d.

11. Hilton Greer, "Prose Writers of Texas: xxxx Winifred Sanford Distinguished Realist," *The Dallas Journal*, July 8, 1936.

12. Winifred Sanford, copy of letter to Margaret Cousins, October 9, 1945.

13. Winifred Sanford, "The Monument," *Windfall and Other Stories*, SMU Press, 43.

14. Ibid., 51.

15. Ibid., 53.

16. Peggy Schachter, telephone interview, January 2, 1991.

17. Winifred Sanford, copy of undated letter to William Kane. Internal evidence indicates it was written in December 1925 or January 1926. "Monument" was the first story of Winifred's to be accepted for publication, but the editors of *Woman's Home Companion* waited a year to publish it.

18. Winifred Sanford, copy of letter to M. K. Singleton, September 12, 1962.

19. Winifred Sanford, "Wreck," *Windfall and Other Stories*, SMU Press, 3.

20. Ibid., 3–4.

21. Ibid., 13.

22. Former Manuscript Club members stated that the women were mutually supportive. Whenever a member achieved publication, she shared the news and any advice she might have received, and the entire group celebrated her success.

23. Information about H. L. Mencken that appears in this chapter came from Carl Bode, *Mencken*, 3–45. Quote appears on 4–5.

24. Carl Bode, *Mencken*, 264–269.

CHAPTER FIVE

1. Carl Bode, *Mencken*, 258–263.

2. As quoted in Carl Bode, *Mencken*, 238.

3. As quoted in William H. Nolte, *H. L. Mencken: Literary Critic*, 247.

4. William H. Nolte, *H. L. Mencken: Literary Critic*, 259.

5. Theodore Peterson, *Magazines in the Twentieth Century*, 2nd edition, 122.

6. Gerald Hewes Carson, review of "Wreck," "Current Short Stories," *The Bookman*, March 1925.

7. These observations were based upon readings in the following books and articles: Frederick J. Hoffman, *The Twenties: American Writing in the Postwar Decade*; Carl Bode, *Mencken*; George Douglas, *H. L. Mencken: Critic of American Life*; Charles Fecher, *Mencken: A Study of His Thought*; William Nolte, *H. L. Mencken: Literary Critic*; M. K. Singleton, *H. L. Mencken and the American Mercury Adventure*.

8. H. L. Mencken, "Zola," *The Smart Set*, August 1912, 37.

9. William H. Nolte, *H. L. Mencken: Literary Critic*, 73, 136–137.

10. M. K. Singleton, *H. L. Mencken and the American Mercury Adventure*, 73–78.

11. As quoted in Carl Bode, *Mencken*, 243.

12. George Jean Nathan, letter to Winifred Sanford, October 21, 1924.

13. Winifred Sanford, letter to H. L. Mencken, July 25, 1924.

14. H. L. Mencken, letter to Winifred Sanford, August 3, 1924.

15. As quoted in Singleton, *H. L. Mencken and the American Mercury Adventure*, 212. This quote from Thomas Wolfe's letter to Madeline Boyd on February 15, 1927, appears in footnote 56.

16. Winifred Sanford, copy of letter to William Kane, n.d. Internal evidence indicates that Winifred wrote this letter in 1925 or 1926.

17. Don B. Graham, "Second Reader's Report," SMU Press.

18. Winifred Sanford, letter to Mrs. M. L. (Helen) Toulme, March 31, 1925.

19. Gerald Hewes Carson, review of "Wreck," "Current Short Stories," March 1925.

20. Winifred Sanford, copy of letter to M. K. Singleton, September 12, 1962.

21. H. L. Mencken, letter to Winifred Sanford, March 18, 1925.

22. Winifred Sanford, letter to H. L. Mencken, March 23, 1925.

23. H. L. Mencken, letter to Winifred Sanford, March 28, 1925.

24. Winifred Sanford, "Windfall," *Windfall and Other Stories*, SMU Press, 25–26.

25. Ibid., 32.

26. Ibid., 33.

27. Winifred Sanford, letter to H. L. Mencken, April 5, 1925.

28. Winifred Sanford, letter to H. L. Mencken, July 19, 1925.

29. Winifred Sanford, "Saved," *Windfall and Other Stories*, SMU Press, 38.

30. Ibid., 42.

31. Emerett Sanford Miles, Foreword, *Windfall and Other Stories*, Sanford family edition, xi.

32. Winifred Sanford, letter to H. L. Mencken, July 19, 1925.

33. H. L. Mencken, letter to Winifred Sanford, July 29, 1925.

34. Winifred Sanford, letter to H. L. Mencken, August 6, 1925.

35. Winifred Sanford, "Mary," *Windfall and Other Stories*, SMU Press, 55.

36. Ibid.

37. Ibid., 62.

38. Ibid., 64.

39 Ibid., 65.

40. Ibid., 66.

41. Ibid.

42. Ibid.

43. Winifred Sanford, letter to Mrs. M. L. Toulme, March 31, 1925.

44. Winifred did not mention this trip to New York again in correspondence with her sister or with H. L. Mencken, but she told M. K. Singleton in a letter dated September 14, 1962, that she had visited Mencken in New York City in spring 1925.

45. Winifred Sanford, letter to H. L. Mencken, October 28, 1925.

46. Winifred Sanford, copy of letter to Mrs. Knopf, December 2, 1925.

47. H. L. Mencken, letter to Winifred Sanford, December 21, 1925.

48. Winifred Sanford, letter to H. L. Mencken, January 14, 1926.

49. H. L. Mencken, letter to Winifred Sanford, January 19, 1926.

50. Winifred Sanford, letter to H. L. Mencken, February 9, 1926.

51. Winifred Sanford, letter to H. L. Mencken, June 7 1926.

52. Winifred Sanford, letter to H. L. Mencken August 28, 1926. The ellipses in this quotation appear in the original letter.

53. Winifred Sanford, "Black Child," *Windfall and Other Stories*, SMU Press, 80.

54. Ibid., 81–82. The ellipses in the last line of this quotation appear in the original text.

55. Ibid., 89.

56. Ibid.
57. H. L. Mencken, letter to Winifred Sanford, September 3, 1926.
58. Winifred Sanford, letter to H. L. Mencken. Internal evidence indicates this letter was written in September 1926. The ellipses in this paragraph appear in the original letter.
59. Winifred Sanford, letter to H. L. Mencken, September 20, 1927. The ellipses in this paragraph appear in the original letter.
60. H. L. Mencken, letter to Winifred Sanford, September 24, 1927.

CHAPTER SIX

1. Winifred Sanford, copy of letter to David Lloyd, November 10, 1927.
2. Winifred Sanford, copy of letter to David Lloyd, November 29, 1927.
3. David Lloyd, letter to Winifred Sanford, December 16, 1927.
4. See David Lloyd, letter to Winifred Sanford, February 9, 1928. Winifred made handwritten notes on the front and back of the envelope and this letter.
5. Winifred Sanford, copy of letter to David Lloyd, April 6, 1928.
6. David Lloyd, letter to Winifred Sanford, April 17, 1928. Lloyd wrote two letters to Winifred on the same date. The second one has a 2 by her name at the top of the page.
7. Winifred Sanford, copy of letter to David Lloyd, April 23, 1928.
8. David Lloyd, letter to Winifred Sanford, May 18, 1928. See also David Lloyd, letter to Winifred Sanford 2, May 18, 1928.
9. See H. L. Mencken, letter to Winifred Sanford, April 11, 1928.
10. Winifred Sanford, "Windfall," *Windfall and Other Stories*, SMU Press, 101.
11. Ibid.
12. Ibid., 102.
13. Ibid., 105.
14. Ibid.
15. Ibid., 107.
16. See Winifred Sanford, copy of letter to David Lloyd, April 23, 1928.
17. See Winifred Sanford, copy of letter to S. Omar Barker, May 18, 1940. "Windfall" appeared in: *Best Stories of the Southwest*, edited by Hilton Ross Greer in 1928 and in *Facts and Ideas for Students of English Composition*, edited by John Owen Beaty, Ernest Erwin Leisy, and Mary Lamar in 1930.
18. H. L. Mencken, letter to Winifred Sanford, May 14, 1929.
19. Winifred Sanford, letter to H. L. Mencken, May 24, 1929. See also H. L. Mencken, letter to Winifred Sanford, May 29, 1929.
20. Hilton Greer, "Prose Writers of Texas: XXXX Winifred Sanford Distinguished Realist," *The Dallas Journal*, July 8, 1936.
21. Emerett Sanford Miles, letter to Helen J. Sanford, n.d.
22. H. L. Mencken, letter to Winifred Sanford, May 8, 1930.
23. Winifred Sanford, "Luck," *Windfall and Other Stories*, SMU Press, 114.
24. Ibid., 24.
25. Ibid., 116.
26. Ibid., 121.
27. Ibid.

28. Ibid., 124.

29. Ibid., 127.

30. Winifred Sanford, letter to H. L. Mencken, September 26, 1930. The ellipses in this paragraph appear in the original letter.

31. H. L. Mencken, letter to Winifred Sanford, September 30, 1930.

32. Winifred Sanford, letter to H. L. Mencken, November 18, 1931.

33. Ibid., 140.

34. Ibid., 142–143.

35. Ibid., 146.

36. H. L. Mencken, letter to Winifred Sanford, November 21, 1930.

37. Frank Luther Mott, "The American Mercury," *A History of American Magazines: Volume. 5: Sketches of 21 Magazines, 1905–1930*, 3–26.

38. Robert Innes Center, letter to Winifred Sanford, April 2, 1931.

39. Winifred Sanford, copy of letter to Robert Innes Center, April 27, 1931.

40. Winifred Sanford, copy of letter to A. W. Barmby, April 27, 1931.

41. Information about crude oil prices came from "U.S. Crude Oil Wellhead Acquisition Price by First Purchaser," U.S. Department of Energy Information Administration.

42. Winifred Sanford, "Fever in the South," *Windfall and Other Stories*, SMU Press, 151.

43. Ibid., 153.

44. Ibid., 154. The ellipses in the final sentence of this paragraph appear in the original story.

45. Ibid., 158. The ellipses in the final sentence of this paragraph appear in the original story.

46. Ibid., 160.

47. Ibid., 162.

48. Ibid., 163.

49. Proof that Paget placed "Two Junes" with *Household Magazine* appears in David Lloyd, letter to Winifred Sanford, August 12, 1931. Proof that Paget placed "Fever in the South" with *North American Review* appears in David Lloyd, letter to Winifred Sanford. October 6, 1931.

50. See Kenneth Littauer, letter to Winifred Sanford, July 14, 1931. Proof that Winifred Sanford placed a story entitled "The Wedding" with *Woman's Home Companion* appears in this letter. For the plot of the novel she planned to base on this story, see Winifred Sanford, copy of letter to David Lloyd, May 9, 1932. See also Winifred Sanford, copy of letter to David Lloyd, March 1, 1938. Sanford's reference to publishing a detective novel under a pen name appears in this latter letter.

51. Carl Bode, *Mencken*, 283–284, 292–303, 305.

52. Ibid., 295–299, 300–301.

53. Ibid., 305–306.

CHAPTER SEVEN

1. For details of Wayland Sanford's life in Longview, see *Letters of Wayland Hall Sanford*, 238–256.

2. Winifred Sanford, copy of letter to David Lloyd, May 9, 1932.

3. The College Club later became a chapter of the American Association of University Women.

4. Charles Angoff, letter to Winifred Sanford. This letter is the last known correspondence between Winifred Sanford and a staff member of *The American Mercury*. It is dated March 9 and internal evidence indicates that the year was 1934. The letterhead on the *Mercury* stationery lists Henry Hazlitt—who became editor of the *Mercury* in the latter months of 1933 and resigned six months later—as editor, and Charles Angoff as managing editor.

5. Carl Bode, *Mencken*, 237–238.

6. Wayland Hall Sanford, *Letters of Wayland Hall Sanford*, 245–248.

7. Sanford family members were hesitant to say anything that might reflect negatively upon Wayland Sanford.

8. Winifred Sanford, copy of letter to David Lloyd, May 17, 1932.

9. Winifred Sanford, copy of letter to Robert Innes Center, April 27, 1931.

10. Winifred Sanford and Clyde Jackson, "Derrick Jargon," 335–345.

11. Hilton Greer, "Texas Institute of Letters Will Be Born Nov. 9," *The Dallas Journal*, July 8, 1936.

12. Winifred Sanford, letter to William H. Vann, September 20, 1936.

13. See J. Frank Dobie's letters to William H. Vann: August 1, 1935, February 1, 1936, September 14, 1936, and September 28, 1936.

14. As quoted by William H. Vann, *The Texas Institute of Letters, 1936–1966*, 5.

15. Ibid., 6.

16. Ibid., 27.

17. Ibid., See also Winifred Sanford, letter to William H. Vann, September 20, 1936.

18. Hilton Ross Greer, "Prose Writers of Texas XXXX: Winifred Sanford Distinguished Realist," *The Dallas Journal*, July 8, 1936.

19. Theodore Peterson, *Magazines in the Twentieth Century*, 123.

20. Hilton Greer, letter to William H. Vann, n.d.

21. Robert Adger Law, "Points of View—Education Should Not be Provincial," *Southwest Review*, 480.

22. Stanley Vestal "The Culture Is Here," *Southwest Review*, 478–480.

23. Albert Guerard, "A Mosaic, Not a Synthesis," *Southwest Review*, 481–482.

24. J. Frank Dobie, "True Culture Is Eclectic, but Provincial," *Southwest Review*, 482–483.

25. John William Rogers, "Southwestern Culture Must not Be a Cult," *Southwest Review*, 485–488.

26. Jay B. Hubbell, "A Note on Regionalism," *Southwest Review*, 368.

27. Ernest E. Leisy, "Realism Peferred," *Southwest Review*, 368–369.

28. Karle W. Baker, "More of Regionalism," *Southwest Review*, 490.

29. Rebecca Smith, "Minutes of the 1936 Meeting," *The Texas Institute of Letters*, 9.

30. "Texas Offers Rich Field for Authors, J. Frank Dobie Says," *The Dallas Morning News*, November 10, 1936.

31. Winifred Sanford, letter to William H. Vann, October 12, 1937. The location of the sanatorium where Winifred convalesced is unknown.

32. For information on the history of tuberculosis, see Thomas Dormandy, *The White Death: A History of Tuberculosis*. See also Neil and Janet Craft, "The History of Tuberculosis."

33. "Dallas College Club to Open Activities for Year at Monday Tea," *The Daily Times Herald*, October 2, 1938.

34. William H. Vann, *The Texas Institute of Letters, 1938–1966*, 11.
35. "Institute of Letters Meet to Open Friday," *The Daily Times Herald*, October 16, 1938.
36. Lon Tinkle, A Prefactory Note, *The Texas Institute of Letters, 1936–1966*, v–x.
37. See William H. Vann, *The Texas Institute of Letters, 1936–1966*, 87–92. See also Lou Halsell Rodenberger, Afterword, *Windfall and Other Stories*, SMU Press, 176.

CHAPTER EIGHT

1. Winifred Sanford, copy of letter to M. K. Singleton, September 12, 1962.
2. Winifred Sanford, copy of letter to David Lloyd, March 1, 1938.
3. Winifred Sanford, copy of letter to David Lloyd, September 1, 1938.
4. David Lloyd, letter to Winifred Sanford, November 11, 1938.
5. Carl Bode, Mencken, 367–376.
6. M. A. Orthofer, "Weighing Words Over Last Wishes," *Poets and Writers*, November/December 2003. In this article, Orthofer writes that writers throughout history have attempted to control what works reach the public and what works do not by burning inferior or incomplete compositions and/or by leaving instructions for these writings to be destroyed after the author's death. See also William Merrill Decker, *Epistolary Practices: Letter Writing in America Before Telecommunications*, 25. Decker writes that the more literary or prominent a writer is, the more mindful that writer is that what he or she intends to remain private might be published.
7. See David Lloyd, letter to Winifred Sanford, December 16, 1927. Lloyd told Winifred that the book is rather solemn but is not a manuscript that should be shelved. See also David Lloyd, letter to Winifred Sanford, April 17, 1928. In this letter, Lloyd reassured Winifred by recounting the positive comments that each of the publishing companies that rejected *Arrows of the Almighty* had made. He assured her that the manuscript had received more than the usual amount of attention.
8. Emerett Sanford Miles, Foreword, *Windfall and Other Stories*, SMU Press, xiv.
9. See Winifred Sanford, copy of letter to the editor of *Saturday Evening Post*, August 10, 1945; Winifred Sanford, copy of letter to Frankie McKee Robins, August 28, 1945; Winifred Sanford, copy of letter to Margaret Cousins, November 1, 1945; Winifred Sanford, copy of letter to Miss Stierhem, November 12, 1945. A manuscript copy of "Deep C" currently resides among Winifred Sanford's papers at the Southwestern Writers Collection at Texas State University in San Marcos, Texas.
10. For an overview of changes that took place in American society and culture with the onset of the Great Depression in 1929, see Frederick J. Hoffman, *The Twenties: American Writing in the Postwar Decade*, revised edition, 416–449.
11. Emerett Sanford Miles, Foreword, *Windfall and Other Stories*, SMU Press. Quote appears on xv.
12. See "Vocational, Rehabilitation Program Promoted by Auxiliary to City-County Hospital System," *The Daily Times Herald*, May 4 1947. See also "Alumnae Honor Two at Luncheon," *The Dallas Morning News*, February 18, 1962.
13. M. K. Singleton, *H. L. Mencken and the American Mercury Adventure*, 76.
14. Angoff, *H. L. Mencken: A Portrait from Memory*, 111.
15. Ibid.

16. Ibid., 112.

17. Winifred Sanford, copy of letter to M. K. Singleton, September 12, 1962.

18. Helen Sanford, copy of letter to M. K. Singleton, September 12, 1962.

19. M. K. Singleton, letter to Winifred Sanford, September 18, 1962.

20. Winifred Sanford, copy of letter to M. K. Singleton, September 26, 1962. The ellipses in this quotation appear in the original letter.

21. See William Nolte, *H. L. Mencken: Literary Critic*, xii. See Charles Fecher, *Mencken: A Study of His Thought*, 88. See also Carl Bode, *Mencken*, 238–240.

CHAPTER NINE

1. Winifred Sanford, *Windfall and Other Stories*, Sanford family edition.

2. Winifred Sanford, copy of letter to Gertrude Lane, February 29, 1926.

3. Winifred Sanford, "Fools," *Windfall and Other Stories*, Sanford family edition, 68.

4. Ibid., 69.

5. Ibid., 72.

6. Ibid.

7. Don B. Graham, "Second Reader's Report," March 31, 1987.

8. Winifred Sanford. "Fannie Baker," *Windfall and Other Stories*, Sanford family edition, 122–128.

9. Winifred Sanford, "A Victorian Grandmother," *Windfall and Other Stories*, Sanford family edition, 129–134.

10. Ibid., 131–132.

11. Laura Faye Yauger, letter to Winifred Sanford, April 20, 1981.

12. Anne Pence Davis, letter to Winifred Sanford, December 11, 1980.

13. See "Death and Funeral Announcements," *The Dallas Morning News*, March 26, 1983.

14. Rev. John A. Buehrens, "The Service in Memory of Winifred Sanford: March 16, 1890 to March 24, 1983." The poem "Invocation" appears in the Sanford family edition of *Windfall and Other Stories*, iii.

15. Winifred Sanford, "A Victorian Grandmother," *Windfall and Other Stories*, Sanford family edition, 133–134.

16. Suzanne Comer, letter to Helen J. Sanford, April 22, 1987.

17. William T. Pilkington, "First Reader's Report," n.d.

18. Don B. Graham, "Second Reader's Report," March 31, 1987.

19. Brad Hooper, review of *Windfall and Other Stories* by Winifred Sanford, *Booklist*, 1989.

20. Review of *Windfall and Other Stories* by Winifred Sanford, "A Critical Checklist of Current Southwestern Americana," *Books of the Southwest*, 364.

21. S. S. Moorty, "Stories Reveal the Twenties as More Than Gin and Flappers," review of *Windfall and Other Stories* by Winifred Sanford, *Texas Books in Review* 9, no. 2 (1989): 14–15.

22. Judith Rigler, "It was a Brief Career but Really Noteworthy," review of *Windfall and Other Stories* by Winifred Sanford, *Fort Worth Star-Telegram* (July 7, 1989): 6: 7.

23. Clay Reynolds, review of *Windfall and Other Stories* by Winifred Sanford, *Review of Texas Books* 3, no. 4 (1989): 3.

24. Bob J. Frye, review of *Windfall and Other Stories* by Winifred Sanford, *Western American Literature Quarterly* 25, no. 2 (1990): 177–178.

25. Dan Baldwin, review of *Windfall and Other Stories* by Winifred Sanford, *Legacies: A History Journal for Dallas and North Central Texas* 1, no. 1 (1989): 39.
26. Diana Davids Olien, review of *Windfall and Other Stories* by Winifred Sanford, *Southwestern Historical Quarterly* 93, no. 4 (1990): 541–2.
27. Emerett Sanford Miles, letter to Helen J. Sanford, n.d. The title of the article that Miles quotes is "New Writer Is Reticent, but Her Work and Success Speaks for Itself; Mrs. W.H. Sanford." This undated article was published originally in a Wichita Falls newspaper (internal evidence indicates in spring 1925). A former Manuscript Club member gave the undated newspaper clipping to Emerett Sanford Miles when she was living in Wichita Falls, at least twenty years after the article was published, and Miles reproduced a portion of the article in an undated letter to Helen J. Sanford. This letter is also mentioned in Chapter Six and referenced in note 21 of that chapter.
28. Lou Halsell Rodenberger, Afterword, 176.
29. Abby Maxwell, letter to Winifred Sanford, March 20, 1925.
30. See David Lloyd, letter to Winifred Sanford, January 24, 1931. The ellipses that appear in excerpts from this story appear in the original.
31. See Winifred Sanford, copy of letter to the editor of *Saturday Evening Post*, August 10, 1945; Winifred Sanford, copy of letter to Frankie McKee Robins of *McCall's Magazine*, August 28, 1945; Winifred Sanford, copy of letter to Margaret Cousins of *Good Housekeeping*, November 1, 1945; Winifred Sanford, copy of letter to Miss Stierhem of *Today's Woman*, November 12, 1945.
32. Winifred Sanford, copy of letter to Margaret Cousins, October 9, 1945.
33. Margaret Cousins, letter to Winifred Sanford, November 1, 1945.

CONCLUSION

1. For evidence that many Texas writers and scholars have taken a critical view of Texas literature, see J. Frank Dobie's letters to William Vann: August 1, 1935, February 1, 1936, September 14, 1936, and September 28, 1936, and numerous articles and opinion pieces by Texas writers and scholars that were published in *Southwest Review* between July 1929 and July 1932. Also, see Ronnie Dugger, "Dobie, Bedichek, Webb: Workers in the Culture," *The Texas Observer* (August 19, 1983): 18–21. On the first page of this essay, Dugger writes, regarding the state of Texas letters prior to the Dobie-Bedichek-Webb era, "First you have to understand how bleak, how barren, the literary culture of the region was then."

   See especially Larry McMurtry's *In a Narrow Grave: Essays on Texas* (1987). For a listing of more articles on the subject of the inferiority of Texas letters, see Bryce Milligan's review of *Range Wars: Heated Debates and Sober Reflections on the Range of Texas Writing*, edited by Craig Clifford and Tom Pilkington, *The Texas Observer* (April 21, 1989): 19–20.
2. Hawthorne's ambivalent feelings toward the Salem witch trials influenced the writing of some of the finest early American novels, and ambivalent feelings that slavery and the Civil War engendered in young writers of the American South resulted in a flurry of literary productivity now known as the Southern Renaissance.

Aley, Maxwell. Letter to Winifred Sanford, January 18, 1924. Winifred Mahon Sanford Papers. Southwestern Writers Collection. Texas State University, San Marcos.

_____. Letter to Winifred Sanford, March 20, 1925. Winifred Mahon Sanford Papers. Southwestern Writers Collection. Texas State University, San Marcos.

_____. Letter to Winifred Sanford, April 1, 1925. Winifred Mahon Sanford Papers. Southwestern Writers Collection. Texas State University, San Marcos.

_____. Letter to Winifred Sanford, March 5, 1926. Winifred Mahon Sanford Papers. Southwestern Writers Collection. Texas State University, San Marcos.

"Alumnae Honor Two at Luncheon." *The Dallas Morning News*, February 18, 1962, 7.3.

Angoff, Charles. *H. L. Mencken: A Portrait from Memory*. New York: A. S. Barnes, 1956.

_____. Letter to Winifred Sanford, March 9, 1931. Winifred Mahon Sanford Papers. Southwestern Writers Collection. Texas State University, San Marcos.

Baker, Karle Wilson. "More of Regionalism." *Southwest Review* 17, no. 4 (July 1932): 490.

Baldwin, Dan. Review of *Windfall and Other Stories*, by Winifred Sanford. *Legacies: A History Journal for Dallas and North Central Texas* 1, no. 1 (1989): 39.

Barnes, Florence Elberta. *Texas Writers of Today*. Dallas: Tardy Publishing, 1935.

Baum, Arthur W. "The Cities of America: Duluth." *Saturday Evening Post*, April 16, 1949. http://www.turbinecar.com/duluth-1949.htm.

Beaty, John, Ernest Leisy, and Mary Lamar, eds. *Facts and Ideas for Students of English Composition*. New York: F. S. Crofts, 1930.

Bode, Carl. *Mencken*. Carbondale and Edwardsville: Southern Illinois University Press, 1969.

Buehrens, John A. "The Service in Memory of Winifred Sanford: March 16, 1890 to March 24, 1983." Winifred Mahon Sanford Papers. Southwestern Writers Collection. Texas State University, San Marcos.

Carson, Gerald Hewes. Review of "Wreck," by Winifred Sanford. *The Bookman* (March 1925): 58+.

Center, Robert Innes. Letter to Winifred Sanford, April 2, 1931. Winifred Mahon Sanford Papers. Southwestern Writers Collection. Texas State University, San Marcos.

"Cokesbury Book Store in Co-Operation with the Texas Institute of Letters Takes Pleasure in Announcing a Series of Literary Programs." *The Dallas Morning News*, October 16, 1938, 3.11.

Comer, Suzanne. Letter to Helen J. Sanford, April 22, 1987. Winifred Mahon Sanford Papers. Southwestern Writers Collection. Texas State University, San Marcos.

Cousins, Margaret. Letter to Winifred Sanford, October 9, 1945. Winifred Mahon Sanford Papers. Southwestern Writers Collection. Texas State University, San Marcos.

_____. Letter to Winifred Sanford, November 1, 1945. Winifred Mahon Sanford Papers. Southwestern Writers Collection. Texas State University, San Marcos.

Craft, Neil and Janet. "The History of Tuberculosis." (2005): http://www.micklebring.com/oakwood/Ch.18.html.

"Dallas College Club to Open Activities for Year at Monday Tea." *Dallas Daily Times-Herald*, October 2, 1938, 3:12.

Davis, Anne Pence. *The Customer Is Always Right*. New York: Macmillan, 1940.

_____. Letter to Winifred Sanford, December 11, 1980. Winifred Mahon Sanford Papers. Southwestern Writers Collection. Texas State University, San Marcos.

"Death and Funeral Announcements." *The Dallas Morning News*, March 26, 1983, B:20.

Decker, William Merrill. *Epistolary Practices: Letter Writing in America Before Telecommunications*. Chapel Hill: University of North Carolina Press, 1998, 25.

Dobie, J. Frank. Letter to William H. Vann, August 1, 1935. Texas Institute of Letters Records. Southwestern Writers Collection. Texas State University, San Marcos.

_____. Letter to William H. Vann, February 1, 1936. Texas Institute of Letters Records. Southwestern Writers Collection. Texas State University, San Marcos.

_____. Letter to William H. Vann. September 14, 1936. Texas Institute of Letters Records. Southwestern Writers Collection. Texas State University, San Marcos.

_____. Letter to William H. Vann, September 28, 1936. Texas Institute of Letters Records. Southwestern Writers Collection. Texas State University, San Marcos.

_____. "True Culture is Eclectic, but Provincial." *Southwest Review* 14 (1929): 482–483.

"Dobie Speaker at Institute Session." *Dallas Daily Times-Herald*, November 10, 1936, 2:10.

Dormandy, Thomas. *The White Death: A History of Tuberculosis*. New York: New York University Press, 1999.

Douglas, George H. *H. L. Mencken: Critic of American Life*. Hamden: Archon Books, 1978.

Dugger, Ronnie. "Dobie, Bedichek, Webb: Workers in the Culture." *The Texas Observer* (August 19, 1983): 18–21.

Duluth Central High School Yearbook, 1907.

Dvorken, Margaret. Interview by author. Wichita Falls, February 16, 1991.

Fecher, Charles. *Mencken: A Study of His Thought*. New York: Alfred A. Knopf, 1978.

Freeman, Cynthia, Director of Archives of the Texas State Bar Association. Telephone interview by author. April 22, 1991.

Frye, Bob J. Review of *Windfall and Other Stories*, by Winifred Sanford. *Western American Literature* 25, no. 2 (1990): 177–178.

Gelzer, Jay. "The Wedding." *Woman's Home Companion* (June 1934): 6+.

Gordon, Mary Sanford. Telephone interview by author. April 22, 1989.

Graham, Don B. "Second Reader's Report." Dallas, SMU Press, March 31, 1987.

_____. "The Short Story in Texas." In *South by Southwest: 24 Stories from Modern Texas*, edited by Don B. Graham, xi–xix. Austin: University of Texas Press, 1986.

Graham, Don B., James Ward Lee, and William T. Pilkington. *The Texas Literary Tradition*. Austin: University of Texas Press, 1983.

Greer, Hilton Ross, ed. *Best Short Stories from the Southwest*. Dallas: Southwest Press, 1928.

_____. Letter to William H. Vann, n.d. Texas Institute of Letters Records. Southwestern Writers Collection. Texas State University, San Marcos.

_____. "Poets of Texas: XXVI Fay M. Yauger Distinguished Ballad-Maker." *The Dallas Journal*, March 1935, 1.6.

_____. "Poets of Texas: XXXVII Fania Kruger Different and Effective." *The Dallas Journal*, June 5, 1935, 2.2.

_____. "Prose Writers of Texas: XXXX Winifred Sanford Distinguished Realist." *The Dallas Journal*, July 8, 1936, 2.1.

_____. "Texas Institute of Letters Will be Born Nov. 9." *The Dallas Journal*, n.d. Vertical files. History and Archives, Dallas Public Library, Dallas.

Grider, Sylvia Ann, and Lou Halsell Rodenberger, eds. *Let's Hear It: Stories by Texas Women Writers*. College Station: Texas A&M University Press, 2003.

Grider, Sylvia Ann, and Lou Halsell Rodenberger, eds. *Texas Women Writers: A Tradition of Their Own*. College Station: Texas A&M University Press, 1997.

Guerard, Albert. "A Mosaic, Not a Synthesis." *Southwest Review* 17 (July 1929): 481–482.

"Henry S. Mahon Dies Suddenly: Well Known Attorney Is Victim of Heart Trouble—Funeral Tomorrow." *Duluth News Tribune*, June 20, 1908, n.p. Duluth Public Library, Duluth.

Hindman, Jenny Louise. Interview by author. Wichita Falls, February 6, 1991.

Hoffman, Frederick J. *The Twenties: American Writing in the Postwar Decade*. Rev. ed. New York: The Free Press, 1962.

Hooper, Brad. Review of *Windfall and Other Stories*, by Winifred M. Sanford. *Booklist* 85, no. 9 (1989): 1093.

"H. S. Mahon is Called." *Duluth Herald*, June 29, 1908, n.p. Duluth Public Library, Duluth.

Hubbell, Jay B. "A Note on Regionalism." *Southwest Review* 17, no. 3 (April 1932): 368.

"Institute of Letters Meet to Open Friday." *Dallas Daily Times-Herald*, October 16, 1938, 3:16.

Jackson, Sarah Ragland. *Texas Woman of Letters: Karle Wilson Baker*. College Station: Texas A&M University Press, 2005.

Law, Robert Adger. "Points of View—Education Should Not Be Provincial." *Southwest Review* 14 (July 1929): 480.

Lee, James Ward. *Adventures with a Texas Humanist*. Fort Worth: Texas Christian University Press, 2004.

Leisy, Ernest E. "Realism Preferred." *Southwest Review* 17, no. 3 (April 1932): 368–369.

Lewis, Sinclair. "The American Fear of Literature." Nobel Lecture, December 12, 1930. Nobel Lectures: 13 (July 2010): http://www.nobelprize.org.

Littauer, Kenneth. Letter to Winifred Sanford, July 14, 1931. Winifred Mahon Sanford Papers. Southwestern Writers Collection. Texas State University, San Marcos.

Lloyd, David. Letter to Winifred Sanford, December 16, 1927. Winifred Mahon Sanford Papers. Southwestern Writers Collection. Texas State University, San Marcos.

_____. Letter to Winifred Sanford, February 9, 1928. Winifred Mahon Sanford Papers. Southwestern Writers Collection. Texas State University, San Marcos.

_____. Letter to Winifred Sanford, April 17, 1928. Winifred Mahon Sanford Papers. Southwestern Writers Collection. Texas State University, San Marcos.

_____. Letter to Winifred Sanford, May 18, 1928. Winifred Mahon Sanford Papers. Southwestern Writers Collection. Texas State University, San Marcos.

_____. Letter to Winifred Sanford, January 24, 1931. Winifred Mahon Sanford Papers. Southwestern Writers Collection. Texas State University, San Marcos.

_____. Letter to Winifred Sanford, August 12, 1931. Winifred Mahon Sanford Papers. Southwestern Writers Collection. Texas State University, San Marcos.

_____. Letter to Winifred Sanford, October 6, 1931. Winifred Mahon Sanford Papers. Southwestern Writers Collection. Texas State University, San Marcos.

_____. Letter to Winifred Sanford, November 11, 1938. Winifred Mahon Sanford Papers. Southwestern Writers Collection. Texas State University, San Marcos.

Mahon, Winifred Balch. Enrollment Card, 1911. University of Michigan, Ann Arbor, Michigan.

_____. "England and the Home-Rule Question." South Atlantic Quarterly (October 1913): 356–368.

"Manuscript Club Proves Methods by Successes." Wichita Falls Daily Times, n.d. Private collection of Peggy Schachter.

The Manuscript: Published By and For the Wichita Falls Penwomen's Club I. January 22, 1925. Winifred Mahon Sanford Papers. Southwestern Writers Collection. Texas State University, San Marcos.

McMurtry, Larry. In a Narrow Grave: Essays on Texas. Albuquerque: University of New Mexico Press, 1987.

Mencken, H. L. Letter to Winifred Sanford, August 3, 1924. Winifred Mahon Sanford Papers. Southwestern Writers Collection. Texas State University, San Marcos.

_____. Letter to Winifred Sanford, October 21, 1924. Winifred Mahon Sanford Papers. Southwestern Writers Collection. Texas State University, San Marcos.

_____. Letter to Winifred Sanford, October 30, 1924. Winifred Mahon Sanford Papers. Southwestern Writers Collection. Texas State University, San Marcos.

_____. Letter to Winifred Sanford, March 18, 1925. Winifred Mahon Sanford Papers. Southwestern Writers Collection. Texas State University, San Marcos.

_____. Letter to Winifred Sanford, March 28, 1925. Winifred Mahon Sanford Papers. Southwestern Writers Collection. Texas State University, San Marcos.

_____. Letter to Winifred Sanford, April 10, 1925. Winifred Mahon Sanford Papers. Southwestern Writers Collection. Texas State University, San Marcos.

_____. Letter to Winifred Sanford, July 29, 1925. Winifred Mahon Sanford Papers. Southwestern Writers Collection. Texas State University, San Marcos.

_____. Letter to Winifred Sanford, December 21, 1925. Winifred Mahon Sanford Papers. Southwestern Writers Collection. Texas State University, San Marcos.

_____. Letter to Winifred Sanford, January 19, 1926. Winifred Mahon Sanford Papers. Southwestern Writers Collection. Texas State University, San Marcos.

_____. Letter to Winifred Sanford, June 7, 1926. Winifred Mahon Sanford Papers. Southwestern Writers Collection. Texas State University, San Marcos.

_____. Letter to Winifred Sanford, September 3, 1926. Winifred Mahon Sanford Papers. Southwestern Writers Collection. Texas State University, San Marcos.

_____. Letter to Winifred Sanford, October 2, 1926. Winifred Mahon Sanford Papers. Southwestern Writers Collection. Texas State University, San Marcos.

_____. Letter to Winifred Sanford, August 20, 1927. Winifred Mahon Sanford Papers. Southwestern Writers Collection. Texas State University, San Marcos.

_____. Letter to Winifred Sanford, September 24, 1927. Winifred Mahon Sanford Papers. Southwestern Writers Collection. Texas State University, San Marcos.

_____. Letter to Winifred Sanford, February 28, 1928. Winifred Mahon Sanford Papers. Southwestern Writers Collection. Texas State University, San Marcos.

_____. Letter to Winifred Sanford, April 11, 1928. Winifred Mahon Sanford Papers. Southwestern Writers Collection. Texas State University, San Marcos.

_____. Letter to Winifred Sanford, May 14, 1929. Winifred Mahon Sanford Papers. Southwestern Writers Collection. Texas State University, San Marcos.

_____. Letter to Winifred Sanford, May 29, 1929. Winifred Mahon Sanford Papers. Southwestern Writers Collection. Texas State University, San Marcos.

_____. Letter to Winifred Sanford, May 8, 1930. Winifred Mahon Sanford Papers. Southwestern Writers Collection. Texas State University, San Marcos.

_____. Letter to Winifred Sanford, September 30, 1930. Winifred Mahon Sanford Papers. Southwestern Writers Collection. Texas State University, San Marcos.

_____. Letter to Winifred Sanford, November 21, 1930. Winifred Mahon Sanford Papers. Southwestern Writers Collection. Texas State University, San Marcos.

_____. "Sahara of the Bozart." In *The American Scene: A Reader*, edited by Huntington Cairns, 156–168. New York: Alfred A. Knopf, 1965.

_____. "Zola." *The Smart Set* 37 (August 1912): 154.

Meyer, Susan E. *America's Great Illustrators*. New York: Harry N. Abrams, 1978.

Michiganensian Nineteen Thirteen. Ann Arbor.

Miles, Emerett Sanford. "About the Author" for *Windfall and Other Stories*, by Winifred Sanford, vii–xi. Privately published. Dallas, 1980.

_____. Foreword for *Windfall and Other Stories*, by Winifred Sanford, ix–xv. Dallas: SMU Press, 1988.

_____. Interview by author. Dallas, April 22, 1991.

_____. Letter to Helen J. Sanford, n.d. Private Collection of Helen J. Sanford.

_____. Telephone interview by author. February 14, 1991.

Mladinov, Mary. Administrative Secretary for Phi Beta Kappa. Letter to the author. September 20, 1991.

Moorty, S. S. "Stories Reveal the Twenties as More Than Gin and Flappers." Review of *Windfall and Other Stories*, by Winifred Sanford. *Texas Books in Review* 9, no. 2 (Summer 1989): 14–15.

Mott, Frank Luther. "The American Mercury." *A History of American Magazines: Vol. 5: Sketches of 21 Magazines, 1905–1930.* Cambridge: Harvard University Press, 1968, 3–26.

Mulligan, Bryce. "The Range of Texas Writing." Review of *Heated Debates and Sober Reflections on the Range of Texas Writing,* by Craig Clifford. *The Texas Observer* (April 21, 1989) 19–20.

Nathan, George Jean. Letter to Winifred Sanford, October 21, 1924. Winifred Mahon Sanford Papers. Southwestern Writers Collection. Texas State University, San Marcos.

_____. Letter to Winifred Sanford, October 30, 1924. Winifred Mahon Sanford Papers. Southwestern Writers Collection. Texas State University, San Marcos.

Nolte, William. *H. L. Mencken: Literary Critic.* Seattle: University of Washington Press, 1966.

O'Brien, Edward J., ed. *The Best Short Stories of 1925 and the Yearbook of the American Short Story.* New York: Dodd, Mead, 1926.

"Obituaries, Helen Jefferson Sanford." *The Dallas Morning News,* June 18, 2006, C:13B.

Olien, Diana Davids. Review of *Windfall and Other Stories,* by Winifred Sanford. *Southwestern Historical Quarterly* 93, no. 4 (1990): 541–542.

Orthofer, M. A. "Weighing Words Over Last Wishes." *Poets and Writers,* November–December 2003. http://www.pw.org/content/weighing_words_over_last_wishes.

Perry, William, ed. *21 Texas Short Stories.* Austin: University of Texas Press, 1954.

Peterson, Theodore. *Magazines in the Twentieth Century.* 2nd ed. Urbana: Illinois University Press, 1964.

Pilkington, William T. "First Reader's Report." Dallas, SMU Press, n.d.

_____. *Imagining Texas: The Literature of the Lone Star State.* Boston: American Press, 1981.

"Points of View." *Southwest Review* 17 (July 1929): 474.

Porter, Katherine Anne. Interview by Barbara Thompson Davis. *The Paris Review* 29 (Winter–Spring 1963): http://www.theparisreview.org/interviews/4569/the-art-of-fiction-no-29-katherine-anne-porter.

"Probing the Purpose of a Literary Group." *Dallas Daily Times-Herald,* March 12, 1967, D:9.

Pulford, Max A. Letter to Wayland Sanford, n.d. Private Collection of Helen J. Sanford.

Review of *Windfall and Other Stories,* by Winifred Sanford. *Books of the Southwest: A Critical Checklist of Current Southwest Americana* 364 (1989): 12.

Reynolds, Clay. Review of *Windfall and Other Stories,* by Winifred Sanford. *Review of Texas Books* 3, no. 4 (1989): 3.

Rigler, Judith. "It Was a Brief Career but Really Noteworthy." Review of *Windfall and Other Stories,* by Winifred Sanford. *Fort Worth Star-Telegram,* July 23, 1989, 6:7.

Rodenberger, Lou Halsell. Afterword for *Windfall and Other Stories,* by Winifred Sanford, 173–179. Dallas: Southern Methodist University Press, 1988.

_____, ed. *Her Work: Stories by Texas Women.* Bryan: Shearer Publishing, 1982.

_____. "Sanford, Winifred Balch Mahon." *Handbook of Texas Online.* Texas State Historical Association. Texas Historical Society. http://www.tshaonline.org/handbook/online. Retrieved 1999.

Rogers, John William. "Southwestern Culture Must not Be a Cult." *Southwest Review* 17 (July 1929): 485–488.

Rundell, Walter, Jr., *Early Texas Oil: A Photographic History, 1836–1936.* College Station: Texas A&M University Press, 1977.

Sanford, Annette. *Lasting Attachments.* Dallas: SMU Press, 2001.

Sanford, Helen. Interview by author. Dallas, February 14, 1989.

_____. Copy of Letter to M. K. Singleton, September 12, 1962. Private Collection of Helen J. Sanford.

_____. Letter to Betty Wiesepape, July 3, 1993.

_____. "Pedigree Chart." Sanford family private collection.

Sanford, Wayland Hall. *Letters of Wayland Hall Sanford*, edited by Helen J. Sanford. Privately published. Dallas, 1999.

"Sanford, Wayland Hall Service Records." Department of Veterans Affairs. Waco, Texas.

Sanford, Winifred, and Clyde Jackson. "Derrick Jargon." *Southwest Review* 19 (April 1934): 335–345.

Sanford, Winifred. "Invocation." *The Manuscript: Published by and for the Wichita Falls Penwomen's Club I.* January 22, 1925, iii.

_____. Copy of letter to Mrs. Alfred A. Knopf, December 2, 1925. Winifred Mahon Sanford Papers. Southwestern Writers Collection. Texas State University, San Marcos.

_____. Copy of letter to A. W. Barmby, April 27, 1931. Winifred Mahon Sanford Papers. Southwestern Writers Collection. Texas State University, San Marcos.

_____. Copy of letter to C. Paget, November 29, 1927. Winifred Mahon Sanford Papers. Southwestern Writers Collection. Texas State University, San Marcos.

_____. Copy of letter to David Lloyd, November 10, 1927. Winifred Mahon Sanford Papers. Southwestern Writers Collection. Texas State University, San Marcos.

_____. Copy of letter to David Lloyd, December 16, 1927. Winifred Mahon Sanford Papers. Southwestern Writers Collection. Texas State University, San Marcos.

_____. Copy of letter to David Lloyd, April 6, 1928. Winifred Mahon Sanford Papers. Southwestern Writers Collection. Texas State University, San Marcos.

_____. Copy of letter to David Lloyd, April 23, 1928. Winifred Mahon Sanford Papers. Southwestern Writers Collection. Texas State University, San Marcos.

_____. Copy of letter to David Lloyd, May 9, 1932. Winifred Mahon Sanford Papers. Southwestern Writers Collection. Texas State University, San Marcos.

_____. Copy of letter to David Lloyd, May 17, 1932. Winifred Mahon Sanford Papers. Southwestern Writers Collection. Texas State University, San Marcos.

_____. Copy of letter to David Lloyd, March 1, 1938. Winifred Mahon Sanford Papers. Southwestern Writers Collection. Texas State University, San Marcos.

_____. Copy of letter to David Lloyd, September 1, 1938. Winifred Mahon Sanford Papers. Southwestern Writers Collection. Texas State University, San Marcos.

_____. Copy of letter to Frankie McKee Robins, August 28, 1945. Winifred Mahon Sanford Papers. Southwestern Writers Collection. Texas State University, San Marcos.

_____. Copy of letter to Gertrude Lane, February 29, 1926. Winifred Mahon Sanford Papers. Southwestern Writers Collection. Texas State University, San Marcos.

_____. Letter to H. L. Mencken, July 25, 1924. H. L. Mencken Papers. Manuscript and Archives Division. New York Public Library. Astor, Lenox, and Tilden Foundation, New York.

_____. Letter to H. L. Mencken, March 23, 1925. H. L. Mencken Papers. Manuscript and Archives Division. New York Public Library. Astor, Lenox, and Tilden Foundation, New York.

_____. Letter to H. L. Mencken, April 5, 1925. H. L. Mencken Papers. Manuscript and Archives Division. New York Public Library. Astor, Lenox, and Tilden Foundation, New York.

_____. Letter to H. L. Mencken, July 19, 1925. H. L. Mencken Papers. Manuscript and Archives Division. New York Public Library. Astor, Lenox, and Tilden Foundation, New York.

_____. Letter to H. L. Mencken, August 6, 1925. H. L. Mencken Papers. Manuscript and Archives Division. New York Public Library. Astor, Lenox, and Tilden Foundation, New York.

_____. Letter to H. L. Mencken, October 28, 1925. H. L. Mencken Papers. Manuscript and Archives Division. New York Public Library. Astor, Lenox, and Tilden Foundation, New York.

_____. Letter to H. L. Mencken, January 14, 1926. H. L. Mencken Papers. Manuscript and Archives Division. New York Public Library. Astor, Lenox, and Tilden Foundation, New York.

_____. Letter to H. L. Mencken, February 9, 1926. H. L. Mencken Papers. Manuscript and Archives Division. New York Public Library. Astor, Lenox, and Tilden Foundation, New York.

_____. Letter to H. L. Mencken, March 9, 1926. H. L. Mencken Papers. Manuscript and Archives Division. New York Public Library. Astor, Lenox, and Tilden Foundation, New York.

_____. Letter to H. L. Mencken, August 28, 1926. H. L. Mencken Papers. Manuscript and Archives Division. New York Public Library. Astor, Lenox, and Tilden Foundation, New York.

_____. Letter to H. L. Mencken, September 20, 1927. H. L. Mencken Papers. Manuscript and Archives Division. New York Public Library. Astor, Lenox, and Tilden Foundation, New York.

_____. Letter to H. L. Mencken, May 24, 1929. H. L. Mencken Papers. Manuscript and Archives Division. New York Public Library. Astor, Lenox, and Tilden Foundation, New York.

_____. Letter to H. L. Mencken, September 26, 1930. H. L. Mencken Papers. Manuscript and Archives Division. New York Public Library. Astor, Lenox, and Tilden Foundation, New York.

_____. Letter to H. L. Mencken, November 18, 1931. H. L. Mencken Papers. Manuscript and Archives Division. New York Public Library. Astor, Lenox, and Tilden Foundation, New York.

_____. Copy of letter to Margaret Cousins, October 9, 1945. Winifred Mahon Sanford Papers. Southwestern Writers Collection. Texas State University, San Marcos.

_____. Copy of letter to Margaret Cousins, November 1, 1945. Winifred Mahon Sanford Papers. Southwestern Writers Collection. Texas State University, San Marcos.

_____. Copy of letter to M. K. Singleton, September 12, 1962. Winifred Mahon Sanford Papers. Southwestern Writers Collection. Texas State University, San Marcos.

_____. Copy of letter to M. K. Singleton, September 26, 1962. Winifred Mahon Sanford Papers. Southwestern Writers Collection. Texas State University, San Marcos.

_____. Letter to Mrs. M. L. Toulme, February 1, 1920. Winifred Mahon Sanford Papers. Southwestern Writers Collection. Texas State University, San Marcos.

_____. Letter to Mrs. M. L. Toulme, March 31, 1925. Winifred Mahon Sanford Papers. Southwestern Writers Collection. Texas State University, San Marcos.

_____. Copy of letter to Robert Innes Center, April 27, 1931. Winifred Mahon Sanford Papers. Southwestern Writers Collection. Texas State University, San Marcos.

_____. Copy of letter to the editor of the *Saturday Evening Post*, August 10, 1945. Winifred Mahon Sanford Papers. Southwestern Writers Collection. Texas State University, San Marcos.

_____. Copy of letter to S. Omar Barker, May 18, 1940. Winifred Mahon Sanford Papers. Southwestern Writers Collection. Texas State University, San Marcos.

_____. Copy of letter to Miss Stierhem, November 12, 1945. Winifred Mahon Sanford Papers. Southwestern Writers Collection. Texas State University, San Marcos.

_____. Letter to William H. Vann, September 20, 1936. Texas Institute of Letters Records. Southwestern Writers Collection. Texas State University, San Marcos.

_____. Letter to William H. Vann, October 12, 1937. Texas Institute of Letters Records. Southwestern Writers Collection. Texas State University, San Marcos.

_____. Copy of letter to William Kane, n.d. Winifred Mahon Sanford Papers. Southwestern Writers Collection. Texas State University, San Marcos.

_____. "Memories." Unpublished manuscript. Winifred Mahon Sanford Papers. Southwestern Writers Collection. Texas State University, San Marcos.

_____. "Memories 2." Unpublished manuscript. Winifred Mahon Sanford Papers. Southwestern Writers Collection. Texas State University, San Marcos.

_____. "Star in the East." Unpublished manuscript. Winifred Sanford Papers. Southwestern Writers Collection. Texas State University, San Marcos.

_____. "The Method of Irony." *The Editor* 72, no. 10 (March 6, 1926): 150–151.

_____. "Two Junes." *Household Magazine*, (November 1931): 4–5.

_____. *Windfall and Other Stories*. Privately published. Dallas, 1980.

_____. *Windfall and Other Stories*. Dallas: SMU Press, 1988.

_____. "Writing the Short Story." *Southwester* (October 1935): 26–27.

"Sanford, Winifred M.: Death and Funeral Announcements." *The Dallas Morning News*, March 26, 1983, B:20.

Schachter, Peggy. Interview by author. Dallas, January 2, 1991.

_____. Interview by author. Dallas, February 11, 1991.

Singleton, M. K. *H. L. Mencken and The American Mercury Adventure*. Durham: Duke University Press, 1962.

_____. Letter to Winifred Sanford. September 18, 1962.

Smith, Bert Kruger. Telephone interview by author. January 30, 1991.

_____. Telephone interview by author. July 6, 1993.

Smith, Rebecca. "Minutes of the 1936 Meeting." Texas Institute of Letters Records. Southwestern Writers Collection. Texas State University, San Marcos.

"Texas Offers Rich Field for Authors, J. Frank Dobie Says." *The Dallas Morning News*, November 10, 1936, 4.1.

Tinkle, Lon. "A Prefactory Note." *History of the Texas Institute of Letters, 1936–1966*, by William Vann, v–x. Austin: Encino Press, 1967.

Ultan, Lloyd, and Barbara Unger. *Bronx Accent: A Literary and Pictorial History of the Borough.* New Brunswick: Rutgers University Press, 2000.

Ultan, Lloyd, and Gary Hermalyn. *The Bronx in the Innocent Years, 1890–1925.* 2nd ed. New York: Bronx County Historical Society, 1991.

University of Michigan class record for Winifred Sanford, 1938. University of Michigan, Ann Arbor, Michigan.

"U.S. Crude Oil Wellhead Acquisition Price by First Purchaser." U.S. Department of Energy Information Administration, Dallas.

Vann, William H. *The Texas Institute of Letters, 1936–1966.* Austin: Encino, 1967.

Vestal, Stanley. "The Culture Is Here." *Southwest Review* 17 (July 1929): 478–480.

"Vocational, Rehabilitation Program Promoted by Auxiliary to City-County Hospital System." *Dallas Daily Times-Herald,* May 4, 1947, 5:1.

Wilson, Carroll. "Who Really Cares About Poetry?" *City: Wichita Falls.* Wichita Falls: Communication Development Services (February 1991): 25–27.

Wolfe, Thomas. *Letters of Thomas Wolfe,* edited by Elizabeth Nowell. New York: Charles Scribner, 1956.

"Woman Author Feted Here." *The Dallas Morning News,* October 21, 1938, 1.13.

Wood, James Playsted. *Magazines in the United States: Their Social and Economic Influence.* 2nd ed. New York: Ronald Press, 1956.

Yauger, Laura Faye. Letter to Betty Wiesepape, February 3, 1991.

_____. Letter to Betty Wiesepape, December 17, 1991.

_____. Letter to Winifred Sanford, April 20, 1981. Winifred Mahon Sanford Papers. Southwestern Writers Collection. Texas State University, San Marcos.

Yergan, Daniel. *The Prize: The Epic Quest for Oil, Money, and Power.* New York: Simon & Schuster, 1991.

Milton Keynes UK
Ingram Content Group UK Ltd.
UKHW040728270823
427541UK00001B/3